VARIETY
COMEDY
MOVIES

COMEDY
MOVIES

ILLUSTRATED REVIEWS OF THE CLASSIC FILMS

MALLARD
PRESS

Half-title page: *A playground traitor gets the third degree in* **The Belles of St Trinians.**

Title page: *Daryl Hannah making waves as a modern-day mermaid in* **Splash.**

ACKNOWLEDGMENTS
Editor: Julian Brown
Design Editor: Leigh Jones
Designer: Jenny England
Jacket designer: Ashley Western
Production Controller: Nick Thompson
Picture researcher: Jenny Faithfull

Photographic acknowledgments
The Ronald Grant Archive 1, 14, 15, 17, 18 left, 20 bottom, 21, 23 bottom, 29, 30, 32, 34, 38, 40, 44 top, 47, 51, 53, 56, 59, 63, 64, 70, 72, 74, 77, 78, 79, 81, 83 bottom, 86 top, 88, 91, 93 top, 98 top, 98 bottom, 107 bottom, 113, 115, 121; The Kobal Collection 2-3, 6, 8, 10, 11, 12 top, 18 right, 20 top, 22 left, 22 right, 23 top, 25, 26, 28, 31 top, 31 bottom, 36, 37, 39, 41, 43, 44 bottom, 45, 46 left, 46 right, 48, 50, 57, 60, 62, 66, 67, 71, 75, 83 top, 84, 86 bottom, 89, 95, 100, 101, 103, 104, 106, 107 top, 109 top, 109, 111, 112, 116, 117, 118, 120, 122, 125, 127; Octopus Publishing Group Ltd 12 bottom, 16, 55, 65, 93 bottom.

MALLARD PRESS
An Imprint of BDD Promotional Book Company, Inc.
666 Fifth Avenue
New York, N.Y. 10103

"Mallard Press" and its accompanying design and logo are trademarks of BDD Promotional Book Company, Inc.

Copyright © 1992 Variety Inc.

First published in the United States of America
in 1992 by The Mallard Press
by arrangement with The Hamlyn Publishing Group Limited,
a division of Reed International Books,
Michelin House, 81 Fulham Road, London SW3 6RB, England

ISBN 0-792-45787-0

Produced by Mandarin Offset
Printed in China.

GLOSSARY

The following is a guide to 80 years of *Variety* 'slanguage' as occurs in the reviews selected; it is not exhaustive and is intended especially for non-American and more general readers.

Variety's snazzy coinages are a goulash of publishing and showbiz/movie jargon, foreign words, Yiddish, street slang, contractions and acronyms that since the mid-1930s have since acquired a reputation and life of their own.

Many of the words have long vanished from use in the paper (along with the slang that inspired them); new ones are still being invented by writers. The only rule is that they sound 'right' and carry on the tradition of sharp, tabloid, flavourful prose.

As a further aid for general readers we have also included some words that are simple movie jargon or archaic slang rather than pure *Variety* language.

a.k.	ass-kisser	helm(er)	direct(or)	org	organization	stepping	dancing
a.k.a.	also known as	histrionics	performance(s)	ozoner	drive-in theatre	stew	drinking bout
ankle	alcoholic	histrionically	performance-wise	p.a.	press agent	sudser	soap opera
anent	regarding	hoke	hokum	pactee	contract player	super	super-production
avoirdupois	weight	hoke up	over-act	Par	Paramount	switcheroo	(plot) twist
b.b.	big business	hoofology	dancing	pen	penitentiary; prison	tab	tabloid
beer stube	bar	hotcha	excellent			tapster	tap-dancer
belter	boxer	hoyden(ish)	tomboy(ish)	Pennsy	Pennsylvania	ten-twent-thirt/10-20-30	amateurish (acting)
burley	burlesque, music hall	ink	sign	photog	photographer		
		i.r.	inquiring or investigative reporter	pic	picture; movie	terp(ing)	danc(ing)
bow	debut; praise			plat	platinum blonde	terpsichore	dancing
b.r.	bankroll; sum of money	jitterbug	(1940s) jazz dance(r); nervous person	p.m.	professional model	thesp(ing)	actor, act(ing)
						thespically	performance-wise
cannon	gun			p.o.v.	point of view	thespics	acting
carny	carnival	kayo	knockout	p.r.	public relations	tint(ed)	colour(ed)
Chi	Chicago	legit(imate)	theatrical, theatre, stage	prexy	(company) president	tintuner	showbiz musical
chili	Mexican					topkick	boss
chirp(er)	sing(er)	legiter	stage play	profesh	profession	topper	boss
chopsocky	martial arts (film)	legituner	stage musical	programmer	B-movie fodder	topline(r)	star
chore	job; routine assignment	lense(r)	photograph(er)	pug	boxer	trick work	special effects
		limn	portray	quondam	one time	trouping	acting
chump	crazy (in love)	lingo	dialogue	ridic	ridiculous	tube	TV
cleff(er)	compose(r)	longhair	intellectual; high brow	rod-man	gunman	20th	20th Century-Fox
click	hit; success			RR	railroad; railway	U	Universal
coin	money; finance	lower case	minor (quality)	s.a.	sex appeal	unreel	play
contempo	contemporary	manse	mansion	sauce	alcohol	unspool	play
d.a.	district attorney	meg(aphoner)	direct(or)	schtick	comic routine(s)	upper case	major (quality)
dick	detective	megger	director	scripter	scriptwriter	vaude	vaudeville
doughboy	infantry soldier	meller	melodrama(tic)	sec	secretary	vet	veteran
dualer	double-billed feature film	milquetoast	meek man	sheet	screen; newspaper	vignetting	describing
		nabes	suburbs			vis-a-vis	(romantic/sexual/billing) partner
femme	female; woman	negative cost	production cost	shutterbug	photographer		
flap	flapper	nitery	nightclub	slugfest	fight	warbling	singing
flivver	car	oater	Western	smokeater	fireman	WB	Warner Bros.
gat	gun	ofay	white man	sock(eroo)	excellent; powerful	w.k.	well-known
gob	sailor	oke	okay			yahoo	redneck
Gotham	New York	one-shot	one-off	solon	lawmaker	yak	joke
gyp	swindler; cheat	o.o.	once-over	speak	speakeasy	yclept	played by
habiliments	clothing	opp	opposite	spec	spectacle	yock	joke

COMEDY MOVIES
CONTENTS

INTRODUCTION

Variety is the world's premier entertainment newspaper. Founded in 1905, its film reviews run from 1907 and cover virtually the entire history of 20th-century cinema, with the freshness both of reviews written at the time of release and of *Variety's* incisive house style.

Comedy Movies is a collection of over 300 reviews of some of the most memorable comedy films of all time. Because of space, the selection has been limited to movies made in the English language. In editing the reviews down (often from many times their original length) much detail has unavoidably been lost. But we have tried to preserve the useful basics – a snappy intro, plot essentials, assessments of the main performances and technical merits, and any interesting background.

Reviewers' box-office predictions have been cut out, as well as plot revelations. Minor changes have been made so that the reviews 'read' from a modern viewpoint, and any now-meaningless contemporary references and prejudices (especially during the two world wars and the McCarthy period) have been toned down or deleted.

Any rewriting has been kept to the absolute minimum to preserve the flavour and opinions of the originals, although until the mid-1930s, when *Variety* reviews began to take on their current shape, editing has had to be considerably heavier.

American spellings and *Variety's* 'language' have been retained (see Glossary); any annotations to the reviews have been put in square brackets. Although *Variety* recently began to include accents on foreign names, this book adheres to tradition by omitting them.

Assembling credits for each film has often involved extra research, and this in turn has been limited by the usual constraints of time and money. *Variety* only started regularly to publish cast lists and limited technical credits in the mid-1920s; fuller credits began from the late 1930s. Mistakes and misprints have been corrected where possible; real names put in square brackets after pseudonyms; and the latest version of people's names used throughout for consistency in the present format.

The following are the main criteria used:

★ **Film title** The original title in country of origin (or 'majority' country, in the case of co-productions). The form of the title is that used on the print itself, not that on secondary material like posters or press handouts. Subsidiary titles (a growing trend since the 1980s) are put on a separate line. Films are listed in strict A-Z order, letter by letter, ignoring all word-breaks and punctuation; those starting with numerals are positioned as if the figures were spelt out. All films included have received a theatrical showing at some time in their life.

★ **Year** The year of first public release in its country of origin (or, with co-productions, 'majority' country). Sneaks, out-of-town tryouts and festival screenings don't count; end-of-year Oscar-qualifying runs do. Establishing some films' opening dates is still problematical.

★ **Running time** The hardest nut to crack. Except when it's obvious the reviewer has been shown a rough-cut, *Variety's* original running times are used. For silent films a very approximate conversion has been made, based on the number of reels or on information contained in the review. Films tend to get shorter over the years as they're trimmed, cut for TV and generally mangled; more recently there has been a trend towards issuing longer versions for TV or video. No running time should be taken as gospel.

★ **Colour** All films in colour, partly in colour, or tinted carry the symbol ◇. Some in the last two categories are now only shown in black-and-white but still carry the colour symbol as this denotes their original form,

★ **Silent** Where a film was made without sound it is indicated with the symbol ⊗.

★ **Video** A nightmare, Films which have been released on video (at one time or another) carry the following symbols: Ⓥ = available in both the US and the UK; ⬥ = available in the US only; and ⊽ = available in the UK only. But given the differences from country to country, and the rapid pace of deletions, don't necessarily expect to find a copy in your local store. Catalogue numbers are of little practical use, so have not been included.

★ **Director** The film's officially credited director or co-directors. Some productions are in fact the work of several hands (especially during Hollywood's studio era); only well-known uncredited contributions are noted in square brackets. Second unit or dance-number directors are occasionally included if their contribution merits it.

★ **Country of origin** The second hardest nut. The rule here has been where the money actually came from, rather than where a film was shot, what passport the director had, or what language the cast spoke in. With co-productions, the first country listed is the 'majority' one (which decides its official title – see above). In the case of many British and American movies, especially since the 1950s, deciding whether some are **UK/US**, **US/UK**, or even **UK** or **US** is virtually impossible.

★ **Cast lists** For space reasons, these have been limited to a maximum of six, not necessarily in their original order of billing. Early appearances by later stars are often included for interest's sake, even though they may only be bit-parts. For consistency, actors who later changed names are listed by their latest moniker.

★ **Academy awards/nominations** The date is that of the Oscar award not of the ceremony (generally held the following spring).

Bill Murray starring in his own directing debut Quick Change *as a dynamite-rigged bank robber.*

ABBOTT AND COSTELLO MEET DR. JEKYLL AND MR. HYDE

1953, 76 mins, ◐ *Dir* Charles Lamont   US

★ *Stars* Bud Abbott, Lou Costello, Boris Karloff, Craig Stevens, Helen Westcott, Reginald Denny

A rousing good time for Abbott & Costello fans is contained in this spoof on fiction's classic bogey-man [from stories by Sidney Fields and Grant Garrett]. The fat & thin comics combat Boris Karloff as the fictional dual personality in the

There's double trouble lurking when Bud and Lou meet Boris in their Jekyll and Hyde spoofer.

very broad doings, and Karloff's takeoff on the character adds to the chuckles dished out by A & C. Helen Westcott, ward of, and coveted by, the good Dr Jekyll, supplies excellent femme appeal in a romance with Craig Stevens, a reporter, while Reginald Denny, harassed Scotland Yard inspector, and John Dierkes, the doctor's zombie-like assistant, help the fun.

Bounced off Denny's police force because of their bungling, Abbott & Costello figure they might be able to get their jobs back if they catch the monster that is terrorizing Hyde Park. Comedic chills and thrills ensue as the pair track down the monster and wind up with its alter ego, Dr Jekyll.

ABBOTT AND COSTELLO MEET FRANKENSTEIN

1948, 82 mins, ◐ *Dir* Charles T. Barton   US

★ *Stars* Bud Abbott, Lou Costello, Lon Chaney, Bela Lugosi, Glenn Strange, Lenore Aubert

The comedy team battles it out with the studio's roster of bogeymen in a rambunctious fracas that is funny and, at the same time, spine-tingling. Stalking through the piece to add menace

are such characters of horror as the Frankenstein Monster, the Wolf Man and Dracula. Loosely-knit script depicts a Monster growing weak. His master, Dracula, decides to transfer Costello's brain to the Frankenstein creation. As a lure, the bat-man uses wiles of Lenore Aubert to soften the fat man and ma-neuver him into proper setup. Through it all runs the Wolf Man as a sympathetic character who tries to warn the heroes against the plot but, unfortunately, proves a bit of a menace himself whenever the moon rises and changes him into a killer.

ABBOTT AND COSTELLO MEET THE INVISIBLE MAN

1951, 82 mins, *Dir* Charles Lamont   US

★ *Stars* Bud Abbott, Lou Costello, Nancy Guild, Arthur Franz, Adele Jergens, Sheldon Leonard

The team's stock double-takes and bewhiskered gags are still fulsome, but the hackneyed quips achieve a new gloss in this entry. Credit for the comics' renaissance goes primarily to the story that Hugh Wedlock Jr and Howard Snyder fashioned from H.G. Wells' *The Invisible Man*. With three other writers screenplaying, the yarn is tied around the efforts of fighter Arthur Franz to clear himself of a murder rap. He hires private eyes Abbott and Costello to help him in his mission. When Franz injects himself with a serum which possesses powers of invisibility, a flock of amusing sequences are touched off. The best of these is a scene in which Costello kayoes the champ (with the invisible man's help).

Franz does a crisp job as the 'invisible' boxer, while Sheldon Leonard is well cast as the heavy. Nancy Guild por-trays Franz's girl with a tender affection and, in contrast to her demureness, is the blowziness Adele Jergens injects into her role as a come-on for the fixers.

ADAM'S RIB

1949, 103 mins, ◉ *Dir* George Cukor   US

★ *Stars* Spencer Tracy, Katharine Hepburn, Judy Holliday, Tom Ewell, David Wayne, Jean Hagen

Adam's Rib is a bright comedy success, belting over a succession of sophisticated laughs. Ruth Gordon and Garson Kanin have fashioned their amusing screenplay around the age-old battle of the sexes.

Setup has Spencer Tracy as an assistant d.a., married to femme attorney Katharine Hepburn. He believes no woman has the right to take shots at another femme. Hepburn believes a woman has the same right to invole the unwritten law as a man. They do courtroom battle over their theories when Tracy is assigned to prosecute Judy Holliday.

This is the sixth Metro teaming of Tracy and Hepburn, and their approach to marital relations around their own hearth is delightfully saucy. A better realization on type than

Holliday's portrayal of a dumb Brooklyn femme doesn't seem possible.

THE ADMIRABLE CRICHTON

1957, 93 mins, ◇ *Dir* Lewis Gilbert   UK

★ *Stars* Kenneth More, Diane Cilento, Cecil Parker, Sally Ann Howes, Martita Hunt, Jack Watling

Staged many times since its original production in London in 1902, and filmed in the silent days [1919] as *Male and Female*, this story of a butler who becomes master on a desert island is a sound starrer for Kenneth More.

A peer of one of England's stately homes takes his three daughters off on a yachting cruise with a few friends and domestic staff. They are shipwrecked and marooned on an uncharted island, and dig themselves in awaiting rescue. Crichton (More), the impeccable butler, is obliged to take complete control, because of the inefficiency of the other castaways. He now gives, not takes orders, and establishes himself as benevolent dictator.

Although More lacks the accepted stature of an English butler, his personality makes a more human and sympathetic figure of the servant who has a firmer sense of snob values than his master. Cecil Parker, alternately genial and pompous as the father, is perhaps more in keeping with the period.

THE ADVENTURE OF SHERLOCK HOLMES' SMARTER BROTHER

1975, 91 mins, ◇ *Dir* Gene Wilder   UK

★ *Stars* Gene Wilder, Madeline Kahn, Marty Feldman, Dom DeLuise, Leo McKern, Roy Kinnear

Gene Wilder joins Mel Brooks in that elusive pantheon of madcap humor, by virtue of Wilder's script, title characterization and directorial debut, all of which are outstanding.

Wilder's script sends the famous Holmes (played by Douglas Wilmer) and Dr Watson (Thorley Walters) ostensi-bly out of England, in order to fool Prof Moriarty (Leo McKern). Latter has a plot going with Dom DeLuise, the most unlikely blackmailing opera freak of the season, to ob-tain some official state papers stolen from nobleman John Le Mesurier.

Holmes' strategy is to use his younger brother, played by Wilder, as a decoy, backstopped by Feldman, a police-man blessed with a photographic memory. Together, this fearless duo fumbles its way to ultimate success.

Wilder's directorial debut is a marvel in many ways, not the least his almost determined economy of footage; the film's 91 minutes never linger too long on a single vignette.

Kahn is terrific and the entire cast is great. The film is a total delight.

Marty Feldman keeping a wary eye open in The Adventures of Sherlock Holmes' Smarter Brother.

THE ADVENTURES OF BARRY MCKENZIE

1972, 117 mins, ◇ *Dir* Bruce Beresford   AUSTRALIA

★ *Stars* Barry Crocker, Barry Humphries, Paul Bertram, Dennis Price, Avice Landon, Peter Cook

Satirist Barry Humphries has put his talents to a film, as co-author and co-star. The result is what one would expect if the Marx Brothers were put into an Aussie-brand *Carry On* pic. It's based on a comic strip [*The Wonderful World of Barry McKenzie*], written by Humphries, around a very Aussie character in London known as Bazza.

Barry Crocker plays title role of the gauche young Aussie visiting Britain for the first time. His turns of phrases are witty and original, often with a bawdy twinge, and although much is in the Australian vernacular (frequently invented by Humphries), few are likely to miss the drift of the remarks.

THE ADVENTURES OF FORD FAIRLANE

1990, 104 mins, ◇ Ⓥ *Dir* Renny Harlin   US

★ *Stars* Andrew Dice Clay, Wayne Newton, Priscilla Presley, Morris Day, Lauren Holly, Robert Englund

Surprisingly funny and expectedly rude, this first starring vehicle by vilified standup comic Andrew Dice Clay has a decidedly lowbrow humor that is a sort of modern equivalent of that of the Three Stooges.

Clay plays Ford Fairlane, a private eye specializing in cases involving rock acts (hence his overused nickname, 'the rock & roll detective'). He gets drawn into a murder mystery linked to a shock-radio deejay (Gilbert Gottfried, in a hilarious cameo), and a sleazy record executive (Wayne Newton) and his ex-wife (Priscilla Presley).

With its heavy rock bent and the direction of Renny Harlin (*Die Hard 2*), much of *Ford Fairlane* resembles a music video.

Aside from his appeal to rednecks and high-school boys overly impressed by certain four-letter words, Clay's chain-smoking goombah in many ways self-parodies the macho ethic that prize rock 'n' roll, fast cars and cheap bimbos above all else.

The film's most significant find, undoubtedly, is Lauren Holly who brings a lot of flash and charisma to a difficult role as Fairlane's longing girl Friday. Also, Robert Englund (aka Freddy Krueger) plays a sadistic killer, sans makeup.

AIRPLANE!

1980, 88 mins, ◇ Ⓥ *Dir* Jim Abrahams, David Zucker, Jerry Zucker   US

★ *Stars* Robert Hays, Julie Hagerty, Lloyd Bridges, Peter Graves, Leslie Nielsen, Robert Stack

Airplane! is what they used to call a laff-riot. Made by team which turned out *Kentucky Fried Movie*, this spoof of disaster features beats any other film for sheer number of comic gags.

Writer-directors leave no cliche unturned as they lay waste to the *Airport*-style disaster cycle, among other targets. From the clever *Jaws* take-off opening to the final, irreverent title card, laughs come thick and fast.

The plot has former pilot Robert Hays, now terrified of flying due to wartime malfeasance, boarding an LA-to-Chicago flight in pursuit of ex-girlfriend stewardess Julie Hagerty. When all the flight personnel, including sexually-deviant pilot Peter Graves and co-pilot Kareem Abdul-Jabbar, contract food poisoning on board, nervous Hays is called upon to land the aircraft safely, an effort not made easier by fact that air controller Lloyd Bridges is completely crazed.

Air traffic controller Lloyd Bridges picks the wrong day to give up sniffing glue in the hilarious spoof **Airplane.**

AIRPLANE II THE SEQUEL

1982, 85 mins, ◇ Ⓥ *Dir* Ken Finkleman   US

★ **Stars** Robert Hays, Julie Hagerty, Lloyd Bridges, Peter Graves, William Shatner, Chad Everett

It can't be said that *Airplane II* is no better or worse than its predecessor. It is far worse, but might seem funnier had there been no original.

In the first *Airplane*, Jim Abrahams, David Zucker and Jerry Zucker had a fresh satirical crack at that hoary old genre, the airborne disaster film. But they wisely chose not to tackle a sequel, leaving incoming writer-director Ken Finkleman a tough task for his feature debut.

Robert Hays is still solid as the fearful pilot destined to take the controls. Ditto his daffy girlfriend Julie Hagerty. But instead of their hilariously earnest efforts the first time around, they seem (perhaps subconsciously) too aware what they're doing is supposed to be funny.

Peter Graves remains amusing as the captain with a fondness for naughty talk with young boys. Among those with nothing much to do are Raymond Burr, Sonny Bono, Chuck Connors, John Dehner, Rip Torn and Chad Everett. Among those with too much to do is William Shatner.

AND BABY MAKES THREE

1949, 83 mins, *Dir* Henry Levin   US

★ **Stars** Robert Young, Barbara Hale, Robert Hutton, Janis Carter, Billie Burke

Fun starts confusingly but mood warms up as footage unfolds and plot line becomes clear. Robert Young has been divorced by Barbara Hale after being caught in a compromising spot. It's a hurry-up Reno untying and Hale is ready to do a quick re-bound marriage when she faints on the way to the altar. Pregnancy is the diagnosis. This upsets wedding plans with Robert Hutton and complications also develop when Young announces he'll fight for partial custody.

Young is his usual able self in taking care of his part of the footage. Hale delights as the wouldbe mother. Henry Levin's direction gets good movement into the script and comedy touches are neatly devised.

ANIMAL CRACKERS

1930, 97 mins, *Dir* Victor Heerman   US

★ **Stars** Groucho Marx, Harpo Marx, Chico Marx, Zeppo Marx, Lillian Roth, Margaret Dumont

First give Paramount extreme credit for reproducing *Animal Crackers* intact from the stage [musical written by George S. Kaufman, Morrie Ryskind, Harry Ruby and Bert Kalmar], without too much of the songs and musical numbers.

Among the Marx boys there is no preference. Groucho shines; Harpo remains a pantomimic clown who ranks with the highest; Chico adds an unusual comedy sense to his dialog as well as business and piano playing; and Zeppo, if in on a split, is lucky.

Lillian Roth may have been cast here to work out a contract. She can't hurt because the Marxes are there, but if Roth is in for any other reason it doesn't appear. She sings one song in the ingenue role. That song is useless. .Opposite is Hal Thompson, a juve who doesn't prove it here.

ANNIE HALL

1977, 93 mins, ◇ Ⓥ *Dir* Woody Allen   US

★ **Stars** Woody Allen, Diane Keaton, Tony Roberts, Carol Kane, Paul Simon, Colleen Dewhurst

Academy Award 1977: Best Picture

Woody Allen's four romantic comedies with Diane Keaton strike a chord of believability that makes them nearly the 1970s equivalent of the Tracy-Hepburn films. *Annie Hall* is by far the best, a touching and hilarious three dimensional love story.

*Groucho in his natural habitat in the early Marx Brothers'
vehicle* Animal Crackers.

The gags fly by in almost non-stop profusion. but
there is an undercurrent of sadness and pain reflecting a
maturation of style. Allen tells Keaton in the film that he has
a 'very pessimistic view of life', and it's true.

The script is loosely structured, virtually a two-charac-
ter running conversation between Allen and Keaton as they
meet, fall in love, quarrel and break up. Meanwhile, he continues his career as a moderately successful TV-nightclub
comic and she develops a budding career as a singer. The
unhappy ending is an unusually satisfying conclusion.

*Psychiatrist-couch comedy: Woody's Allen's award-
winning confessional* Annie Hall *with Diane Keaton.*

ANY WEDNESDAY

1966, 109 mins, ◇ ⓥ *Dir* Robert Ellis Miller   US

★ *Stars* Jane Fonda, Jason Robards, Dean Jones, Rosemary Murphy, Ann Prentiss, Jack Fletcher

Based on Muriel Resnik's popular legiter, *Any Wednesday* emerges in screen translation as an outstanding sophisticated comedy about marital infidelity. Adaptation and production by Julius J. Epstein is very strong, enhanced by solid direction and excellent performances.

Epstein's zesty adaptation wisely distributes the comedy emphasis among all four principals – Jason Robards, the once-a-week philanderer; Jane Fonda, his two-year Wednesday date; Dean Jones, whose arrival rocks Robards' dreamboat; and Rosemary Murphy, recreating in superior fashion her original Broadway role as Robards' wife.

Interactions between principals are uniformly strong, both in dialog and acting as well as in very effective use of split-screen effects.

Fonda comes across quite well as the girl who can't make up her mind, although she has a tendency to overplay certain bits in what might be called an exaggerated Doris Day manner. Jones impresses as a likable comedy performer whose underlying dramatic ability gets a good showcasing here.

Robards is outstanding as the likable lecher who winds up losing both his mistress and his wife.

THE APARTMENT

1960, 124 mins, ◇ ⓥ *Dir* Billy Wilder   US

★ *Stars* Jack Lemmon, Shirley MacLaine, Fred MacMurray, Ray Walston, Edie Adams, Jack Kruschen

Academy Award 1960: Best Picture

Billy Wilder furnishes *The Apartment* with a one-hook plot that comes out high in comedy, wide in warmth and long in running time. As with *Some Like It Hot*, the broad handling is of more consequence than the package.

The story is simple. Lemmon is a lonely insurance clerk with a convenient, if somewhat antiquated, apartment which has become the rendezvous point for five of his bosses and their amours. In return, he's promoted from the 19th floor office pool to a 27th floor wood-paneled office complete with key to the executive washroom. When he falls in love with Shirley MacLaine, an elevator girl who's playing Juliet to top executive Fred MacMurray's Romeo, he turns in his washroom key.

The screenplay fills every scene with touches that spring only from talented, imaginative filmmakers. But where their *Some Like It Hot* kept you guessing right up to fade-out, *Apartment* reveals its hand early in the game. Second half of the picture is loosely constructed and tends to lag.

Apartment is all Lemmon, with a strong twist of MacLaine. The actor uses comedy as it should be used, to evoke a rainbow of emotions. He's lost in a cool world, this lonely bachelor, and he is not so much the shnook as the well-meaning, ambitious young man who lets good be the ultimate victor. MacLaine, in pixie hairdo, is a prize that's consistent with the fight being waged for her affections. Her ability to play it broad where it should be broad, subtle where it must be subtle, enables the actress to effect reality and yet do much more.

THE APRIL FOOLS

1969, 95 mins, ◇ ⓥ *Dir* Stuart Rosenberg   US

★ *Stars* Jack Lemmon, Catherine Deneuve, Peter Lawford, Jack Weston, Myrna Loy, Charles Boyer

Jack Lemmon is both funny and touching as the mild-mannered stockbroker, tied to a nothing of a wife. Given a big promotion by his boss (Peter Lawford), he meets the latter's wife (Catherine Deneuve) at a stultifying cocktail party. She's bored and he doesn't know her real identity but they depart for a night of self-discovery.

In addition to Lemmon, comedians Jack Weston (as his lawyer) and Harvey Korman (as a drinking companion they encounter in the commuter train's drinking car) provide their own brand of laughs and the contrasting styles of the three actors gives the plot most of its action.

Things slow down to a mere simmer, by contrast, in the romantic segments although Deneuve, in her first American film, is worth just looking at.

ARTHUR

1981, 117 mins, ◇ *Dir* Steve Gordon   US

★ *Stars* Dudley Moore, Liza Minnelli, John Gielgud, Geraldine Fitzgerald, Jill Eikenberry

Arthur is a sparkling entertainment which attempts, with a large measure of success, to resurrect the amusingly artificial conventions of 1930s screwball romantic comedies. Dudley Moore is back in top-"*10*" form as a layabout drunken playboy who finds himself falling in love with working-class girl Liza Minnelli just as he's being forced into an arranged marriage with a society WASP.

Central dilemma, which dates back to Buster Keaton at least, has wastrel Moore faced with the choice of marrying white bread heiress Jill Eikenberry or being cut off by his father from $750 million. After much procrastination, he finally agrees to the union, but situation is complicated when, in a vintage (meet cute), he protects shoplifter Minnelli from the authorities and finds himself genuinely falling for someone for the first time in his padded life.

As Moore's eternally supportive but irrepressibly sarcastic valet, John Gielgud gives a priceless performance. Minnelli fills the bill in a less showbizzy and smaller part than usual, but pic's core is really the wonderful relationship between Moore and Gielgud.

arthur

Bubbly Dudley Moore makes millionaire mayhem in the romantic screwball comedy Arthur.

ARTHUR 2 ON THE ROCKS

1988, 113 mins, ◇ Ⓥ *Dir* Bud Yorkin US

★ *Stars* Dudley Moore, Liza Minelli, Geraldine Fitzgerald, Paul Benedict, John Gielgud, Cynthia Sikes

Arthur 2 is not as classy a farce as the original, but still manages to be an amusing romp. Five years into their marriage and living the enviable Park Avenue lifestyle with the kind of digs photographed by Architectural Digest wife Linda (Liza Minnelli) finds she's unable to conceive and goes about adopting a baby.

While Minnelli is gung ho to expand the fold, Arthur's ex-girlfriend's father (Stephen Elliott) seeks to break it apart. Vindictive over having his love-struck daughter stood up at the altar by Arthur last time around, he works up a legal trick to take away the wastrel's $750 million fortune and force him to marry his daughter after all.

Though not critical to the pleasures of watching Moore in one of his best screen roles, it does undermine his performance when he has lesser personalities to tease. Minnelli loses some of her working class sassiness as the downtown-gone-uptown-gone-downtown wife trying to put her house in order, though credit is due her for carrying plot's best scenes.

ASK A POLICEMAN

1939, 83 mins, *Dir* Marcel Varnel UK

★ *Stars* Will Hay, Graham Moffatt, Moore Marriott, Glennis Lorimer, Peter Gawthorne, Charles Oliver

Bits of *Dr Syn* (1937), with George Arliss, and *The Ghost Train* (1931) blend happily with amusing dialog and situations [story by Sidney Gilliatt] usually associated with Will Hay and his two stooges, the fat boy and old man.

A village police station becomes the center of interest when it's discovered there's been no crime there for over 10 years. The sergeant (Hay) in command of two subordinates (Graham Moffatt, Moore Marriott), hearing they're likely to be transferred or fired because of lack of 'business', plans to frame one or two cases.

Planting a keg of brandy on the beach, to stage a smuggler's racket, they discover another, real contraband keg. From then on it's a wild chase between the three witnits and a band headed by the local squire (Charles Oliver) which is carrying on a lucrative haul.

AT THE CIRCUS

1939, 86 mins, ⊕ *Dir* Edward Buzzell   US

★ *Stars* Groucho Marx, Chico Marx, Harpo Marx, Margaret Dumont, Florence Rice, Eve Arden

---

The Marx Bros. revert to the rousing physical comedy and staccato gag dialog of their earlier pictures in *At the Circus*.

Story is slight but unimportant. Kenny Baker, owner of a circus, is harrassed by pursuing James Burke, who wants to foreclose the mortgage he holds on the outfit. When Baker's bankroll is stolen, Chico and Harpo call in Groucho to straighten out the difficulties. Groucho winds up by selling the circus for one performance to Margaret Dumont, Baker's rich aunt and Newport social leader.

Chico does his pianolog in circus car, while Harpo's turn for a harp solo is set up in the menagerie with a production and choral background. A colored kid band and adult chorus (from Hollywood company of *Swing Mikado*) are used here.

AVANTI!

1972, 143 mins, ◇ ⊕ *Dir* Billy Wilder   US

★ *Stars* Jack Lemmon, Juliet Mills, Clive Revill, Edward Andrews, Gianfranco Barra, Franco Angrisano

---

Billy Wilder has taken the Samuel Taylor Broadway play and given it his own peculiar treatment. In casting Jack Lemmon as an American corporation executive come to Italy to claim the body of his father, killed when he drove his car off a high cliff, he has the perfect foil for the building situations, marking the fifth time pair have teamed up in a picture.

Scripted by Wilder and I.A.L. Diamond, two basic themes are nicely blended to lend motivation. There is the sort-of romance between Lemmon and Juliet Mills and the endless Italian governmental red tape which cues all of the film's action.

Basic situation takes form as Lemmon discovers another person also met her death in the tragic accident, his father's longtime English mistress with whom he's been carrying on a clandestine love affair for past 12 years. He meets a chubby English dumpling (Mills) whom he learns is the daughter of the lady in question also heading to claim her mother's body.

Lemmon displays his usual aptitude in a frantic role, here a hardboiled American exec who is gradually drawn

into the aura in which his father had found himself. Mills, who is said to have put on 25 pounds for character, which demands chubbiness, is a happy choice, endowing part with warmth and understanding.

THE BAD NEWS BEARS

1976, 102 mins, ◇ ⊕ *Dir* Michael Ritchie   US

★ *Stars* Walter Matthau, Tatum O'Neal, Vic Morrow, Joyce Van Patten, Ben Piazza, Jackie Earle Haley

---

The Bad News Bears is an extremely funny adult-child comedy film. Walter Matthau stars to perfection as a bumbling baseball coach in the sharp production about the foibles and follies of little-league athletics. Tatum O'Neal also stars as Matthau's ace pitcher.

Michael Ritchie's film has the correct balance of warmth and empathy to make the gentle social commentary very effective.

Premise finds activist politico Ben Piazza having won a class action suit to admit some underprivileged kids to an otherwise upwardly-mobile WASP suburban little league schedule.

Piazza recruits Matthau, a one-time minor leaguer now cleaning swimming pools to coach the slapdash outfit. O'Neal and Jackie Earle Haley reluctantly join their juvenile peers to spark the team to a second place win.

Coach Walter Matthau (right) talks tactics with little-league baseballers The Bad News Bears.

Guerilla tactics or plain monkey business - Woody Allen in revolutionary role in Bananas.

BANANAS

1971, 82 mins, ◇ Ⓥ *Dir* Woody Allen   US

★ **Stars** Woody Allen, Louise Lasser, Carlos Montalban, Natividad Abascal, Jacobo Morales, Miguel Suarez

Bananas is chockfull of sight gags, one-liners and swiftly executed unnecessary excursions into vulgarity whose humor for the most part can't make up for content.

Woody Allen, as bumbling New Yorker working for an automation film, is rejected by his activist sweetheart Louise Lasser who is involved in revolutions, particularly in fictional San Marcos where dictator Carlos Montalban has seized control. Allen, disconsolate, bids farewell to parents Charlotte Rae and Stanley Ackerman while they are performing medical operation. Landing in San Marcos, he is feted by Montalban, who is setting him up as pigeon to be erased supposedly by revolutionary Jacobo Morales' men.

Allen and Mickey Rose have written some funny stuff, and Allen, both as director and actor, knows what to do with it. Scenes between Lasser and comedian have wonderfully fresh, incisive touch. Montalban's dictator is properly arrogant. Morales performs with assurance right up to the point when, drunk with power, he proclaims Swedish the national language.

THE BANK DICK

1940, 69 mins, Ⓥ *Dir* Edward Cline   US

★ **Stars** W.C. Fields, Cora Witherspoon, Una Merkel, Jessie Ralph, Franklin Pangborn, Grady Sutton

Story is credited to Mahatma Kane Jeeves, Fields' own humorous nom de plume. It's a deliberate rack on which to hang the varied Fieldsian comedic routines, many of them repeats from previous pictures but with enough new material inserted to overcome the antique gags. A wild auto ride down the mountainside for the climax is an old formula dating back to the Mack Sennett days, but director Edward Cline has refurbished the episode with new twists that make it a thrill-laugh dash of top proportions.

Fields is the town's foremost elbow bender who injects himself into any situation without invitation. The unexpected hero of a bank robbery, he is rewarded with the job of detective to guard against future holdups. He involves his prospective son-in-law as a temporary embezzler to buy wildcat mining stock, and then holds off the bank examiner via the Mickey Finn route. Repeat bank robbery again results in Fields' accepting hero honors, the reward and sudden riches from a film directing contract.

Several times, Fields reaches into satirical pantomime reminiscent of Charlie Chaplin's best efforts during his Mutual and Essanay days. Directorial guidance by Edward Cline (graduate of the Keystone Kop school) smacks over every gag line and situation to the fullest extent.

Fields has a field day in tabbing the various characters. His own screen name, he is careful to explain, is pronounced Soo-zay, and not Souse, as it appears from English pronunciation.

BAREFOOT IN THE PARK

1967, 104 mins, ◇ ⓥ *Dir* Gene Saks   US

★ *Stars* Robert Redford, Jane Fonda, Charles Boyer, Mildred Natwick, Herbert Edelman, Mabel Albertson

Barefoot in the Park is one howl of a picture. Adapted by Neil Simon from his legit smash, retaining Robert Redford and Mildred Natwick from the original cast, and adding Jane Fonda and Charles Boyer to round out the principals, this is a thoroughly entertaining comedy delight about young marriage. Director Gene Saks makes a sock debut.

Redford is outstanding, particularly adept in light comedy. Fonda is excellent, ditto Natwick, her mother. A genuine surprise casting is Boyer, as the Bohemian who lives in

Robert Redford and Jane Fonda, a perfect pairing as Manhattan newlyweds in Barefoot in the Park.

the attic above the newlyweds' top-floor flat. With only one slight flagging pace – about 30 minutes from the end, when Redford and Fonda have their late-night squabble – pic moves along smartly.

THE BED SITTING ROOM

1970, 90 mins, ◇ ⓥ *Dir* Richard Lester   UK

★ *Stars* Rita Tushingham, Ralph Richardson, Peter Cook, Dudley Moore, Spike Milligan, Michael Hordern

A play by Spike Milligan and John Antrobus serves as an ideal springboard for an offbeat anti-war film by Richard Lester which, miraculously, manages to convey its grim message with humor.

Sketch-like pic catches glimpses and comments of the 20-odd survivors of a London shredded by an A-bomb as they dig out of their holes to try and cope with the grey new world before they, too, become animals.

In the manner of vaude blackouts, they soon meld into a general mosaic of stiff-upper-lip acceptance of new conditions, some fizzlers but others very amusing.

Ralph Richardson is superb in a relatively brief stint as the diehard traditionalist who eventually 'becomes' the title's

B

bed-sitting room, but all in a carefully-chosen roster of British character thesps who contribute stellar bits in almost impossibly difficult roles.

BEDAZZLED

1967, 104 mins, ◇ ⊙ *Dir* Stanley Donen   UK

★ *Stars* Peter Cook, Dudley Moore, Eleanor Bron, Raquel Welch, Robert Russell, Barry Humphries

Bedazzled is smartly-styled and typical of certain types of high British comedy. It's a fantasy of a London short-order cook madly in love with a waitress, who is offered seven wishes by the Devil in return for his soul.

Stanley Donen production is pretty much the work of two of its three stars, Peter Cook and Dudley Moore. Pair scripted from Cook's original story, and Moore also composed music score. Eleanor Bron is third star, plus Raquel Welch, whose brief appearance is equalled only by her scant attire.

Mephistophelean overtones are inserted in this modern-day Faust legend tacked onto Moore, who would give his soul to possess Margaret, the waitress (Bron). Cook (Mephistopheles), parading under the mundane name of George Spiggot, appears mysteriously in Moore's flat as he flubs a suicide attempt and grants all of the cook's wishes.

BEDTIME STORY

1941, 83 mins, *Dir* Alexander Hall   US

★ *Stars* Fredric March, Loretta Young, Robert Benchley, Allyn Joslyn, Eve Arden, Helen Westley

Picture is a combo of slick scripting, fast-paced direction and excellent performances. Richard Flournoy provides plenty of laugh embellishment to the original story by

Dudley Moore (right) swops chef's hat for nun's habit in Bedazzled, with Peter Cook's Satan never far away.

Horace Jackson and Grant Garrett; director Alexander Hall keeps his foot on the speed throttle from start to finish; and Fredric March teams with Loretta Young for a pair of topnotch performances in the starring spots.

Despite the light and fluffy tale unreeled, maximum entertainment is provided in the breezy exposition of the marital problems of producer-playwright March and his star-wife Young. After seven years of marriage and struggle, pair are top successes in their respective endeavors.

The wife desires to retire to their farm in Connecticut, while the energetic March hatches a new play in which he wants Young to star. Both Young and the audience keep intrigued by the inventive devices concocted by the playwright in trying to swing his wife into the new play.

BEING THERE

1979, 130 mins, ◇ *Dir* Hal Ashby   US

★ *Stars* Peter Sellers, Shirley MacLaine, Melvyn Douglas, Jack Warden, Richard Basehart

Being There is a highly unusual and an unusually fine film. A faithful but nonetheless imaginative adaptation of Jerzy

Peter Sellers as the illiterate gardener Chance who is taken for a homespun philosopher in Being There.

Kosinski's quirky comic novel, pic marks a significant achievement for director Hal Ashby and represents Peter Sellers' most smashing work since the mid-1960s.

Kosinski's story is a quietly outrageous fable which takes Sellers from his position as a childlike, unblinking naif who can't read or write to that of a valued advisor to an industrial giant and ultimately to the brink of a presidential nomination.

Tale possesses political, religious and consumer society undertones, but by no means is an overly symbolic affair trying to impress with its deep meanings.

Sellers' performance stands as the centerpiece of the film, and it's a beauty.

Shirley MacLaine is subtle and winning, retaining her dignity despite several precarious opportunities to lose it. If such is possible in a picture dominated by Sellers, Melvyn Douglas almost steals the film with his spectacular performance as the dying financial titan.

BELLE OF THE NINETIES

1934, 75 mins, *Dir* Leo McCarey   US

★ **Stars** Mae West, Roger Pryor, John Mack Brown, Katherine DeMille, John Miljan

Mae West's opera, *Belle of the Nineties*, is as ten-twent-thirt as its mauve decade time and locale. The melodramatics are put on a bit thick, including the arch-villain who is an arch-renegade, a would-be murderer, a welcher, an arsonist and everything else in the book of ye good old-time mellers.

The original songs by Sam Coslow and Arthur Johnston are 'My Old Flame', 'American Beauty' and 'Troubled Waters'. Duke Ellington's nifty jazzique is a natural for the Westian song delivery.

Just like she makes stooges of almost anybody assigned to bandy talk with her, West dittoes with her principal support, including Roger Pryor, the fave vis-a-vis, John Mack Brown as the good time Charlie, and John Miljan, a villyun of darkest mien. Katherine DeMille as the spurned gambler's sweetheart looks better and suggests better opportunities than the prima facie script accords her.

THE BELLES OF ST. TRINIAN'S

1954, 91 mins, Ⓥ *Dir* Frank Launder   UK

★ **Stars** Alastair Sim, Joyce Grenfell, George Cole, Hermione Baddeley, Betty Ann Davies, Renee Houston

Inspired by Ronald Searle's British cartoons about the little horrors of a girls' school, *The Belles of St. Trinian's* makes an excellent start but never lives up to the opening reel.

By way of a story, Frank Launder and Sidney Gilliat have concocted an involved yarn about a plot to steal the favorite horse in a big race which is foiled by the girls in the fourth form after a battle royal with the sixth form.

Unrestrained direction by Launder is matched by the

lively and energetic performances by most of the cast. As both the headmistress and her bookmaker brother, Alastair Sim rarely reaches comedy heights. Joyce Grenfell, however, as a police spy posing as a games teacher, is good for plenty of laughs. Best individual contribution is by George Cole, playing a wide-shouldered wiseguy, who acts as selling agent for the homemade gin brewed in the school lab, and also as go-between for the girls and the local bookie.

THE BELLS GO DOWN

1943, 86 mins, *Dir* Basil Dearden   UK

★ **Stars** Tommy Trinder, James Mason, Philip Friend, Mervyn Johns

Like *Fires Were Started* this film depicts the activities of life in the London Auxiliary Fire Service. But the first one out was more legitimate in that it was portrayed by actual members of the service.

Viewed as a mere low comedy, *The Bells Go Down* ambles along amiably. There is a running commentary patterned on the lines of those made familiar by Quentin Reynolds, and the fire scenes alternate with the wisecracking of Tommy Trinder, which are often without provocation. Thrillingly effective conflagration scenes deserve a large share of the honors.

Trinder enacts a lovable East Side young man whose mother runs a fish-and-chip shop, and who owns a racing greyhound that never wins until his comrades have gone broke backing the pooch.

The supporting cast is very well chosen, with Mervyn Johns ofering a scintillating portrayal. James Mason, as a fireman, scores as usual; Beatrice Varley, as Trinder's mother, and fully a score of others can be set down as efficient support. Direction, production and photography are praiseworthy.

BETSY'S WEDDING

1990, 98 mins, ◇ Ⓥ *Dir* Alan Alda   US

★ **Stars** Alan Alda, Madeline Kahn, Molly Ringwald, Ally Sheedy, Anthony LaPaglia, Joe Pesci

From a bolt of ordinary cloth Alan Alda fashions a thoroughly engaging matrimonial romp in *Betsy's Wedding*. Most of the action comes from the clash of personalities and wills as unconventional daughter Betsy (Molly Ringwald) announces her plans to wed boyfriend Jake (Dylan Walsh), and everyone jumps into the act.

Overreaching dad (Alda) wants a big, wonderful Italian Jewish wedding, and plans accelerate into a one-upmanship contest when Jake's wealthy WASP parents try to take the reins. To finance the bash, Alda, a contractor, unwittingly throws in with some funny-money Italian business partners, as arranged by his double-dealing brother-in-law (Joe Pesci).

Setting a buoyant, anything-could-happen tone from the outset, Alda as director creates what he's striving for: a feeling

Alan Alda (right) gives away daughter Molly Ringwald in the knock-about nuptuals of Betsy's Wedding.

of being caught up in the warm craziness of this family, as all its vivid characters push and tug to impose their will on the proceedings. His punchy, inpertinent script is equally good.

BIG

1988, 102 mins, ◇ Ⓥ   *Dir* Penny Marshall   US

★ *Stars* Tom Hanks, Elizabeth Perkins, John Heard, Jared Rushton, Robert Loggia, David Moscow

A 13-year-old junior high kid Josh (David Moscow) is transformed into a 35-year-old's body (Tom Hanks) by a carnival wishing machine in this pic which unspools with enjoyable genuineness and ingenuity.

Immediate dilemma, since going back to school is not an option and his mom thinks he's an intruder and doesn't buy into the explanation that he's changed into a man, is to escape to anonymous New York City and hide out in a seedy hotel.

Pretty soon, the viewer forgets that what's happening on screen has no basis in reality. The characters are having too much fun enjoying life away from responsibility, which begs the question why adults get so serious when there is fun to be had in almost any situation.

Hanks plays chopsticks on a walking piano at F.A.O. Schwarz with a man who turns out to be his boss (Robert Loggia) and as a result of this freespirited behavior is promoted way beyond his expectations, but it's what he does with all his newfound self-worth that propels this 'dramedy'.

Greatest growth comes from his involvement with co-worker Elizabeth Perkins, though by no means is he the only one getting an education.

BIG BUSINESS

1988, 97 mins, ◇ Ⓥ   *Dir* Jim Abrahams   US

★ *Stars* Bette Midler, Lily Tomlin, Fred Ward, Edward Herrmann, Michele Placido

Big Business is a shrill, unattractive comedy which stars Bette Midler and Lily Tomlin, who play two sets of twins mixed up at birth. They have distinctly different comic styles, with the former's loud brashness generally dominating the latter's sly skittishness.

Robert Loggia and Tom Hanks indulge in some nifty footwork in the walking piano scene in Big.

A mishap at a rural hospital pairs off the daughters of a hick couple with the sprigs of a major industrialist and his society wife. Jump to New York today, where dynamic Moramax Corp board chairman Sadie Shelton (Midler) is forced to tolerate her scatterbrained, sentimental sister Rose (Tomlin) while trying to push through the sale of a subsidiary firm in their birthplace of Jupiter Hollow.

To try to thwart the sale at a stockholders' meeting, another Sadie and Rose, of the Ratcliff clan, leave Jupiter Hollow for the big city. As soon as they arrive at the airport, the complications begin.

Of the four performances by the two leads, the one easiest to enjoy is Midler's as venal corporate boss. Dressed to the nines and sporting a mincing but utterly determined walk, Midler tosses off her waspish one-liners with malevolent glee, stomping on everyone in her path.

There are moments of delight as well in her other characterization as a country bumpkin who has always yearned for the material pleasures of Babylon. Tomlin has her moments, too, but her two sweetly flakey, nay-saying characters for a while seem so similar.

A rock-exploiter with a new twist, **Bill and Ted's Excellent Adventure** *is time-travel aimed at a strictly teen market.*

THE BIG STEAL

1990, 100 mins, ◇   *Dir* Nadia Tass   AUSTRALIA

★ *Stars* Ben Mendelsohn, Claudia Karvan, Steve Bisley, Marshall Napier, Tim Robertson

The third feature from husband-and-wife team Nadia Tass and David Parker has a low-key charm that's appealing, and a couple of riotously funny scenes.

Ben Mendelsohn is Danny, a shy 18-year-old who wants two things: to own a Jaguar and to date Joanna (Claudia Karvan). Danny's father (Marshall Napier in a rich comic performance) gives him a car for his birthday, but it's a 1963 Nissan Cedric the family has owned for years. Danny trades this in for a 1973 Jag in time for his first date.

Trouble is that car dealer Gordon Farkas (Steve Bisley giving a splendidly sleazy performance) is a crook who's switched engines on Danny. He and his mates decide to hit back by lifting the engine from Farkas' Jag while he's having a drunken time at a sex club.

Teens here are incredibly unsophisticated compared to 18-year-olds in Hollywood teen comedies, and that's part of the film's charm. Mendelsohn and Karvan are quite sweet in their roles.

BILL & TED'S EXCELLENT ADVENTURE

1989, 90 mins, ◇ Ⓥ   *Dir* Stephen Herek   US

★ *Stars* Keanu Reeves, Alex Winter, George Carlin, Terry Camilleri, Dan Shor

Keanu Reeves (Ted) and Alex Winter (Bill) play San Dimas 'dudes' so close they seem wired together.

Preoccupied with plans for 'a most triumphant video'

to launch their two-man rock band, The Wyld Stallyns, they're suddenly, as Bill put it, 'in danger of flunking most heinously' out of history.

George Carlin appears as a cosmic benefactor who offers them a chance to travel back through history and gather up the speakers they need for an awesome presentation.

Through brief, perilous stops here and there, they end up jamming Napoleon, Billy The Kid, Sigmund Freud, Socrates, Joan of Arc, Genghis Khan, Abraham Lincoln and Mozart into their time-traveling phone booth.

Each encounter is so brief and utterly cliched that history has little chance to contribute anything to this pic's two dimensions.

Reeves, with his beguilingly blank face and loose-limbed, happy-go-lucky physical vocabulary, and Winter, with his golden curls, gleefully good vibes and 'bodacious' vocabulary, propel this adventure as long as they can.

BILLY LIAR

1963, 98 mins, Ⓥ   *Dir* John Schlesinger   UK

★ *Stars* Tom Courtenay, Julie Christie, Wilfred Pickles, Mona Washbourne, Finlay Currie, Rodney Bewes

Based on a West End hit play by Keith Waterhouse (who wrote the novel) and Willis Hall, *Billy Liar* is an imaginative, fascinating film. It is perhaps unfair to label the film as entirely realistic, since it moves into a world of Walter Mitty-like fantasy, and that is its only weakness. These scenes are lacking in impact.

Billy Liar (Tom Courtenay) is a day-dreaming young man who leads an irresponsible life as a funeral director's clerk. He fiddles the petty cash, he is at war with his parents, he has become involved with two young women who share an engagement ring. Above all, he is an incorrigible liar, dreaming dreams and, whenever possible, retreating into an

*The fantasy faces of **Billy Liar** (Tom Courtney), day-dreaming his way through an otherwise mundane life.*

*Matthew Broderick (second right) in Neil Simon's **Biloxi Blues**, based on his own experiences as a serviceman.*

---

invented world where he is the dictator of an imagined slice of Ruritania.

Courtenay who took over from Albert Finney in the legit version of *Billy Liar*, has a hefty part and is rarely off the screen. Of the three girls with whom he is involved, Julie Christie is the only one who really understands him. Christie turns in a glowing performance. Helen Fraser and Gwendolyn Watts provide sharply contrasting performances as the other young women in Billy Liar's complicated, muddled existence.

Mona Washbourne, as his dim mother, Wilfred Pickles, playing a hectoring, stupid father, and grandmother Ethel Griffies also lend considerable color.

BILOXI BLUES

1988, 106 mins, ◇ Ⓥ   *Dir* Mike Nichols   US

★ *Stars* Matthew Broderick, Christopher Walken, Matt Mulhern, Corey Parker, Markus Flanagan

---

Biloxi Blues is an agreeable but hardly inspired film version of Neil Simon's second installment of his autobiographical trilogy, which bowed during the 1984–85 season. Even with high-powered talents Mike Nichols and Matthew Broderick

aboard, World War II barracks comedy provokes just mild laughs and smiles rather than the guffaws Simon's work often elicits in the theater.

Film is narrated from an adult perspective by Simon's alter ego, Eugene Morris Jerome (Broderick), an aspiring writer called up for service in the waning months of the war.

With 10 weeks of boot camp ahead of them, it's not at all sure that Eugene and his cohorts will ever see action, but that doesn't prevent their basic training from being a living hell relieved only by an excursion into town to party and look for ladies.

Playing a character perched precisely on the point between adolescence and manhood, Broderick is enjoyable all the way.

Penelope Ann Miller is adorable as the girl who inspires love at first sight in Eugene at a dance, while the most intriguing performance comes from Christopher Walken as the weird sergeant.

BIRD ON A WIRE

1990, 110 mins, ◇ Ⓥ   *Dir* John Badham   US

★ *Stars* Mel Gibson, Goldie Hawn, David Carradine, Bill Duke, Joan Severance, Stephen Tobolowsky

---

Frank Capra's *It Happened One Night* established the format, but John Badham is stuck with a terrible script on this 1990s version. Only the chemistry of Goldie Hawn and Mel Gibson makes the film watchable.

Gibson plays a shnook who's been hiding out for 15 years under an FBI witness relocation program. He gave testimony on a drug deal and the man he fingered (David Carradine) is just out of prison. Contrived and thoroughly unconvincing plot cog has Gibson discovered incognito by old flame Hawn at the Detroit gas station where he works just as Carradine and partner Duke catch up with him. Resulting shootout throws Hawn and Gibson together on the lam for the rest of the pic.

Rekindling of duo's romance is best thing about the repetitive chase format, set in numerous US locations but

COMEDY MOVIES

Airborne action helps keep up the pace in the Mel Gibson-Goldie Hawn comedy chaser Bird on a Wire.

shot almost entirely in British Columbia. Main kudos goes to British designer Philip Harrison, who's allowed to run hog wild in a largescale climax set at a zoo exhibit depicting a Brazilian rain forest.

BLAME IT ON RIO

1984, 110 mins, ◇ ⑨ *Dir* Stanley Donen   US

★ **Stars** Michael Caine, Joseph Bologna, Valerie Harper, Michelle Johnson, Jose Lewgoy, Demi Moore

Central premise of a secret romance between Michael Caine and the love-smitten daughter of his best friend (Joe Bologna) while the trio vacations together in torrid Rio may

be adventurous comedy. Zany comedic conflict, however, is offputting, even at times nasty, in this essentially dead-ahead comedy that sacrifices charm and a light touch for too much realism.

Newcomer Michelle Johnson comes off as callow and disagreeably spoiled in key role of buxom daughter lusting after dad's best buddy.

Caine and Bologna play colleagues in a Sao Paulo coffee company whose marriages are toppling – Bologna is getting a divorce and Caine's wife (Valerie Harper) tells Caine while couple is packing for Rio that she's splitting for Bahia in a separate vacation.

Director Stanley Donen gets sharp, comic performances from Caine and Bologna.

BLAZING SADDLES

1974, 93 mins, ◇ ⑨ *Dir* Mel Brooks   US

★ **Stars** Cleavon Little, Gene Wilder, Slim Pickens, David Huddleston, Mel Brooks, Madeline Kahn

Blazing Saddles spoofs oldtime westerns with an avalanche of one-liners, vaudeville routines, campy shticks, sight gags, satiric imitations and comic anachronisms. Pic is essentially a raunchy, protracted version of a television comedy skit.

Although Cleavon Little and Gene Wilder head a uniformly competent cast, pic is handily stolen by Harvey Korman and Madeline Kahn. Kahn is simply terrific doing a Marlene Dietrich lampoon.

Gene Wilder and Cleavon Little in Blazing Saddles, Mel Brooks' classic sagebrush send-up.

Rest of cast is fine, although Little's black sheriff doesn't blend too well with Brooks' Jewish-flavored comic style. Wilder is amusingly low-key in a relatively small role.

BLIND DATE

1987, 93 mins, ◇ ⓥ *Dir* Blake Edwards   US

★ **Stars** Kim Basinger, Bruce Willis, John Larroquette, William Daniels

Bruce Willis abandons his mugging TV personality in favor of playing an animated, amiable, hard-working, ambitious financial analyst in LA.

Stuck without a date for a company function, he reluctantly agrees to ask his brother's wife's cousin (Kim Basinger) to accompany him. His first impression: she's darling. His first mistake: he's not supposed to let her drink and ignores the advice. Two sips of champagne later, she's out of control.

Theme of pure mayhem works well because of chemistry between the main trio of actors, Willis, Basinger and her spurned ex-beau (John Larroquette).

Basinger is cool when sober and wacky when drunk. Her part is really secondary to Willis', who starts out a befuddled date with the manners of a gentleman and ends up not only befuddled, but crazy for the woman.

It's really the psychotic Larroquette who drives this romp. While Willis tries to control his date (or at least figure her out), Larroquette is hot on his tail trying to get her back. Their skirmishes are hilarious.

Pic is essentially a running string of gags with snippets of catchy dialog in-between.

THE BLISS OF MRS. BLOSSOM

1968, 93 mins, ◇ *Dir* Joseph MacGrath   UK

★ **Stars** Shirley MacLaine, Richard Attenborough, James Booth, Freddie Jones, William Rushton, Bob Monkhouse

The Bliss of Mrs. Blossom is a silly, campy and sophisticated marital comedy, always amusing and often hilarious in impact. Shirley MacLaine stars as a wife with two husbands – Richard Attenborough, the legal and night-time spouse, and James Booth, who lives in the attic. Script covers the laugh spectrum from throwaway verbal and sight gags through broad comedy to satirical pokes at old-fashioned film romances.

MacLaine, bored but adoring wife, calls Attenborough, a noted brassiere manufacturer, for help when her sewing machine breaks down. Only plant worker available is the bumbling Booth, who is seduced by MacLaine. He refuses to leave the attic, and MacLaine gets to liking the cozy arrangement. Gumshoes Freddie Jones and William Rushton pursue Booth's 'disappearance' over the course of many years.

Although basically a one-joke story, idea is fleshed out most satisfactorily so as to take undue attention away from the premise.

The performances are all very good, and Richard Attenborough's in particular.

BLITHE SPIRIT

1945, 96 mins, ◇ *Dir* David Lean   UK

★ **Stars** Rex Harrison, Constance Cummings, Kay Hammond, Margaret Rutherford, Hugh Wakefield, Joyce Carey

Inasmuch as this is largely a photographed copy of the stage play [by Noel Coward], the camerawork is outstandingly good and helps to put across the credibility of the ghost story more effectively than the flesh and blood performance does.

Acting honors go to Margaret Rutherford as Mme Arcati, a trance medium who makes you believe she's on the level. There is nothing ethereal about this 200-pounder. Her dynamic personality has all the slapdash of Fairbanks Sr in his prime.

Kay Hammond, as dead Wife No 1, brings to the screen a faithful repetition of the performance she has been giving in the flesh for nearly four years. As a spoiled darling with murder in her heart for Wife No 2, she is as much a smiling menace as she is wistfully wraithlike.

As Ruth, the very much alive Wife No 2, Constance Cummings more than holds her own in an altogether capable cast – until her death in the automobile accident engineered by Elvira. As a ghost, However, Cummings is not at all convincing. As Charles Condomine, twice married novelist, Rex Harrison repeats his stage performance, which is so flawless as to merit some critics' charge of under-acting.

Direction by David Lean is workmanlike

THE BLUES BROTHERS

1980, 133 mins, ◇ ⓥ *Dir* John Landis   US

★ **Stars** John Belushi, Dan Aykroyd, James Brown, Ray Charles, Carrie Fisher, Aretha Franklin

If Universal had made it 35 years earlier, *The Blues Brothers* might have been called *Abbott & Costello in Soul Town.* Level of inspiration is about the same now as then, the humor as basic, the enjoyment as fleeting. But at $30 million, this is a whole new ball-game.

Enacting Jake and Elwood Blues roles created for their popular concert and recording act, John Belushi and Dan Aykroyd use the slenderest of stories – attempt to raise $5,000 for their childhood parish by putting their old band back together – as an excuse to wreak havoc on the entire city of Chicago and much of the Midwest.

Film's greatest pleasure comes from watching the likes of James Brown, Cab Calloway, Ray Charles and especially Aretha Franklin do their musical things.

Given all the chaos, director and, with Aykroyd, co-writer, John Landis manages to keep things reasonably controlled and in a straight line. Pic plays as a spirited tribute by

John Belushi (left) and Dan Aykroyd as the soul-singing Jake and Elwood - the **Blues Brothers.**

white boys to black musical culture, which was inspiration for the Blues Brothers act in the first place.

BOB & CAROL & TED & ALICE

1969, 104 mins, ◇ ⊘ *Dir* Paul Mazursky   US

★ *Stars* Natalie Wood, Robert Culp, Elliott Gould, Dyan Cannon, Horst Ebersberg, Lee Bergere

The story concerns a young documentary filmmaker (Robert Culp) and his wife (Natalie Wood) who make a visit to an institute in Southern California which supposedly helps people expand their capacities for love and understanding. When our friends are back in their swank surroundings, chatting with friends, Elliott Gould and wife Dyan Cannon, the comedy begins and never lets up until the final scenes when the sociological effects of this pseudo-liberal thinking come into play.

The acting is superb. Cannon proves an expert comedienne. She and Gould practically steal the film, although admittedly they have the best lines. Wood and Culp give equally fine performances.

The film is almost flawless, presenting the issues in a pleasing, entertaining and thought-provoking manner.

BOEING BOEING

1965, 102 mins, ◇ *Dir* John Rich   US

★ *Stars* Tony Curtis, Jerry Lewis, Dany Saral, Christine Schmidtmer, Suzanna Leigh, Thelma Ritter

Boeing Boeing is an excellent modern comedy about two newshawks with a yen for airline hostesses. First-rate performances and direction (by John Rich) make the most of a very good script.

The fanciful dream of a dedicated bachelor is realized in this adaptation of a Marc Camoletti play in which Paris-based US newsman Tony Curtis has no less than three airline gals on a string.

Director John Rich has done a topnotch job in overcoming what is essentially (except for a few Paris exteriors) a one-set, one-joke comedy. Curtis is excellent and neatly restrained as the harem keeper whose cozy scheme approaches collapse when advanced design Boeing aircraft (hence, the title) augur a disastrous overlap in femme availability.

Rich has also brought out a new dimension in Lewis, herein excellent in a solid comedy role as Curtis' professional rival who threatens to explode the plan.

The outstanding performance is delivered by Thelma Ritter, Curtis' harried housekeeper who makes the necessary domestic changes in photos, clothing and menu so that the next looker will continue to believe that she, alone, is mistress of the flat.

THE BOHEMIAN GIRL

B

1936, 80 mins, ⬤ *Dir* James W. Horne, Charles Rogers   US

★ *Stars* Stan Laurel, Oliver Hardy, Thelma Todd, Antonio Moreno, Jacqueline Wells, James Finlayson

The Bohemian Girl is a comedy with little or no comedy. Laurel and Hardy are snatch-purses with an 18th-century band of roving gypsies. In retaliation for the flogging of a fellow-member (Antonio Moreno), caught red-handed in an attempted burglary, the gypsies steal the child of a nobleman and bring her up as one of their own. In the end the customary tell-tale medallion saves the peeress and restores her to her daddy.

There are no credits for screen adaptation. Responsibility is thrown back upon Michael Balfe who wrote the original opera in 1843 and should be permitted to rest in peace. He composed the score; original librettists also not credited – or blamed.

Chained to such a scenario, the picture has the additional liability of inept direction. Thelma Todd who goes

*A musical comedy from a pre-movie era, **The Bohemian Girl** was a rare costume piece for Ollie and Stan.*

through the motions of singing (a mere bit) with the voice track poorly synchronized to her lips, seems strangely unlike herself. (A good deal of her footage, fortunately for her rep, was cut out just prior to release).

THE BONFIRE OF THE VANITIES

1990, 125 mins, ◇ ⓥ *Dir* Brian De Palma   US

★ *Stars* Tom Hanks, Bruce Willis, Melanie Griffith, Kim Cattrall, Morgan Freeman, F. Murray Abraham

Brian de Palma's take on Tom Wolfe's *The Bonfire of the Vanities* is a misfire of inanities. Wolfe's first novel boasted rich characters and teeming incident that proved highly alluring to filmmakers. Unfortunately, De Palma was not the man for the job. It doesn't take long to turn off and tune out on this glitzy $45 million-plus dud.

Early sequences of marital discord between Wall Street maestro Sherman McCoy (Tom Hanks) and wife Judy (Kim Cattrall) possess a grating, uncertain quality, and film never manages to locate a consistent tone. McCoy is having an affair with Southern bombshell Maria Ruskin (Melanie Griffith), and clearly stands as a symbol for Success, 1980s style. Monkeywrench arrives in the form of an automobile mishap one night in deepest Bronx.

Seemingly threatened by two black youths, Maria backs Sherman's Mercedes into one of them, slightly injuring him. When the kid falls into a coma, the machinery of law, politics and journalism begins grinding. The rich man's status makes him an ideal scapegoat for multifarious social ills, as well as for the personal agendas of the city's most shameless operators, most prominently, Peter Fallow (Bruce Willis), a down-and-out alcoholic reporter who parlays the McCoy story into fame and fortune.

Unfortunately, the caricatures are so crude and the 'revelations' so unenlightening of the human condition, that the satire appears about as socially incisive as a *Police Academy* entry.

BORN YESTERDAY

1950, 102 mins, ◉ *Dir* George Cukor   US

★ *Stars* Broderick Crawford, Judy Holliday, William Holden, Howard St John, Frank Otto, Larry Oliver

Academy Award 1950: Best Picture (Nomination)

The bright, biting comedy of the Garson Kanin legit hit adapts easily to film.

Judy Holliday repeats her legit success here as femme star of the film version. Almost alone, she makes *Born Yesterday*.

Holliday delights as she tosses off the malaprops that so aptly fit the character. Even though considerable amount of the dialog is unintelligible, its sound and her artful delivery smite the risibilities. William Holden is quietly effective as the newspaperman hired to coach her in social graces so she will better fit in with her junkman's ambitious plans.

Broderick Crawford, as the selfmade dealer in junk, comes off much less successfully, however. The actual and implied sympathy is missing, leaving it just a loud-shouting, boorish person.

BOY, DID I GET A WRONG NUMBER!

1966, 98 mins, ◇ ◉ *Dir* George Marshall   US

★ *Stars* Bob Hope, Elke Sommer, Phyllis Diller, Cesare Danova, Marjorie Lord, Kelly Thordsen

Bob Hope enters the realm of near-bedroom farce as he finds a near-unclad film star on his hands in a lake cottage and his ever-loving spouse continually appearing on the scene. If the action sometimes seems to get out of hand it really doesn't matter, for Phyllis Diller is there too, to help him hide the delectable Elke Sommer from the missus.

Hope plays his role straight for the most part, making the most of the situation. George Marshall's direction sparks events in proper perspective, wisely allowing his characters to go their separate ways in their own particular styles. Sommer, who knows her way through a comedy scene either with or without clothes, elects the latter state for most of

her thesping, raimented mostly in a shirt. Diller is immense as the nosy domestic responsible for the majority of the funny lines that abound throughout the fast unfoldment.

BREAKING AWAY

1979, 100 mins, ◇ ⓥ *Dir* Peter Yates   US

★ *Stars* Dennis Christopher, Dennis Quaid, Daniel Stern, Jackie Earle Haley, Barbara Barrie, Robyn Douglass

Academy Award 1979: Best Picture (Nomination)

Though its plot wins no points for originality, *Breaking Away* is a thoroughly delightful light comedy, lifted by fine performances from Dennis Christopher and Paul Dooley. The story is nothing more than a triumph for the underdog through sports, this time cycle racing.

Christopher, Dennis Quaid, Daniel Stern and Jackie Earle Haley are four recent high-school graduates with no particular educational ambitions, yet stuck in a small college town – and a fairly snooty college at that. But Christopher is a heck of a bike rider and such an adulator of Italian champions that he pretends to be Italian himself, even at home.

Pretending to be an Italian exchange student, Christopher meets pretty co-ed Robyn Douglass (an able film debut for her) and this ultimately brings the boys into conflict with the big men on campus that must finally be resolved in a big bike race.

The relationship among the four youths is warm and funny, yet full of different kinds of conflicts. Quaid is very good as the ex-quarterback facing a life with no more cheers; Haley is good as a sawed-off romantic; and Stern is superb as a gangly, wise-cracking mediator.

Though the film sometimes seems padded with too much cycle footage, the climax is exciting, even though predictable.

BREAKING IN

1989, 91 mins, ◇ ⓥ *Dir* Bill Forsyth   US

★ *Stars* Burt Reynolds, Casey Siemaszlo, Sheila Kelley, Lorraine Toussant, Albert Salmi, Harry Carey

Burt Reynolds plays Ernie Mullins, a 61-year-old, graying, professional burglar with a gammy leg and the beginning of a pot belly, in this charming buddy-caper movie.

He teams up with young Mike Lefebb (Casey Siemaszko), a garage hand who likes to break into houses to raid the fridge and read the mail, when they both hit the same place one night. They become partners, with the old-timer teaching the youngster the tricks of the trade.

What follows is a gentle comedy, filled with incisive observation, which builds to a wry conclusion which won't set well with action fans.

Reynolds plays the old-timer with a relaxed charm that's wholly delightful. Siemaszko is fine, too, as the initially

nervous and ultimately relaxed and confident young criminal. Sheila Kelley is fun as a prostie who favors colored condoms and likes to be known as an actress.

BREWSTER'S MILLIONS

1985, 97 mins, ◇ Ⓥ *Dir* Walter Hill   US

★ *Stars* Richard Pryor, John Candy, Lonette McKee, Stephen Collins, Jerry Orbach, Pat Hingle

It's hard to believe a comedy starring Richard Pryor and John Candy is no funnier than this one is, but director Walter Hill has overwhelmed the intricate genius of each with constant background action, crowd confusions and other endless distractions.

All the frenetic motion, unfortunately, never disguises the fact that the writers haven't done much of distinction with the familiar story [a 1902 novel by George Barr McCutcheon] that has been produced in many forms, dating back to a 1906 stage version. [Previous film versions were in 1914, 1921, 1935, 1945 and 1961.]

In one incarnation or another, the yarn always involves somebody who stands to inherit a huge fortune, but first must squander a small one over a short time. In order to

enjoy the fantasy, the audience must be given good reason to root for the hero.

Though Pryor plays it likably enough, he never seems particularly deserving of the fun, excitement and brief luxury he falls into in having to spend $30 million in 30 days, much less the $300 million inheritance he stands to receive if he succeeds.

BRIDE FOR SALE

1949, 87 mins, *Dir* William D. Russell   US

★ *Stars* Claudette Colbert, Robert Young, George Brent, Max Baer, Gus Schilling

Bride for Sale is a lot of escapist nonsense that manages to be generally amusing, and sometimes hilariously so. Screwball angles are played up for laughs, the pacing is good and the playing enjoyable, making it entirely acceptable for light entertainment.

Kingpinning the slapstick are Claudette Colbert, Robert Young and George Brent. Colbert does glib work as a tax expert for the accounting firm conducted by Brent. She figures to find the perfect husband, with suitable bankroll, by casing the returns the firm makes out. Brent wants to keep her on the job so enlists aid of Young to make like an eligible male, and woo the maiden.

On that basis of fun, William D. Russell's direction marches the plot and the players along a broad path of antics.

John Candy (left) and Richard Pryor with **Brewster's** **Millions** *just waiting for them if they spend wisely.*

BRINGING UP BABY

1938, 102 mins, Ⓥ   *Dir* Howard Hawks   US

★ *Stars* Katharine Hepburn, Cary Grant, Charlie Ruggles, Barry Fitzgerald, May Robson, Walter Catlett

This harum-scarum farce comedy, Katharine Hepburn's first of the type, is constructed for maximum of laughs. Opposite her is Cary Grant, who is perfectly at home as a farceur after his work in *The Awful Truth* (1937).

Wacky developments [story by Hagar Wilde] include pursuit by an heiress of a zoology professor who expects to wed his femme assistant in the museum on the same day that he plans to complete a giant brontosaurus; a pet leopard, 'Nissa', who makes a playmate of 'Asta', a redoubtable Scots terrier; a wealthy woman who may endow the professor's museum with $1 million; an escaped wild leopard from the circus; a stupid town constable; a forgetful ex-big game hunter; a scientifically-minded brain specialist; and lastly a tippling gardener.

Hepburn is invigorating as the madcap deb. Grant, who thinks more of recovering the priceless missing bone for his uncompleted brontosaurus than his impending wedding and the companionship of the playful heiress, performs his role to the hilt. Charlie Ruggles, as the former African game hunter, does wonders with a minor characterization brought in late in the picture.

Chief shortcoming is that too much time is consumed with the jail sequence. Prime reason for it, of course, is that it gives Hepburn a chance to imitate a gunmoll.

BROADWAY DANNY ROSE

1984, 86 mins, Ⓥ   *Dir* Woody Allen   US

★ *Stars* Woody Allen, Mia Farrow, Nick Apollo Forte, Milton Berle, Sandy Baron, Corbett Monica

Broadway Danny Rose is a delectable diversion which allows Woody Allen to present a reasonably humane, and amusing gentle character study without sacrificing himself to overly commercial concerns.

Allen is perfect playing the part of a small-time, good-hearted Broadway talent agent, giving his all for a roster of hopeless clients.

Agent's career is fondly recalled here by a group of Catskill comics (all played by themselves) sitting around over coffee, focusing mainly on Allen's attempt to revive the career of an aging, overweight, boozing lounge singer, beautifully played by Nick Apollo Forte.

One of Forte's many problems that Allen must deal with is a floozy of a girlfriend. And it's truly one of the picture's early delights that this sunglassed bimbo is actually on screen for several minutes before most of the audience catches on that she's Mia Farrow.

Through Forte and Farrow, Allen becomes the target of a couple of hit men.

Katharine Hepburn and Cary Grant in **Bringing Up Baby,** *a zany screwball comedy typical of the late Thirties.*

BUCK PRIVATES

1941, 82 mins, Ⓥ   *Dir* Arthur Lubin   US

★ *Stars* Lee Bowman, Alan Curtis, Bud Abbott, Lou Costello, Jane Frazee

Geared at a zippy pace, and providing lusty and enthusiastic comedy of the broadest slapstick, *Buck Privates* is a hilarious laugh concoction. Supplied with a compact script and spontaneous direction by Arthur Lubin, Abbott and Costello have a field day in romping through a lightly frameworked yarn that makes little attempt to be serious or credible. Aiding considerably is the appearance of the Andrews Sisters, who do their regularly competent harmonizing of several tuneful melodies.

Abbott and Costello are inducted into the army and assigned to camp. The madcap and zany antics of Costello are displayed in numerous comedy and knock-about sequences that – although the material is familiar – click for solid laughs through the timing of the gags and situations. There's a light thread of romantic triangle between rich boy, Lee Bowman; comely camp hostess, Jane Frazee; and former chauffeur Alan Curtis.

BUONA SERA, MRS. CAMPBELL

1968, 111 mins, ◇   *Dir* Melvin Frank   ITALY

★ *Stars* Gina Lollobrigida, Shelley Winters, Phil Silvers, Peter Lawford, Telly Savalas, Janet Margolin

Buona Sera, Mrs. Campbell is a very entertaining comedy with solid, personal, human values. Story is about an Italian woman who has conned three American bed partners from World War II into support of her and an illegitimate daughter for more than 20 years.

Gina Lollobrigida, Shelley Winters, Phil Silvers, Peter Lawford, Telly Savalas and Lee Grant head an excellent cast.

Story is economically laid forth: Lollobrigida has fooled her neighbors into believing daughter Janet Margolin was by a deceased US Air Force pilot. However, a reunion of the airmen, in the town where they were based, precipitates a potential crisis, since, in truth, the real father could have been Silvers, Lawford or Savalas.

Performances are strong: Lollobrigida, no comedy actress, is one here. Winters and Grant are great; Silvers and all the others are just right.

THE 'BURBS

1989, 103 mins, ◇ Ⓥ *Dir* Joe Dante   US

★ **Stars** Tom Hanks, Bruce Dern, Carrie Fisher, Rick Ducommun, Corey Feldman

Director Joe Dante funnels his decidedly cracked view of suburban life through dark humour in *The 'Burbs*. The action never strays beyond the cozy confines of the nightmarish block everyman Ray (Tom Hanks) inhabits along with an uproarious assemblage of wacky neighbours.

Poor Ray has a week off and just wants to spend it quietly at home with his wife Carol (Carrie Fisher). Instead, he's drawn into an increasingly elaborate sleuthing game involving the mysterious Klopeks, who reside in a 'Munsters'-esque house rife with indications of foul play.

Ray's more familiar neighbors are equally bizarre: the corpulent Art (Rick Ducommun), convinced the Klopeks are performing satanic sacrifices; Rumsfield (Bruce Dern), a shell-shocked ex-GI; Walter (Gale Gordon), who delights in letting his dog relieve himself on Rumsfield's lawn; and Ricky (Corey Feldman) a teenager who sees all the strange goings-on as viewing fodder for parties with his friends.

Hanks does a fine impersonation of a regular guy on the verge of a nervous breakdown, while Dern adds another memorable psychotic to his resume. The big breakthroughs, however, are Ducommun, superb in his role, and Wendy Schaal as Dern's airhead wife.

Close to the hedge - The 'Burbs exposes the urban jungle behind the picket fences and neat lawns of suburbia.

BUS STOP

1956, 96 mins, ◇ Ⓥ *Dir* Joshua Logan   US

★ **Stars** Marilyn Monroe, Don Murray, Arthur O'Connell, Betty Field, Eileen Heckart, Hope Lange

William Inge's rowdy play about a cowboy and a lady (sic) gets a raucous screen treatment. Both the scripter and director, George Axelrod and Joshua Logan respectively, were brought from the legit field to get the Inge comedy on film and, with a few minor exceptions, bring the chore off resoundingly.

New face Don Murray is the exuberant young cowhand who comes to the city to win some rodeo money and learn about women.

Marilyn Monroe fans will find her s.a. not so positive, but still potent, in her *Bus Stop* character, but this goes with the type of well-used saloon singer and would-be actress she portrays. Monroe comes off acceptably, even though failing to maintain any kind of consistency in the Southern accent.

Murray is a 21-year-old Montana rancher who comes to Phoenix for the rodeo, meets and kisses his first girl and literally kidnaps her. The girl, a 'chantoosie' in a cheap restaurant patronized by rodeo performers, is reluctant about marriage, but by the time Murray ropes her, shouts at her, and gets beat up for her, she gives in, both because love has set in, as well as physical exhaustion.

Arthur O'Connell milks everything from his spot as Murray's friend and watchdog and Betty Field clicks big as the amorous operator of the roadside bus stop.

CACTUS FLOWER

1969, 103 mins, ◇ Ⓥ *Dir* Gene Saks   US

★ **Stars** Walter Matthau, Ingrid Bergman, Goldie Hawn, Jack Weston, Rick Lenz, Vito Scotti

Cactus Flower drags, due to sloppy direction by Gene Saks and the miscasting of Walter Matthau opposite Ingrid Bergman.

The plot is minimal and the lines are somewhat stilted and hollow, but if the direction was tighter and the mood kept light and airy it might have worked.

Matthau is cast as a dentist ready to marry his young mistress who enlists the aid of his stuffy but organized secretary. This too, might have worked had they found a suitable foil for him. Bergman, more believable in her role as the nurse, is too reserved and sophisticated opposite Matthau.

There are some laughs and Goldie Hawn, as the Greenwich Village kook with whom Matthau contemplates marriage, makes a credible screen debut.

Above: *Classic Monroe: Don Murray holds Marilyn aloft in Joshua Logan's rodeo romp* Bus Stop.

Below: *A prickly business - dentist Walter Matthau needles nurse Ingrid Bergman in* Cactus Flower.

CADDYSHACK

1980, 90 mins, ◇ Ⓥ   *Dir* Harold Ramis   US

★ *Stars* Chevy Chase, Rodney Dangerfield, Bill Murray, Michael O'Keefe, Ted Knight

In its unabashed bid for the mammoth audience which responded to the anti-establishment outrageousness of *National Lampoon's Animal House*, this vaguely likable, too-tame comedy falls short of the mark.

This time, the thinly plotted shenanigans unfold against the manicured lawns and posh backdrop of a restricted country club, generally pitting the free-living youthful caddies against the uptight gentry who employ them.

Stock characters include Chevy Chase as resident golf-pro; club prexy and jurist Ted Knight; and Rodney Dangerfield as the perfectly cast and very funny personification of antisocial, nouveau riche grossness.

Beyond Chase, prime lure is Bill Murray as a foul-habited, semi-moronic groundskeeper, constantly aroused by the older femme golfers.

CALIFORNIA SPLIT

1974, 108 mins, ◇ ⓥ *Dir* Robert Altman   US

★ *Stars* George Segal, Elliott Gould, Ann Prentiss, Gwen Welles, Edward Walsh, Joseph Walsh

California Split is an aimless, strung-out series of vignettes starring George Segal and Elliott Gould as compulsive gamblers. The film is technically and physically handsome, all the more so for being mostly location work, but lacks a cohesive and reinforced sense of story direction.

The pic is well cast – Segal and Gould contrast well, while Ann Prentiss and Gwen Welles play happy hookers to good effect. Bert Remsen, an Altman stock player, herein does a drag number. Edward Walsh (the writer's father) is very good as a mean poker adversary, and the writer himself has a good scene as Segal's loan shark.

CALIFORNIA SUITE

1978, 103 mins, ◇ ⓥ *Dir* Herbert Ross   US

★ *Stars* Alan Alda, Michael Caine, Bill Cosby, Jane Fonda, Walter Matthau, Elaine May

Neil Simon and Herbert Ross have gambled in radically altering the successful format of *California Suite* as it appeared on stage. Instead of four separate playlets, there is now one semi-cohesive narrative revolving around visitors to the Beverly Hills Hotel.

Alan Alda and Jane Fonda portray a divorced couple wrangling over possession of their child, while Michael Caine and Maggie Smith play a showbiz couple with varying sexual tastes holed up at the Bev-Hills prior to the Academy Awards. Walter Matthau has to explain his unwitting infidelity to spouse Elaine May in a third segment, and Richard Pryor and Bill Cosby, accompanied by their wives (Gloria Gifford and Sheila Frazier), manage to turn a vacation into a series of disastrous mishaps.

Walter Matthau seeks the help of a higher authority amid the hotel hokum of **California Suite.**

Ross and Simon have set up as counterpoint to the more tragicomic episodes (those involved Alda and Fonda, and Caine and Smith) some farcical moments around Matthau and blitzed floozy Denise Galik, along with the Pryor-Cosby shenanigans. The technique is less than successful, veering from poignant emotionalism to broad slapstick in sudden shifts.

Fonda demonstrates yet another aspect of her amazing range, although her brittle quips with Alda seem very stage-bound. Smith and Caine interplay wonderfully, as do Pryor and Cosby. The latter duo get the worst break, however, as their seg is chopped up, spread around and generally given short shrift.

CALL ME BWANA

1963, 93 mins, ◇ *Dir* Gordon Douglas   UK

★ *Stars* Bob Hope, Anita Ekberg, Edie Adams, Lionel Jeffries, Percy Herbert

Bob Hope's gags are tossed off in his usual slick fashion. And a great number of them are slyly but pointedly directed at Anita Ekberg's stimulating sculpture. The visual situations and incidents need spacing out a little more but they invariably crop up just in time to disguise the occasional repetition of plot.

Hope has built up a phoney reputation as an intrepid explorer of the jungles of Darkest Africa, by writing successful books based on old, secret diaries of his uncle. Actually, the nearest the timid character has ever been to Africa is to visit his aunt in Cape Cod. When an American moon-probe capsule is lost in the jungle and it's necessary to locate it before foreign powers get their thieving mitts on it, Hope is detailed for the task because of his supposed expert knowledge of the locale.

Overall, there's enough fun to keep this bubbling along merrily. There is Hope going through bravery tests to escape the native tribe, getting mixed up with a rogue elephant, a lion in his tub, having his pants repaired by Ekberg while he's wearing 'em (and with the poisoned needle from his suicide kit), and eventually becoming airborne in the moon-capsule.

Though most of the responsibility falls on Hope and his personality, Edie Adams gives a pleasantly unobtrusive performance and La Ekberg, though an unlikely Mata Hari, is a sound and decorative foil for Hope. Only the most fastidious carper will protest that the jungle often reeks of Pinewood Studio.

CAN SHE BAKE A CHERRY PIE?

1983, 90 mins, ◇ ⓥ *Dir* Henry Jaglom   US

★ *Stars* Karen Black, Michael Emil, Michael Margotta, Frances Fisher, Martin Frydberg

Henry Jaglom follows his *Sitting Ducks* [1981] with a similar opus. This is once again a talky comedy, in which the scripter-director puts his characters in a number of sitcom situations, feeds them the opening lines of their scenes and lets them embroider the rest on their own.

Starting from the basic premise that human beings suffer from their inability to communicate with their fellow men, Jaglom builds up a romance of sorts between a fresh divorcee who is still not emotionally rid of her husband, and a man who has been living on his own for some years.

Characters are built very much around the personality of the two main actors, Karen Black giving a beautiful performance, humorous, edgy, nervous and implying deep fears and pains hidden barely under the surface, and Michael Emil brings back many of the peculiarities of his part in *Sitting Ducks*.

CARBON COPY

1981, 92 mins, ◇ *Dir* Michael Schultz   US

★ **Stars** George Segal, Susan Saint James, Denzel Washington, Jack Warden, Paul Winfield, Dick Martin

Carbon Copy is a comedy which attempts to deal with racial issues much in the way that *Watermelon Man* did. This time the story is rooted in reality. *Carbon Copy* has business executive George Segal faced with the arrival of a long-lost and heretofore unknown son whom he describes as 'Hickory Bronze.'

Segal attempts to pass off son Denzel Washington as a social experiment in his all-white suburb, but paternal instincts force him to reveal the truth to his straight-laced wife Susan Saint James. Abruptly, he loses his job, credit cards and Saint James throws him out of the house.

Suddenly, without allies, Segal is forced to accept the lot of the racial minorities. Cut off from his money and powerful contacts, he accepts manual labor jobs and begins to experiment and appreciate the lot of his son. The Segal character, a Jew, could hide behind a name, but his son can't adopt a new color.

Segal is particularly effective as he begins to realize just how complacent he is under his liberal values.

Carbon Copy is admittedly a fairytale, just as the Capra films of the 1930s were. However, director Michael Schultz maintains a convincing balance between the film's broad humor and its genuinely poignant moments.

CAREER OPPORTUNITIES

1991, 85 mins, ◇ ▼ *Dir* Bryan Gordon   US

★ **Stars** Frank Whaley, Jennifer Connelly, Dermot Mulroney, Kieran Mulroney, Barry Corbin, John Candy

Writer-producer John Hughes' followup to *Home Alone* lacks the spit-polish and magic of the blockbuster but still has plenty of absorbing characters, smart, snappy dialog and delightful stretches of comic foolery.

Like *Home Alone*, story has a young man on his own to defend a fortress against bungling burglars, but in this case he's a 21-year-old trapped in a job he hates (night janitor at a discount store) and pitted against gun-toting hoods out to clean out, not clean up, the store.

Jim (Frank Whaley) is a ne'er-do-well fast talker and nonstop liar bounced from as many deadend jobs as his humble hometown of Munroe, Ill, has to offer. He's been given his last chance to succeed by his blue-collar father – or get kicked out of the house.

That's when he discovers he's not alone. Darkly voluptuous Josie (Jennifer Connelly), princess daughter of the town land baron, is locked in after falling asleep during a shoplifting spree.

Trapped together, the misfits discover each other, and, in the type of scenes Hughes writes best, sort out their differences and common ground from their horrifying high school years. But the guntoting hoods (Dermot and Kieran Mulroney) show up and they must turn their specialties to more immediate escape.

CARLTON-BROWNE OF THE F.O.

1959, 87 mins, ▼ *Dir* Jeffrey Dell, Roy Boulting   UK

★ **Stars** Terry-Thomas, Peter Sellers, Luciana Paoluzzi, Thorley Walters, Ian Bannen, Raymond Huntley

The F.O. in the title stands for Foreign Office and the film is a crazy peck at the indiscretions of foreign diplomacy. Much of the dialog is brilliantly witty. There are some excellent situations and some first-class prods at dignity. But the comedy tends to get out of hand and, at times, develops merely into a series of not totally relevant sketches.

The pic concerns the mishaps that happen to a Foreign Office junior official when an ex-colony of Britain's – Gaillardia – becomes news. Rich mineral deposits are indicated on the tiny island. Learning that other Great Powers are sniffing around the island, Carlton-Browne (Terry-Thomas) is dispatched to sort things out. Peter Sellers plays the Gaillardian blackguard of a prime minister with relish. But the Sellers personality tends to throw the part off-balance.

Best of the major performances come from Raymond Huntley, as a pompous Foreign Office minister, and Ian Bannen, who, as the young king suddenly brought to the throne, brings a most engaging charm and humor to his role.

CARRY ON CLEO

1964, 92 mins, ◇ ▼ *Dir* Gerald Thomas   US

★ **Stars** Sidney James, Kenneth Williams, Kenneth Connor, Charles Hawtrey, Joan Sims, Amanda Barrie

Intended as a parody of the expensive *Cleopatra*, this entry from the *Carry On* stables relies on the bludgeon rather than the rapier, so isn't entirely successful in its purpose.

Accent in this frolic is less on situation than on dialog and so there is less action to hold the audience. Talbot Rothwell's dialog is unabashedly corny but this doesn't much

Hengist (Kenneth Connor) and Caesar (Kenneth Williams) meet Cleopatra (Amanda Barrie) in Carry On Cleo.

matter. But it is also unusually bristling with plodding double entendres. Gags, both verbal and visual, suffer from repetition and few are as neat as Julius Caesar's woeful complaint, 'Infamy! Infamy! Everybody's got it in for me!'

The practised cast of Old Regulars are also, mainly, up to form, with Sidney James as Mark Anthony and Kenneth Connor as Hengist the Wheelmaker particularly prominent as they disport among the vestal virgins. Kenneth Williams has a few twittering moments as Caesar but again irritatingly overplays. Charles Hawtrey's main function is to look incongruous and carry the weight of some of the least subtle sex patter.

On the femme side, Joan Sims is a hearty gal as Caesar's wife, Sheila Hancock is a shrill one as Hengist's spouse. Best discovery is Amanda Barrie as the poor man's Cleopatra. Her takeoff of the Queen of the Nile gets nearer to the tongue-in-cheek sense of what filmmakers were aiming at than any of her more experienced colleagues.

CARRY ON DOCTOR

1968, 95 mins, ◇ ⑰ *Dir* Gerald Thomas   UK

★ *Stars* Frankie Howerd, Sidney James, Kenneth Williams, Charles Hawtrey, Jim Dale, Barbara Windsor

Usual unabashed mixture of double meanings, down-to-earth vulgarity, blue jokes about hypodermic syringes, etc., and slapstick situations. This time the Carry On team returns to hospital life for its farcical goings-on.

Inevitably, the gags and situations waver in comic impact but the general effect is artless yocks in which audience participation is carried to fullest extent, in that part of the fun is anticipating the verbal and physical jokes.

Added zest is given by the inclusion of Frankie Howerd as a quack 'mind-over-matter' doctor who becomes a reluctant patient. Howerd's brilliantly droll sense of comedy is given plenty of scope.

Among the grotesque patients are Sidney James, very funny as a cheerful malingerer; Bernard Bresslaw, Charles Hawtrey (more subdued than usual) and Peter Butterworth. The hospital staff is equally energetic and resourceful in providing simple-minded yocks, with Kenneth Williams as a supercilious chief physician.

CARRY ON, SERGEANT

1958, 85 mins, ⑰ *Dir* Gerald Thomas   UK

★ *Stars* William Hartnell, Bob Monkhouse, Shirley Eaton, Eric Barker, Dora Bryan, Kenneth Connor

Carry On, Sergeant is an army farce [from a story by R.F. Delderfield, *The Bull Boys*] exploiting practically every army gag, but while some of the writing is careless and there is no attempt to develop a reasonable story, it is by no means sloppily produced.

William Hartnell is a training sergeant who is about to retire from the service and has one more chance to fulfill his life ambition, which is to train the champion troop of the intake. Moreover, he has a $140 bet on the outcome. He is handed a bunch of rookies which is believable only in farce. The barrack-room attorney, the young man in love, the hypochondriac malingerer, the man always out of step . . . in fact, the repertory company of trainees. There's the sergeant with the bark, the fussy officer.

Kenneth Connor steals most of the honors as the hypochondriac being chased by a love-starved army waitress, played characteristically by Dora Bryan. He has a shade too much to do, but never misses a trick. Bob Monkhouse, called up on his wedding day, Shirley Eaton as his frustrated wife who crops up in camp, Eric Barker as a fussy officer, William Hartnell as the gravelly-voiced sergeant and Bill Owen as his faithful corporal add their quota.

CARRY ON SPYING

1964, 87 mins, *Dir* Gerald Thomas   UK

★ *Stars* Kenneth Williams, Bernard Cribbins, Charles Hawtrey, Barbara Windsor, Eric Pohlmann, Eric Barker

---

The Society for Total Extinction of Non-Conforming Humans (STENCH for short) has grabbed a secret formula and the British Operational Security Headquarters (BOSH in brief) tackles the job of getting back Formula X and outwitting its arch-enemy, Doctor Crow. Through shortage of personnel, the assignment is handed to Simkins (Kenneth Williams), an agent in charge of training new spies, and three of his pupils.

Best knockabout sequences take place on the Orient Express, in a Viennese restaurant, a murky quarter of the Casbah and in the Automatum Plant where the inept foursome nearly come to a sticky end, but are rescued by good luck and the intervention of a beautiful spy.

Kenneth Williams' brand of camp comedy, while very funny in smallish doses, can pall when he has a lengthy chore as here. But Bernard Cribbins brings some useful virility to his fatuous role, Charles Hawtrey contributes his now familiar performance as the guileless one and Barbara Windsor proves a well-upholstered and perky heroine as the girl spy with a photogenic memory.

CAR WASH

1976, 97 mins, ◇ ⊕ *Dir* Michael Schultz   US

★ *Stars* Franklyn Ajaye, Sully Boyar, Richard Brestoff, George Carlin, Irwin Corey, Ivan Dixon

---

Car Wash uses gritty humor to polish clean the souls of a lot of likable street people.

The setting is Sully Boyar's downtown car wash,

where the colorful ethnic crew contends as much with oddball customers as with themselves.

Perhaps the best known of the players is Richard Pryor, shining it on as a fancy-dressed preacher, complete with flashy car and retinue that includes The Pointer Sisters. Pryor's license plate spells out 'tithe', a sure evocation of the real-life character he suggests.

Woven into the main proceedings is the lonely sidewalk vigil of a streetwalker, Lauren Jones, which, combined with Bill Duke's equally sensitive portrayal of a frightened black militant, keeps the film in fine balance of humanism.

CASINO ROYALE

1967, 131 mins, ◇ ⊛ *Dir* John Huston, Ken Hughes, Val Guest, Robert Parrish, Joe McGrath   UK

★ *Stars* Peter Sellers, Ursula Andress, David Niven, Orson Welles, Woody Allen, William Holden

---

Wacky comedy extravaganza, *Casino Royale* is an attempt to spoof the pants off James Bond. The $12 million film is a conglomeration of frenzied situations, gags and special effects, lacking discipline and cohesion. Some of the situations are very funny, but many are too strained.

Based freely on Ian Fleming's novel, the story line defies sane description. Sufficient to say that the original James Bond (David Niven), now knighted and living in eccentric retirement, is persuaded back into the Secret Service to help cope with a disastrous situation.

Niven seems justifiably bewildered by the proceedings, but he has a neat delivery of throwaway lines and enters into the exuberant physical action with pleasant blandness. Peter Sellers has some amusing gags as the gambler, the chance of dressing up in various guises and a neat near-seduction scene with Ursula Andress.

CHARLEY'S AUNT

1941, 90 mins, *Dir* Archie Mayo   US

★ *Stars* Jack Benny, Kay Francis, Anne Baxter, Edmund Gwenn, Richard Haydn, James Ellison

---

Like Niagara Falls, *Charley's Aunt* stands the test of time. Jack Benny playing with enthusiasm and romping merrily and crazily along the route, takes fullest advantage of laugh opportunities.

Under expert direction of Archie Mayo, there's no letdown in the fast pace maintained for rollicking results. Many situations are double-barrelled for laughs – first when the audience is given advance tipoff on what's going to happen; and a roar when it actually occurs. Only deft timing by both director and comedian can achieve that result, and the Benny-Mayo team works in perfect synchronization.

Picture closely follows the stage farce [by Brandon Thomas] in unfoldment, carrying Oxford background of 1890. Perennial student Benny is forced to masquerade as

Charley's rich aunt from Brazil to provide chaperonage while Charley (Richard Haydn) and James Ellison have their girl friends for lunch and marriage proposals. The old-fashioned female getup tosses Benny into a series of complications that fall on him in torrents.

THE CHEAP DETECTIVE

1978, 92 mins, ◇ ⑦   *Dir* Robert Moore   US

★ **Stars** Peter Falk, Ann-Margret, Eileen Brennan, Sid Caesar, Stockard Channing, James Coco

The Cheap Detective, which might also be called *Son Of Casablanca*, is a hilarious and loving takeoff on all 1940s Warner Bros private eye and foreign intrigue mellers.

The time is 1940, San Francisco, where clumsy gumshoe Peter Falk is accused of murdering his partner, whose wife Marsha Mason (in early Janet Leigh curls) has been Falk's mistress. Detective Vic Tayback and assistants regularly blunder into matters.

Madeline Kahn, with as many smart clothes changes as she has aliases, appears in Falk's office. She's in league with John Houseman (Sydney Greenstreet to the core), Paul Williams (Elisha Cook Jr was never like this) and Dom DeLuise (a fat Peter Lorre) in search of ancient treasure – a dozen diamond eggs.

Amidst the confusing threads of mystery, Falk is regularly affronted by the overly explicit descriptions of sexual torture inflicted on all the dames. But at fadeout he's got a lot more going for him than Bogart did in the final dissolve.

A CHUMP AT OXFORD

1940, 63 mins,   *Dir* Alfred Goulding   US

★ **Stars** Stan Laurel, Oliver Hardy, James Finlayson, Forrester Harvey, Peter Cushing, Sam Lufkin

Stan Laurel and Oliver Hardy's farce is mildly comical without offending. Time-worn gags clutter up the earlier footage and only when Laurel and Hardy, as new initiates into Oxford, actually move into the dean's home does the action speed up.

Early episodes have Laurel as a maid and Oliver Hardy as butler in a rich man's home. It looks as though it had been tacked on in order to make up footage. James Finlayson is the wealthy host in this episode but not given any cast credit.

A dinner party brings in all the familiar dress-tearing, pastry-flinging, corkpopping and shot-gun gags. Even that venerable nifty where the cop says 'you are liable to blow my brains out' and then exhibits the bullet-marked seat of his trousers is left in.

But once the comedians land in England they fare better. Outside of the lost-in-the-woods stunt and ghost-at-midnight routine, the gagging and all-round material brightens up here considerably.

CITIZENS BAND

1977, 98 mins, ◇ ⑦   *Dir* Jonathon Demme   US

★ **Stars** Paul Le Mat, Candy Clark, Ann Wedgeworth, Bruce McGill, Marcia Rodd, Charles Napier

Plot peg is the truck accident of philandering husband Charles Napier, who's got Ann Wedgeworth in Dallas and Marcia Rodd in Portland, both with homes and children.

While he is recovering at the hands of Alix Elias (whose charms are mobile), the two suspicious women arrive in a small town where Paul Le Mat and estranged brother Bruce McGill are both courting Candy Clark. Roberts Blossom is the boy's irascible widower-father. Linking all their lives is the CB radio, buzzing away like a verbal Muzak.

The CB dialog exemplifies the good-natured horsing around that marks those channels, at the same time the serious emergency traffic that often saves lives.

CITY SLICKERS

1991, 112 mins, ◇ ⑦   *Dir* Ron Underwood   US

★ **Stars** Billy Crystal, Daniel Stern, Bruno Kirby, Patricia Wettig, Helen Slater, Jack Palance

The setup is sheer simplicity, as Billy Crystal, coming to grips with the doldrums of midlife thanks to his 39th birthday, is convinced by his wife (Patricia Wettig) and two best friends (Daniel Stern, Bruno Kirby) to take off for two weeks on a ranch driving cattle across the west.

The childhood fantasy comes to life in a number of ways, perhaps foremost in the presence of gnarled trail boss

Card-punchers turned cow-punchers, Billy Crystal and his fellow greenhorns go west in City Slickers.

Curly (Jack Palance), a figure always seemingly backlit in larger-than-life silhouettes.

The other cowboy wannabes include a father-and-son dentist team (Bill Henderson, Phill Lewis), fraternal ice-cream tycoons (David Paymer, Josh Mostel), a beautiful woman (Bonnie Rayburn) who braved the trip on her own. A series of increasingly absurd events lead the central trio toward an ultimate challenge that turns the vacation into a journey of self-discovery.

Crystal gets plenty of chance to crack wise while he, Stern and Kirby engage in playful and not-so-playful banter – Stern coming off a recently (and publicly) failed marriage while the womanizing Kirby grapples with his own fear of fidelity. Director Ron Underwood (who made his feature debut on *Tremors*) generally keeps the herd moving at a fine pace.

CLOCKWISE

1986, 97 mins, ◇ Ⓥ *Dir* Christopher Morahan   UK

★ *Stars* John Cleese, Alison Steadman, Penelope Wilton, Stephen Moore, Joan Hickson, Sharon Maiden

Clockwise is a somewhat uneven comic road film. John Cleese plays the headmaster of a secondary school whose main trait, obsessive timewatching, turns out to be a strategy to dam up the natural disarray of his personality.

Film's plot is triggered when Stimpson (Cleese) misses the train for a headmaster's conference over which he has

Clock-watching school chief John Cleese in the British black comedy Clockwise.

been invited to preside. Immediately panic-struck, he seeks some other way to get to the meeting on time.

The best moments depict his gradually going to pieces as he struggles to complete his journey in the company of an abducted schoolgirl (Sharon Maiden) and former girlfriend (Penelope Wilton).

Clockwise would be a bore were it not for Cleese's comic ability, which derives from broad expressive gesticulations and expressions which mark the simple man still trying to control his world long after he has gone over the edge. Christopher Morahan's direction, in his first feature since the late 1960s, is adequate.

COMING TO AMERICA

1988, 116 mins, ◇ Ⓥ *Dir* John Landis   US

★ *Stars* Eddie Murphy, Arsenio Hall, John Amos, James Earl Jones, Shari Headley, Eriq LaSalle

Coming to America starts on a bathroom joke, quickly followed by a gag about private parts, then wanders in search of something equally original for Eddie Murphy to do for another couple of hours. It's a true test for loyal fans.

Murphy has no difficulty creating a pampered young prince of Zamunda who would like a chance to live a little real life and select his own bride instead of being forced into a royal marriage of convenience. Murphy even makes the prince sympathetic and genuine, complete to his stilted English. He and courtly sidekick Arsenio Hall venture to Queens to find a queen.

Longing for someone to love him for himself, Murphy discovers beautiful Shari Headley and goes to work mopping

Eddie Murphy (left), with Arsenio Hall, is an African aristocrat looking for a bride in Coming to America.

floors in father's hamburger emporium to be near her.

She, no surprise, already has a well-to-do, insufferable boyfriend (Eriq LaSalle) that dad is anxious for her to marry. How does a janitor capture the heart of such a maiden?

A CONNECTICUT YANKEE

1931, 93 mins, *Dir* David Butler   US

★ *Stars* Will Rogers, William Farnum, Myrna Loy, Maureen O'Sullivan, Frank Albertson, Mitchell Harris

The [Mark Twain] story was originally turned down by Doug Fairbanks, after which Fox made it with Harry Myers. It was released late in 1920. The staff working on this sound version must have run off the silent print plenty. William Conselman gets the credit for the modern adaptation, but there's no telling how many writers worked on the script. Neither the beginning nor the end is entirely satisfactory, especially the finish. But the main section is a dream, and there are more than sufficient laughs to compensate.

Opening has Will Rogers as a smalltown radio store proprietor, called to a mysterious house to install a battery. An armored figure falls over, knocks Rogers out and thence into the dream. The change back to the modern story and finish is decidedly weak.

Rogers' main cast support comes from William Farnum as King Arthur. Mitchell Harris as Merlin, the magician, and Brandon Hurst playing the menace. Myrna Loy does not do much with her femme heavy, while Maureen O'Sullivan has nothing much more than a bit. Frank Albertson, supplying the other half of the love interest, appears to be at a loss in not being able to chatter at his generally furious rate.

COOKIE

1989, 93 mins, ◇ Ⓥ *Dir* Susan Seidelman   US

★ *Stars* Peter Falk, Dianne Wiest, Emily Lloyd, Michael V. Gazzo, Brenda Vaccaro

Half-baked, bland and flat as a vanilla wafer, *Cookie* rolls out the tired marriage of comedy and organized crime to produce a disorganized mess with little nutritional or comedic value.

The story gets set in motion, such as it is, when mobster Dino Capisco (Peter Falk) is released from prison after 13 years, rejoining his wife (Brenda Vaccaro), mistress (Dianne Wiest) and the headstrong daughter he had with the latter, played by Emily Lloyd.

Sadly, about the only thing Lloyd gets to do here is prove she can affect a New York accent and chew gum at the same time. Thrown together with Falk as his driver, the two fail to build any of the warmth or even grudging admiration they display in the final reel.

The film ultimately turns into an elaborate scheme by which Falk can get even with his treacherous former partner (played by Michael V. Gazzo), and the payoff is hardly worth the protracted build-up.

Only Dianne Wiest emerges in top form with her brassy portrayal of a weepy red-haired gun moll in the Lucille Ball mode.

THE COUCH TRIP

1988, 98 mins, ◇ Ⓥ *Dir* Michael Ritchie   US

★ *Stars* Dan Aykroyd, Walter Matthau, Charles Grodin, Donna Dixon, Richard Romanus

The Couch Trip is a relatively low-key Dan Aykroyd vehicle that restores some of the comic actor's earlier charm simply by not trying too hard. Relying as much on character as shtick, Aykroyd is a likable everyman here out to right the minor indignities and injustices in the world.

As an obstreperous prisoner biding his time in a Cicero, Ill, loony bin, Aykroyd trades places with his attending shrink, Dr Baird (David Clennon), and moves to LA to fill in for radio therapist Dr Maitlin (Charles Grodin) who is having a mental breakdown of his own.

Screenplay [from the novel by Ken Kolb] doesn't break any new ground in suggesting that there is a thin line between the certifiably crazy and the certifiably sane, but it still manages some gentle jabs at the pretensions of the psychiatric profession.

As a mock priest and another fringe member of society, Walter Matthau is Aykroyd's soulmate, but the connection between the men is too thinly drawn to have much meaning. Donna Dixon, stunningly beautiful though she is, is impossible to swallow as a brilliant psychiatrist, particularly since her duties include signaling commercial breaks on radio and standing around posing.

Welcome to the madhouse! Mental patient Dan Aykroyd joins the crazy world of radio in **The Couch Trip.**

COUSINS

1989, 110 mins, ◇ ⓥ *Dir* Joel Schumacher   US

★ *Stars* Ted Danson, Isabella Rossellini, Sean Young, William Petersen, Lloyd Bridges, Norma Aleandro

As derivative as it is, *Cousins* still is a hugely entertaining Americanized version of the French film *Cousin, cousine*, with nearly the same insouciant tone as the Jean-Charles Tacchella comedy of 1975. It's been spiced with a dash of 1980s social commentary and a dollop of Italian ethnic flavoring.

Isabella Rossellini and Ted Danson's sappy, overly sentimental series of rendezvous are well compensated by their relatives' caustic comments, irreverent asides and other antics at the three weddings, one funeral and other functions all attend during the course of the picture.

Object of most of the ridicule is William Petersen, the unctuous BMW car salesman and Don Juan pretender who starts everything off in the opening wedding scene drooling at Danson's flamboyantly dressed wife (Sean Young).

It's obvious enough that Rossellini, the martyred Madonna type who knows of her husband's philandering, represents prudishness and purity as much as Young, dressed in outlandish high-fashion ruffles of red and black, represents the opposite.

What's most fun is to get everyone else's thoughts on the matter. There's Rossellini's wealthy mother Edie (Norma Aleandro), cranky old Aunt Sofia (Gina De Angelis) and Danson's son Mitchell (Keith Coogan), who has a penchant for videotaping family gatherings.

Best of all is Lloyd Bridges, Danson's irascible, sporting uncle, who has as much pep in his step and gleam in his eye for Aleandro as the two main couples have combined.

CRAZY PEOPLE

1990, 90 mins, ◇ ⓥ *Dir* Tony Bill   US

★ *Stars* Dudley Moore, Daryl Hannah, Paul Reiser, Mercedes Ruehl, J.T. Walsh, David Paymer

Crazy People combines a hilarious dissection of advertising with a warm view of so-called insanity. Pic had a rocky production history as two weeks into lensing John Malkovich was replaced by Dudley Moore, and screenwriter Mitch Markowitz ceded his directing chair to Tony Bill. Finished film is a credit to all hands.

Moore toplines as a burnt-out ad man working with fast-talking Paul Reiser (perfect as a type commonplace in business) for a tyranical boss, J.T. Walsh. Under deadline pressure, he turns in campaigns that attempt a more honest approach.

This raises more than eyebrows, but when Moore hands in 'Most of our passengers get there alive' to promote United Air Lines, the film jumpcuts emphatically to Bennington Sanitarium, his new home.

Director Bill envisions this looney bin as an idyllic retreat, with a natural, warm and beautiful Daryl Hannah as Moore's nutty playmate there. The visual mismatch (she towers over the diminutive star) pays off.

Markowitz's ingenious twists overcome the gag-driven nature of the film. Moore's oddball ads accidentally get printed and create a consumer rush. Walsh hires Moore back and soon the inmates are virtually running the asylum.

'CROCODILE' DUNDEE

1986, 102 mins, ◇ ⓥ *Dir* Peter Faiman   AUSTRALIA

★ *Stars* Paul Hogan, Linda Kozlowski, John Meillon, Mark Blom, Michael Lombard, David Gulpilil

As the title character, Paul Hogan limns a laconic if rather dim Australian crocodile hunter who achieves some notoriety after surviving an attack by a giant croc. New York reporter Linda Kozlowski journeys to the Northern Territory to cover the story.

Plot bogs down somewhat as Hogan and Kozlowski trudge through the outback. However, proceedings are intermittently enlivened by John Meillon who is slyly humorous as Dundee's manager and partner in a safari tour business.

Rather implausibly, Kozlowski persuades Hogan to return to Gotham with her. Here he is initiated into the delights of the Big Apple.

Director Peter Faiman, essaying his first theatrical venture after an impressive career in Australian TV, directing Hogan's shows among others, has problems with the pacing and a script that has its flat, dull spots.

Hogan is comfortable enough playing the wry, irreverent, amiable Aussie that seems close to his own persona, and teams well with Kozlowski, who radiates lots of charm, style and spunk.

CROCODILE DUNDEE ⑮

Aussie TV comic Paul Hogan turns on his animal charm in the outback-to-America caper 'Crocodile' Dundee.

'CROCODILE' DUNDEE II

1988, 111 mins, ◇ ⑰   *Dir* John Cornell   US

★ **Stars** Paul Hogan, Linda Kozlowski, Charles Dutton, Hechter Ubarry

'Crocodile' Dundee II is a disappointing followup to the disarmingly charming first feature with Aussie star Paul Hogan. Sequel is too slow to constitute an adventure and has too few laughs to be a comedy.

Story unfolds with Hogan making a passable attempt to find gainful employment at just about the time Linda Kozlowski's ex-lover is killed in Colombia for taking photos of a cocaine king as he shoots one of his runners. The nefarious Rico (Hechter Ubarry is much too cute for this role) learns the photos were sent to Kozlowski and in a flash he sets up an operation in a Long Island fortress with a handful of stereotypical Latino henchmen to get the incriminating evidence back. Hogan has the photos, which means Rico has Kozlowski kidnaped.

Using outback strategy, that is, getting the punks to yelp like a pack of wild dogs, Hogan gains entrance and frees his woman. Kozlowski basically does little but wait at the sidelines as Hogan flies into action.

CROSSING DELANCEY

1988, 97 mins, ◇ ⑰   *Dir* Joan Micklin Silver   US

★ **Stars** Amy Irving, Reizl Bozyk, Peter Riegert, Jeroen Krabbe, Sylvia Miles

In an unexpectedly enjoyable way, *Crossing Delancey* addresses one of the great societal issues of our day – the dilemma of how the 30-ish, attractive, successful, intelligent and unmarried female finds a mate she can be happy with.

Off-off-Broadway fans may remember the title from playwright Susan Sandler's semi-autobiographical 1985 comedy about how her loving, old-worldly and slightly overbearing Lower East Side NY Jewish grandmother engages the services of a matchmaker to find her a suitable marriage partner.

Amy Irving is the dutiful granddaughter who works in a pretentious Manhattan bookstore by day, keeps her own apartment and always finds time to make frequent visits to her precious Bubbie (Yiddish actress Reizl Bozyk).

Matchmaker (Sylvia Miles) brings Irving together with an unlikely candidate, pickle maker Sam Posner (Peter Riegert). The major set-ups focus on Irving's torn affections between the rakish, smooth-talking charm of pulp novelist Anton Maes (Jeroen Krabbe), who gives good readings on rainy days at the bookstore, and earnest, straight-forward, vulnerable Riegert, who unabashedly holds his heart in his hand for her. To the credit of most of the actors, the sentimentality doesn't sink the story.

CURSE OF THE PINK PANTHER

1983, 109 mins, ◇ Ⓥ *Dir* Blake Edwards   UK

★ *Stars* Ted Wass, David Niven, Robert Wagner, Herbert Lom, Capucine, Roger Moore

The eighth in the hit comedy series, *Curse of the Pink Panther* resembles a set of gems mounted in a tarnished setting. Abetted by screen newcomer Ted Wass' flair for physical comedy, filmmaker Blake Edwards has created genuinely funny sight gags but the film's rickety, old-hat story values waste them.

Lensed simultaneously with *Trail of the Pink Panther*, *Curse* boasts all-new footage but virtually repeats the prior release's storyline. Instead of a newshen tracking down the missing Inspector Clouseau, this time Interpol's Huxley 600 computer (an uppity machine named Aldous) is secretly programmed by Clouseau's boss (Herbert Lom) to select the world's worst detective to search for his unwanted employee.

NY cop Clifton Sleigh (Ted Wass) is the bumbling man for the job, simultaneously trying to discover who has stolen (again) the Pink Panther diamond. As with *Trail*, format has him encountering and interviewing characters from earlier films in the series.

Guest stars David Niven (in his final film appearance), Robert Wagner and Capucine have little to do, while pert British blonde Leslie Ash is briefly impressive as a lethally-kicking martial arts partner for Wass.

A DAY AT THE RACES

1937, 100 mins, Ⓥ *Dir* Sam Wood   US

★ *Stars* Groucho Marx, Chico Marx, Harpo Marx, Allan Jones, Maureen O'Sullivan, Margaret Dumont

Surefire film fun and up to the usual parity of the madcap Marxes, even though a bit hectic in striving for jolly moments and bright quips.

Day at the Races is the picture which the late Irving Thalberg started and Max Siegel, Sam Harris' former legit production associate, completed as his initial Hollywood chore at Metro.

Obviously painstaking is the racehorse code-book sequence, a deft switch on the money-changing bit; the long-distance telephoning between the horse doctor (Groucho) and the light-heavy; the midnight rendezvous business between Groucho and Esther Muir, including the paper-handing slapstickery; the orchestra pit hokum, which permits the standard virtuosity by Chico at the Steinway and Harpo at the harp, including a very funny breakaway piano.

Allan Jones and Maureen O'Sullivan sustain the romance and Jones gets his baritone opportunities during a water carnival which is cameraed in light brown sepia.

Esther Muir is a good foil, topped only by Margaret Dumont as the moneyed Mrs Upjohn, who is stuck on Groucho and stands for much of his romantic duplicity, even unto paying off the mortgage on the sanatorium owned by O'Sullivan.

DEAD MEN DON'T WEAR PLAID

1982, 89 mins, Ⓥ *Dir* Carl Reiner   US

★ *Stars* Steve Martin, Rachel Ward, Reni Santoni, Carl Reiner, George Gaynes, Frank McCarthy

Lensed in black-and-white and outfitted with a 'straight' mystery score by Miklos Rozsa and authentic 1940s costumes by Edith Head, this spoof of film noir detective yarns sees Steve Martin interacting with 18 Hollywood greats by way of intercutting of clips from some 17 old pictures.

Thus, when sultry, Rachel Ward enters his seedy LA office to discuss her father's murder, $10-per-day sleuth Martin is able to call Bogart's Philip Marlowe for assistance on the case. And so it goes with such additional tough guys as Burt Lancaster, Kirk Douglas and Edward Arnold and such dames as Barbara Stanwyck, Ingrid Bergman, Veronica Lake, Bette Davis, Lana Turner and Joan Crawford.

Film is most engaging in its romantic sparring between Martin and his gorgeous client, Ward. Latter looks sensational in period garb and is not above such Martinesque gags as

Steve Martin as a Marlowesque sleuth in a spoof homage to the Forties whodunnit **Dead Men Don't Wear Plaid.**

removing bullets from his wounds with her teeth or having her breasts 'rearranged' by the hardboiled detective.

Sporting dark hair and facetious confidence, Martin also looks spiffy in trenchcoat and hat. Only other roles of note see Carl Reiner essentially essaying Otto Preminger as a Nazi, and Reni Santoni as a zealous Peruvian officer.

DESIGN FOR LIVING

1933, 90 mins, *Dir* Ernst Lubitsch   US

★ *Stars* Fredric March, Gary Cooper, Miriam Hopkins, Edward Everett Horton, Franklin Pangborn, Isabel Jewell

Ben Hecht's screen treatment has transmuted Noel Coward's idea better than Coward's original play. It's a competent job in every respect. What matter it – or perhaps it does – if Hecht threw Coward's manuscript out the window and set about writing a brand new play? The dialog is less lofty, less epigramatic, less artificial. There's more reality.

Coward, of course, has contributed a basic premise that's arresting – a girl and two men all of whom are very fond of each other. Edward Everett Horton, as the patient mentor of the girl (or, as the dialog puts it, 'in other words, you never got to first base'), is built up here, as much by the script as his own personal histrionic dominance.

Miriam Hopkins' expert handling of the delicate premise which motivates the other three men is a consummate performance in every respect. She glosses over the dirt, but gets the punch over none the less. She confesses quite naively she is stumped – she likes both Tom and George (Fredric March and Gary Cooper).

Hecht patterns Cooper to a rugged chapeau and March to a more formal top-piece, and Hopkins interprets her reactions in relation to wearing one type of hat or another with the shifting moods.

THE DISORDERLY ORDERLY

1964, 89 mins, ◇ ⓥ *Dir* Frank Tashlin   US

★ *Stars* Jerry Lewis, Glenda Farrell, Everett Sloane, Karen Sharpe, Kathleen Freeman, Susan Oliver

The Disorderly Orderly is fast and madcappish, with Lewis again playing one of his malaprop characters that seem to suit his particular talents.

As the orderly, Lewis is himself almost a mental patient as he takes on all the symptoms of the individual patients in the plush sanitarium where he's employed. Ambitious to be a doctor, he flunked out in medical school because of this particular attribute. He's cured through some fancy script-figuring when Susan Oliver, one of the patients, offers him love and he discovers that he's really in love with Karen Sharpe, a nurse. Sandwiched within this premise is Lewis at work, at play, always in trouble.

Star is up to his usual comicking and Frank Tashlin's direction of his own screenplay is fast and vigorous in main-

taining a nutty mood. Sharpe is pert and cute, Oliver ably transforms from a would-be suicide to a sexpot, and Glenda Farrell, cast as head of the sanitarium, displays the talent which once made her a star.

DIVORCE AMERICAN STYLE

1967, 109 mins, ◇ ⓥ *Dir* Bud Yorkin   US

★ *Stars* Dick Van Dyke, Debbie Reynolds, Jason Robards, Jean Simmons, Van Johnson, Joe Flynn

Comedy and satire, not feverish melodrama, are the best weapons with which to harpoon social mores. An outstanding example of these weapons in action is *Divorce American Style* [from a story by Robert Kaufman], which pokes incisive, sometimes chilling, fun at US marriage-divorce problems.

Amidst wow comedy situations, story depicts the break-up after 15 years of the Van Dyke-Debbie Reynolds marriage, followed by the economic tragedies exemplified by Jason Robards and Jean Simmons, caught in a vicious circle of alimony and remarriage problems.

Shelley Berman and Dick Gautier, two chummy lawyers, spotlight the occasional feeling by litigants that their personal problems are secondary to the games their attorneys play.

THE DIVORCE OF LADY X

1938, 92 mins, ◇ ⓥ *Dir* Tim Whelan   UK

★ *Stars* Merle Oberon, Laurence Olivier, Binnie Barnes, Ralph Richardson, Morton Selten, Gus McNaughton

Alexander Korda's Technicolored comedy is rich, smart entertainment, a comedy built around several situations and a wrong-identity hoax. Picture takes unusually long in getting going into brisk action and the repetitions during the first half hour are many.

Robert E. Sherwood's deft writing is apparent in the screenplay job he did along with Lajos Biro, author of the play [*Counsel's Opinion*] from which the pic was evolved. Comedy lines have that Sherwood sting.

Merle Oberon attends a costume ball in a London hotel and after the manager can't persuade an annoyed young lawyer (Laurence Olivier) to part with some space in his suite, Oberon maneuvers in and wheedles him out of his bed.

Next day girl vamooses before chap can find out much about her; he's convinced she's married. On arrival at his office, he is plagued by a college classmate to get the latter a divorce. He claims his wife spent the night with an unknown man in the same hotel, after attending the same dance. Girl continues to interest the chap and when she knows the sort he believes her to be maintains the ruse.

Oberon impresses. Olivier does his role pretty well, retarded somewhat by an annoying bit of pouting business. Two key performances which sparkle are those of Ralph

Richarson and Morton Selten. Former plays the man who wants the divorce; latter Oberon's grandfather, who is the judge sitting on most of the cases the young lawyer pleads.

DOCTOR AT LARGE

1957, 104 mins, ◇ ⓥ *Dir* Ralph Thomas UK

★ **Stars** Dirk Bogarde, Muriel Pavlow, Donald Sinden, James Robertson Justice, Shirley Eaton, Michael Medwin

This continues the adventures of the young medico who qualified in *Doctor in the House* and got his first appointment in *Doctor at Sea*. This time round he's on a job hunting spree and the film depicts his experiences and adventures while working for a mean provincial doctor and in a fashionable Park Lane practice.

The yarn develops with a blending of light comedy and a dash of sentiment, with punch comedy lines providing timely shots in the arm. They're welcome when they come, but they're too irregular.

Role of the young doctor again is played by Dirk Bogarde. The story opens at St Swithin's hospital where Bogarde hopes to achieve his vocational ambitions to prac-

tice surgery. But he falls foul of James Robertson Justice, who is the hospital's chief consultant. To gain experience (and pay the rent), he begins his job hunting trail.

Bogarde, of course, is the mainstay of the story, but Justice again emerges as the standout character, even though his role is reduced to more modest proportions.

DOCTOR AT SEA

1955, 93 mins, ◇ ⓥ *Dir* Ralph Thomas UK

★ **Stars** Dirk Bogarde, Brigitte Bardot, Brenda De Banzie, James Robertson Justice, Maurice Denham, Michael Medwin

As their first British venture in VistaVision, the Rank studios play safe with a sequel to *Doctor in the House,* but *Doctor at Sea* does not rise to the same laugh-provoking heights as its predecessor.

James Robertson Justice is a gruff ship's captain on whose freighter the young medico has his first appointment

Dirk Bogarde as student doctor Simon Sparrow in **Doctor in the House,** *the story of a London medical school.*

at sea. The ship is obliged to take on board the daughter of the chairman of the line and her friend, a pert and attractive cabaret chanteuse.

By far the most dominating performance of the cast is given by Justice. He towers above the others and is the focal point of every scene in which he appears. Dirk Bogarde plays the medico with a pleasing quiet restraint and Brigitte Bardot has an acting talent to match her charm.

DOCTOR IN THE HOUSE

1954, 92 mins, ◇ ⓥ *Dir* Ralph Thomas   UK

★ **Stars** Dirk Bogarde, Muriel Pavlow, Kenneth More, Donald Sinden, Kay Kendall, James Robertson Justice

A topdraw British comedy, *Doctor in the House* is bright, diverting entertainment, intelligently scripted, and warmly played.

Background to the story is the medical school of a London hospital. Within 92 minutes, the film spans the five years in the life of a student group.

The new recruit to the school is Dirk Bogarde, who is taken under the protective wing of three old-timers who had all failed their preliminary exams. Kenneth More, Donald Sinden and Donald Houston make up a contrasted quartet who seem to have ideas on most subjects but not how to qualify as a medico.

Much of the comedy incident has been clearly contrived but it is nonetheless effective, particularly in the scenes featuring James Robertson Justice as a distinguished surgeon and More.

DOWN AND OUT IN BEVERLY HILLS

1986, 97 mins, ◇ ⓥ *Dir* Paul Mazursky   US

★ **Stars** Nick Nolte, Richard Dreyfuss, Bette Midler, Little Richard, Tracy Nelson

Down and Out in Beverly Hills continues Paul Mazursky's love-hate relationship with the bourgeoisie and its institutions, especially marriage. It's a loving caricature of the nouveau riche (Beverly Hills variety) and although it is more of a comedy of manners than a well-developed story, there are enough yocks and bright moments to make it a thoroughly enjoyable outing.

Mazursky and co-writer Leon Capetanos have cleverly taken the basic premise of Jean Renoir's 1932 classic *Boudu Saved from Drowning* and used it as a looking glass for the foibles of the rich and bored.

Head of the household is the aptly named David Whiteman (Richard Dreyfuss). Bette Midler is the lady of the house with their near anorexic daughter Tracy Nelson and son Evan Richards.

In short it's a household of unhappy people and the fly (perhaps flea is more accurate) in the ointment is Nick Nolte as the bum Jerry Baskin. A disheveled and dirty street

Tramp Nick Nolte gets help from wealthy Richard Dreyfuss and Bette Midler in Down and Out in Beverly Hills.

person, Jerry is an artist of sorts, a con artist. For the Whitemans he becomes their idealized bum, the family pet.

THE DREAM TEAM

1989, 113 mins, ◇ ⓥ *Dir* Howard Zieff   US

★ **Stars** Michael Keaton, Christopher Lloyd, Peter Boyle, Stephen Frust, Dennis Boutsikaris

The Dream Team is a hokey comedy that basically reduces mental illness to a grab bag of quirky schtick. Yet with a quartet of gifted comic actors having a field day playing loonies on the loose in Manhattan, much of that schtick is awfully funny.

In an attempt to give his patients a taste of the real world, New Jersey hospital doctor Dennis Boutsikaris decides to treat four of his charges to a day game at Yankee Statium.

Going along for the ride are the certified oddballs: Keaton, who seems to have his wits about him but periodically displays extreme delusions of grandeur, as well as a mean violent streak; Christopher Lloyd, a prissy fuss-budget who enjoys posing as a member of the hospital staff; Peter Boyle, a

Michael Keaton, Stephen Furst, Christopher Lloyd and Peter Boyle as inmates let loose on New York in The Dream Team.

man with a heavy Jesus complex given to undressing at moments of intense spirituality; and Stephen Furst, an uncommunicative simpleton who speaks mainly in baseball jargon.

As soon as they hit the Big Apple, however, the good doctor is seriously injured after witnessing a killing, and the boys are left to their own devices.

Keaton is at his manic best, Lloyd prompts numerous guffaws with his impersonation of a self-serious tidiness freak, and Furst quietly impresses as the sickest and most helpless of the lot.

DUCK SOUP

1933, 70 mins, *Dir* Leo McCarey   US

★ *Stars* Groucho Marx, Chico Marx, Harpo Marx, Zeppo Marx, Margaret Dumont, Louis Calhern

The laughs come often, too often sometimes, which has always been the case with Marx talkers, although in this instance more care appears to have been taken with the timing, since the step-on gags don't occur as frequently as in the past.

In place of the constant punning and dame chasing, *Duck Soup* has the Marxes madcapping through such bits as the old Schwartz Bros mirror routine, so well done in the hands of Groucho, Harpo and Chico that it gathers a new and hilarious comedy momentum all over again.

Story is a mythical kingdom burlesque that could easily have been written by a six-year-old with dust in his eyes, but it isn't so much the story as what goes with and on within it. Groucho is the prime minister. For his customary dowager-foil he has the high, wide and handsome Margaret Dumont, making it perfect for Groucho.

While Groucho soft pedals the verbal clowning for more physical effort this time the other boys also make a quick change. Chico and Harpo omit their musical specialties here, which should make it much easier for the piano and

Chico, Zeppo, Groucho and Harpo in a publicity still for **Duck Soup, considered as the Marx Brothers' best film.**

harp numbers the next time, if needed. Zeppo is simply Zeppo.

Music and lyrics [by Bert Kalmar and Harry Ruby] through which much of the action is in rhyme and song, serve to carry the story along rather than to stand out on pop song merit on their own. Everything's in keeping with the tempo of the production.

EARTH GIRLS ARE EASY

1988, 100 mins, ◇ ⓥ *Dir* Julien Temple   US

★ *Stars* Geena Davis, Jeff Goldblum, Julie Brown, Jim Carrey, Damon Wayans

Earth Girls Are Easy is a dizzy, glitzy fish-out-of-water farce about three horny aliens on the make in LA.

Julie (Geena Davis), a gorgeous Valley Girl, works as a manicurist in high-tech beauty salon operated by Candy (Julie Brown) a Val-Queen supreme who likes good times and good sex.

Meanwhile in outer space, three aliens who look like tie-dyed werewolves are wandering around our solar system going bonkers with randiness. In keeping with the film's hot-pastel, contempo-trash design motif, their spacecraft looks like the inside of a pinball machine. When it lands in Julie's swimming pool, the broken-hearted girl who's just broken off with her nogoodnik lover takes the spacecraft for an oversized hair dryer.

Julie brings this gruesome threesome to Candy's beauty parlor for a complete 'makeover.' They emerge as three

hairless hunky dudes: the captain, Jeff Goldblum and two flaked-out crewman, Jim Carrey and Damon Wayans. The two val-gals and their alien 'dates' take off for a weekend of LA nightlife, where the visitors' smooth adaptation to Coast culture is intended by director Julian Temple and his screenwriters to affectionately skewer Tinseltown lifestyles.

EATING RAOUL

1982, 83 mins, ◇ ⓥ *Dir* Paul Bartel   US

★ *Stars* Paul Bartel, Mary Woronov, Robert Beltram, Susan Salger, Ed Begley Jr, Buck Henry

All poor Paul and Mary Bland want in life is enough money to buy their own restaurant in Valencia, California and call it Paul and Mary's Country Kitchen. But the couple have little real hope of raising the $20,000 they need to make their dreams come true.

To compound matters, the proper couple, who sleep in separate beds and find sex particularly dirty, live in a tacky Hollywood apartment building chock full of all kinds of crazies. When one of the 'low lifes' tries to rape Mary, Paul kills him by a blow to the head with a frying pan.

Alas, the victim had all kinds of money and both Paul and Mary soon realize they have a potential answer to their financial worries. They put an ad in a local sex publication and decide to lure new 'perverts' to their home. That way they can get the money for their restaurant and help clean up society in one sweeping stroke.

The appeal of Paul Bartel's tongue-in-cheek approach is that he manages to take his story to such a ridiculous extreme, remain genuinely funny and successfully tell his perverse story. While the material could offend in some circles, Bartel has a light, deadpan approach that makes what would normally seem repulsive become perfectly acceptable (at least on film).

Unlikely aliens set out on an interstellar mating spree in Earth Girls Are Easy.

Paul Bartel (right) as a would-be restauranteur contemplating cannibalism in the bizarre Eating Raoul.

Class issues in the classroom, as Michael Caine's professor takes on Educating Rita, played by Julie Walters.

EDUCATING RITA

1983, 110 mins, ◇ Ⓥ *Dir* Lewis Gilbert   UK

★ *Stars* Michael Caine, Julie Walters, Maureen Lipman, Jeananne Crowley, Malcolm Douglas, Godfrey Quigley

Producer-director Lewis Gilbert has done a marvelous job of bringing the charming British play, *Educating Rita*, to the big screen. Aided greatly by an expert film adaptation by its playwright, Willy Russell, Gilbert has come up with an irresistible story about a lively lower-class British woman hungering for an education and the rather staid, degenerating English professor who reluctantly provides her with one.

Witty, down-to-earth, kind and loaded with common sense, Rita is the antithesis of the humorless, stuffy and stagnated academic world which she so longs to infiltrate. Julie Walters injects her character with just the right mix of comedy and pathos. Michael Caine is the sadly smart, alcoholic teacher who knows the fundamentals of English literature, but long ago lost the ability to enjoy life the way his uneducated pupil does.

The contradictions of the two characters are at the core of the picture, as Walters goes from dependent housewife to intelligent student and Caine begins to learn what it's like to feel again.

ERIK THE VIKING

1989, 103 mins, ◇ Ⓥ *Dir* Terry Jones   UK

★ *Stars* Tim Robbins, Gary Cady, Mickey Rooney, Eartha Kitt, Terry Jones, John Cleese

The idea of telling the story of a Viking warrior who thought there must be more to life than rape and pillage is an amusing one, and for the most part *Erik the Viking* is an enjoyable film.

Pic opens with Erik (Tim Robbins) falling in love with a girl just as he kills her. Spurred by her death he decides to try and bring the Age of Ragnarok – where men fight and kill – to an end.

He sets off with an unruly band of followers – including the local blacksmith who wants Ragnarok to continue as it helps his sword-making business – and is pursued by Halfdan the Black (John Cleese), the local warlord who quite enjoys Ragnarok and wants it to continue.

American Tim Robbins is fine as the softly spoken and sensitive Erik, and especially seems to enjoy himself in the battle scenes. The film's great strength, though, is the Viking crew, which is full of wonderful characters, such as Tim McInnerny's manic Sven the Berserk, heavily disguised Antony Sher's scheming Loki and best of all Freddie Jones' put-upon missionary.

EVERYTHING YOU ALWAYS WANTED TO KNOW ABOUT SEX** BUT WERE AFRAID TO ASK

1972, 87 mins, ◇ ⓥ *Dir* Woody Allen   US

★ *Stars* Woody Allen, John Carradine, Anthony Quayle, Tony Randall, Burt Reynolds, Gene Wilder

Borrowing only the title and some typically inane questions from Dr David Reuben's oft-ingenuous but widely read overview of sexual matters, Woody Allen writes his sixth screenplay and serves for the third time as his own director.

Pic is divided into seven segments – blackout sketches, really – that presumably are Allen's surrealistic answer to selected questions from the Reuben tome.

One of the episodes is a prolonged piece of nonsense involving a *2001*-inspired mission control centre that is engineering a bout of intercourse in a parked car. Idea of Allen as a reluctant sperm may sound funny on paper, but it plays like an adolescent jape.

Allen's gift is in the depiction of a contemporary intellectual shlump who cannot seem to make it with the chicks always tantalizingly out of reach. That persona could well have served him once more as the focus for a good bit of caustic comedy on today's sexual mores.

Gene Wilder is just one of Woody Allen's case histories in **All You Wanted To Know About Sex...**

THE FAMILY WAY

1967, 114 mins, ◇ *Dir* Roy Boulting   UK

★ *Stars* Hayley Mills, Avril Angers, John Comer, Hywel Bennett, John Mills, Wilfred Pickles

Based on Bill Naughton's warm-hearted play, *All in Good Time*, and adapted by Roy Boulting and Jeffrey Dell, film is the story of an innocent young couple who marry and are unable to consummate their marriage.

The youngsters (Hayley Mills and Hywel Bennett) marry and because of circumstances have to live with the lad's parents. Even the honeymoon is a disaster since a flyaway travel agent cheats them out of their package deal trip to the Continent.

Hayley Mills gets away from her Disney image as the young bride, even essaying an undressed scene. Bennett is excellent as the sensitive young bridegroom. But it is the older hands who keep the film floating on a wave of fun, sentiment and sympathy.

John Mills is first-class in a character role as the bluff father who cannot understand his son and produces the lower working-class man's vulgarity without overdoing it.

Avril Angers as the girl's acid mother and John Comer as her husband are equally effective, but the best performance comes from Marjorie Rhodes as John Mills' astute but understanding wife.

FATHER OF THE BRIDE

1950, 92 mins, ⓥ *Dir* Vincente Minnelli   US

★ *Stars* Spencer Tracy, Joan Bennett, Elizabeth Taylor, Don Taylor, Billie Burke, Russ Tamblyn

Academy Award 1950: Best Picture (Nomination)

Father of the Bride as a pic smites the risibilities just as hard as it did in book form [by Edward Streeter].

Screenplay provides director Vincente Minnelli with choice situations and dialog, sliced right from life and hoked just enough to bring out the comedy flavor. Opening shot is a daybreak scene among the debris created by a wedding reception. Weary, but relieved, Spencer Tracey recounts the sorry lot of a bride's father, emotionally and financially devastating, and gives a case history of the events leading up to his present state.

On the critical side: Minnelli could have timed many of the scenes so that laughs would not have stepped on dialog tag lines. Also he permits the wedding rehearsal sequence to play too long, lessening the comedic effect.

FERRIS BUELLER'S DAY OFF

1986, 103 mins, ◇ ⓥ *Dir* John Hughes   US

★ *Stars* Matthew Broderick, Alan Ruck, Mia Sara, Jeffrey Jones, Jennifer Grey, Cindy Pickett

Ferris Bueller exhibits John Hughes on an off day. Paucity of invention here lays bare the total absence of plot or involving situations.

In a nutshell, the thin premise demonstrates the great lengths to which the irrepressible Ferris Bueller (Matthew Broderick) goes in order to hoodwink his parents and high school principal into thinking he's really sick when, in fact, all he wants to do is play hooky for a day.

Oddly, for a rich kid, Ferris doesn't have a car of his own, so he shanghais his best friend for the day, appropriates the vintage Ferrari of the buddy's father, then spirits his girlfriend out of school and speeds off for downtown Chicago.

Broderick's essential likability can't replace the loony anarchy of Hughes' previous leading man, Anthony Michael Hall. Alan Ruck can't do much with his underwritten second-banana role, and Mia Sara is fetching as Ferris' g.f.

Picture's one saving grace is the absolutely delicious comic performance of Jeffrey Jones as the high school principal, driven nearly out of his mind in his frustrated pursuit of Ferris. With a series of reactions exaggerated to perfection, Jones is pricelessly funny.

FIFTH AVENUE GIRL

1939, 82 mins, ⓥ *Dir* Gregory LaCava   US

★ *Stars* Ginger Rogers, Walter Connolly, Verree Teasdale, James Ellison, Tim Holt

Fifth Avenue Girl, is a cleverly devised comedy drama, expertly guided by Gregory LaCava. Story is basically of Cinderella pattern – always good. Millionaire Walter Connolly, shunned by his family on his birthday, meets Ginger Rogers in Central Park. After a night club celebration, he hires her to pose as a golddigger, and takes her to his Fifth Avenue mansion.

Sock laughs are supplied by situations and surprise dialog. Rogers, bewildered by her sudden catapult into a swank home, carries it all off with a blankness that accentuates her characterization. Connolly deftly handles the assignment of the prosperous manufacturer.

Production is distinctly a LaCava achievement. In motivation, its unfolding lies between the wacky *My Man Godfrey* and the more serious *Stage Door*. But it's good substantial fun. Direction is at a steady and fast tempoed pace without extraneous footage. Excellent photography by Robert de Grasse.

A FISH CALLED WANDA

1988, 108 mins, ◇ ⓥ *Dir* Charles Crichton   US

★ *Stars* John Cleese, Jamie Lee Curtis, Kevin Kline, Michael Palin, Tom Georgeson, Maria Aitken

In *A Fish Called Wanda*, Monty Pythoners John Cleese and Michael Palin get caught up in a double-crossing crime caper with a mismatched and hilarious pair of scheming Yanks, Jamie Lee Curtis and Kevin Kline.

Though it is less tasteless, irreverent and satirical than the Python pics, film still is wacky and occasionally outrageous in its own, distinctly British way.

John Cleese is Archie Leach (Cary Grant's real name) an uptight, respected barrister who becomes unglued when Wanda (Jamie Lee Curtis), the girlfriend of a crook he's defending, comes on to him for no apparent reason.

Curtis fakes it as an American law student looking to learn about English law when really she just wants to get information out of Cleese about some diamonds she's recently heisted with his client George (Tom Georgeson) and two others – her 'brother' Otto (Kevin Kline), who's really no relation and a stuttering animal rights freak Ken (Michael Palin), as the proud owner of a fish tank and a fish named Wanda.

Cleese takes an opportunity to poke fun at something ripe for ridicule – this time, the love-hate rivalry between the Brits and the Yanks. It's funny without being mean, since both sides get their due. Curtis steals the show with her keen sense of comic timing and sneaky little grins and asides. Palin has too limited a role.

Psycho Kevin Kline successfully gets lawyer John Cleese (upside down) to apologise in **A Fish Called Wanda.**

THE FLAMINGO KID

1984, 100 mins, ◇ ⓥ   *Dir* Garry Marshall   US

★ **Stars** Matt Dillon, Richard Crenna, Hector Elizondo, Jessica Walter, Molly McCarthy, Janet Jones

The Flamingo Kid, set in 1963, sports the amusing trappings connected with 18-year-old Matt Dillon working for a summer at the El Flamingo Beach Club in Far Rockaway, NY. At its heart, though, story has to do with the critical choices facing a youth of that age and how they will help determine the rest of one's life.

Taken out of his rundown Brooklyn neighborhood one day to play cards with friends at the club, Dillon ends up getting a job there parking cars. He is soon promoted to cabana boy, and also attracts the attention of blonde UCLA student Janet Jones, with whom he has a skin-deep summer fling, and her uncle Richard Crenna, a sharp-talking sports car dealer.

Dillon does a good job in his fullest, least narcissistic characterization to date.

FLETCH

1985, 96 mins, ◇ ⓥ   *Dir* Michael Ritchie   US

★ **Stars** Chevy Chase, Dana Wheeler-Nicholson, Tim Matheson, Joe Don Baker, Richard Libertini, Geena Davis

What propels this contempo LA yarn about a dissembling newspaper columnist on the trail of a nefarious con man (Tim Matheson) is the obvious and successful byplay between Chevy Chase's sly, glib persona and the satiric brushstrokes of director Michael Ritchie. Their teamwork turns an otherwise hair-pinned, anecdotal plot into a breezy, peppy frolic and a tour de force for Chase.

Most supporting players have little to do, such as M. Emmet Walsh as an inane MD. The film is sparked by some hilarious moments, among them Chase as an unwitting surgeon in attendance at an autopsy conducted by a cackling pathologist and, in the script's funniest scene, Chase donning the guise of a legionnaire in a hall full of VFW stalwarts.

FLETCH LIVES

1989, 95 mins, ◇ ⓥ   *Dir* Michael Ritchie   US

★ **Stars** Chevy Chase, Hal Holbrook, Julianne Phillips, Cleavon Little, R. Lee Ermey, Patricia Kalember

Chevy Chase is perfectly suited to playing a smirking, wisecracking, multiple-identitied reporter in *Fletch Lives*.

Ridiculous and anecdotal plot that transports Chase from his beloved LA base to Louisiana's bayou country to take over his dead aunt's crumbling plantation works for the simple reason that Chase's sly, glib persona is in sync with Michael Ritchie's equally breezy direction.

From Gregory McDonald's popular novel, script works out an excessive and cliche-ridden portrait of a Southern, insular town. Dimwits abound as if inbreeding has been going on since the days of slavery.

The night Chase arrives, he beds the sexy executor/lawyer of his aunt's estate (Patricia Kalember as a convincing belle), who is then murdered while they're slumbering.

Chase tracks the murderer through some inane sequences as only he could do. Film's saving grace is its scathing satirical sketches of fictional televangelist preacher Jimmy Lee Farnsworth.

THE FLIM-FLAM MAN

1967, 104 mins, ◇ ⓥ   *Dir* Irvin Kershner   US

★ **Stars** George C. Scott, Sue Lyon, Michael Sarrazin, Harry Morgan, Jack Albertson, Alice Ghostley

An outstanding comedy starring George C. Scott as a Dixie drifter. Socko comedy-dramatic direction by Irvin Kershner

A PETER ROGER'S PRODUCTION
PHIL SILVERS · KENNETH WILLIAMS · JIM DALE
CHARLES HAWTREY · JOAN SIMS · ANGELA DOUGLAS
IN COLOUR **FOLLOW THAT CAMEL**

A touch of Beau Jest, as the Carry On regulars are joined by Phil Silvers (second left) in **Follow That Camel.**

makes the most of a very competent cast and a superior script. Michael Sarrazin, as Scott's fellow-traveler, makes an impressive feature film bow.

Guy Owen's novel, *The Ballad of the Flim-Flam Man*, has been adapted into a finely balanced screenplay which exploits inherent comedy situations while understating, appropriately, the loneliness of a rootless man. A series of flim-flams are pulled off only on people who seemingly deserve to be stiffed, thus minimizing any complaint that lawlessness is being made attractive.

FOLLOW THAT CAMEL

1967, 95 mins, ◇ ⑦ *Dir* Gerald Thomas   UK

★ *Stars* Phil Silvers, Jim Dale, Peter Butterworth, Charles Hawtrey, Anita Harris, Kenneth Williams

Story line provides adequate excuse for a Carry On foray into the Foreign Legion territory, with a young hero (Jim Dale), accused of cheating at cricket, enlisting with his manservant to exculpate his disgrace. There he encounters Phil Silvers, as a sergeant who invents acts of heroism and is much decorated, Kenneth Williams as the German commanding officer, Charles Hawtrey, as his deft adjutant, and Joan Sims, as a much-cleavage siren. They are involved in running skirmishes with an Arab chieftain, serving a master called Mustapha Leak, and the farrago climaxes in a hilarious battle at a desert fort, after a forced march through waterless wastes.

It all works with considerable bounce, with elements of parody of *Beau Geste*-style movies for those alert to them. All the regular comics are on first-rate form.

A FOREIGN AFFAIR

1948, 113 mins, *Dir* Billy Wilder   US

★ *Stars* Jean Arthur, Marlene Dietrich, John Lund, Millard Mitchell

A Foreign Affair is a witty satire developed around a Congressional investigation of GI morals in Germany. Much of the action is backgrounded against actual Berlin footage.

The humor to which such a theme lends itself has been given a stinging bite, even though presented broadly to tickle the risibilities.

While subject is handled for comedy, Charles Brackett and Billy Wilder have managed to underlay the fun with an expose of human frailties and, to some extent, indicate a passive bitterness among the conquered in the occupied areas.

Jean Arthur is in a topflight characterization as a spinsterish congresswoman, who furnishes the distaff touch to an elemental girl-meets-boy angle in the story. The boy is John Lund, and Marlene Dietrich personifies the eternal siren as an opportunist German femme who furnishes Lund with off-duty diversion. Also, she gives the Dietrich s.a. treatment to three Frederick Hollander tunes, lyrics of which completely express the cynical undertones of the film.

FOREIGN BODY

1986, 108 mins, ◇ Ⓥ *Dir* Ronald Neame   US, UK

★ *Stars* Victor Banerjee, Warren Mitchell, Geraldine McEwan, Denis Quilley, Amanda Donohoe, Anna Massey

Even if *Foreign Body* [based on the novel by Roderick Mann] doesn't have quite the comic and narrative richness of Ronald Neame's Ealing Studios classics, this variation on the 'great impostor' plot device is still an unalloyed pleasure to watch.

Built solidly upon a fluid, comic virtuoso performance by Victor Banerjee, the picaresque fable of an impoverished refugee from Calcutta faking it as a doctor to London's upper crust makes some jaunty points about racism, gullibility and sheer pluck.

Even though he's a deceiver, sincerity is a bedrock trait of the *Foreign Body* hero, Ram Das, and Banerjee is free to romp with bug-eyed zaniness through the improbable adventures of this Asian naif abroad.

THE FORTUNE

1975, 88 mins, ◇ *Dir* Mike Nichols   US

★ *Stars* Jack Nicholson, Warren Beatty, Stockard Channing, Florence Stanley

The Fortune is an occasionally enjoyable comedy trifle, starring Jack Nicholson and Warren Beatty as bumbling kidnappers of heiress Stockard Channing, who is excellent in her first major screen role. Very classy 1920s production values often merit more attention than the plot.

Beatty elopes with Channing but, not yet free of a former wife, Nicholson actually marries her. Trio sets up housekeeping in Los Angeles, and after Channing is disinherited, the guys try to kill her. If lugging around a passed-out intoxicated girl in clumsy murder attempts does not offend sensibilities, then the alleged fun may be passable.

David Shire superbly recreates some old Joe Venuti-Eddi Lang jazz band arrangements.

FOUR'S A CROWD

1938, 91 mins, *Dir* Michael Curtiz   US

★ *Stars* Errol Flynn, Olivia de Havilland, Rosalind Russell, Patric Knowles, Walter Connolly, Hugh Herbert

As a true follower of the dizzy school of comedy, *Four's a Crowd* defies and renounces all relationship to reality. Providing much zest and spice to this dizzy dish [story by Wallace Sullivan] is Walter Connolly's characterization of the eccentric millionaire, whose major interest in life is his miniature electric railway system and a kennel of mastiffs that make tough going for unwanted visitors.

While the film has its arid stretches, there is little letdown in action. Deftly developed is the miniature train race sequence, in which the millionaire's entry meets defeat through the artful placement of a chunk of butter on the tracks. Other laugh cascades derive from Errol Flynn's attempt to carry on twin phone conversations with a couple of insistent dames, and from a double elopement in paralleling cabs with the situation stepped up in a big way by Hugh Herbert's functioning as the cynical justice of the peace. The marriage service builds to a whirlwind finish.

Complications develop from Flynn's efforts to sell the hardboiled Connolly into whitewashing his public-be-damned past by endowing a few clinical foundations. The wily public relations counsel uses his temporary connection as managing ed of Patric Knowles' newspaper to stir up public sentiment against his proposed client.

THE FRESHMAN

1990, 102 mins, ◇ Ⓥ *Dir* Andrew Bergman   US

★ *Stars* Marlon Brando, Matthew Broderick, Bruno Kirby, Penelope Ann Miller, Paul Benedict, Maximilian Schell

Marlon Brando's sublime comedy performance elevates *The Freshman* from screwball comedy to a quirky niche in film history – among films that comment on cult movies.

Mario Puzo and Francis Coppola's *The Godfather* is director Andrew Bergman's starting point. Incoming NYU film student Matthew Broderick is exposed not only to that Paramount film (and its sequel) in pretentious prof Paul Benedict's classroom but meets up with a virtual doppelganger for Don Vito Corleone in the form of mobster Carmine Sabatini (Brando).

The ornate and intentionally screwy plotline has Brando making an irresistible offer to Broderick to work for him part-time as a delivery boy. Broderick's first assignment is transporting a huge (but real) lizard from the airport. Broderick quickly tumbles to the criminality of Brando and his nutty partner Maximilian Schell, but is unable to extricate himself from the situation.

Pic's weakest element is the recurring satire of film studies. Although Benedict is droll as an academic poseur, the mocking of film analysis is puerile and obvious.

Broderick is ably abetted by two previous co-stars: Penelope Anne Miller (*Biloxi Blues*), winning as an offbeat form of mafia princess; and B.D. Wong (who popped up in *Family Business*) as Schell's goofy partner in culinary crime. Technical credits on the mixed New York and Toronto shoot are good, capturing the right amount of Greenwich Village ambience.

THE FRONT PAGE

1974, 105 mins, ◇ *Dir* Billy Wilder   US

★ **Stars** Jack Lemmon, Walter Matthau, Carol Burnen, Susan Sarandon, Vincent Gardenia, David Wayne

The reteaming of Jack Lemmon and Walter Matthau, in a Billy Wilder remake of a famous 1920s period newspaper story, *The Front Page*, with a featured spot by Carol Burnett, sure looks good on paper. But that's about the only place it looks good. The production has the slick, machine-tooled look of certain assembly line automobiles that never quite seem to work smoothly.

The 1928 play by Ben Hecht and Charles MacArthur has, in this third screen version, been 'liberated' from old

*Cop columnists in a verbal battle of wits determining whether truth will triumph on **The Front Page**.*

Production code restraints. The extent of the liberation appears to be in the tedious use of undeleted expletives.

The basic story takes place in a Chicago police press room on the eve of a politically-railroaded execution of a supposed radical who killed a cop in a scuffle.

Matthau and Lemmon again demonstrate their fine screen empathy.

A FUNNY THING HAPPENED ON THE WAY TO THE FORUM

1966, 99 mins, ◇ 🎭 *Dir* Richard Lester   US

★ **Stars** Zero Mostel, Phil Silvers, Buster Keaton, Jack Gilford, Michael Crawford, Annette Andre

A Funny Thing Happened on the Way to the Forum – after the [1962 Stephen Sondheim] stage musicomedy of the same name – will probably stand out as one of the few originals of two repetition-weary genres, the film musical comedy and the toga-cum-sandal 'epic'. Flip, glib and sophisticated, yet rump-slappingly bawdy and fast-paced, *Forum* is a capricious look at the seamy underside of classical Rome through a 20th-century hipster's shades.

Plot follows the efforts of a glib, con-man slave, Pseudolus (Zero Mostel), to cheat, steal or connive his freedom from a domineering mistress, Domina (Patricia Jessel),

and his equally victimized master, the henpecked Senex (Michael Hordern). An unwilling ally, through blackmail, is the timorous toady Hysterium (Jack Gilford), another household slave.

Early instrument of Pseudolus' plot is the callow Hero (Michael Crawford), who, smitten by one of the luscious courtesans peddled by Lycus (Phil Silvers), local flesh supplier, promises Mostel his freedom if he can finagle the 'virgin's' purchase. Plot complications multiply like the film's pratfalls, however, and the winsome object of Hero's passion has already been sold to the egomaniacal Miles (Leon Greene), a legion captain of legendary ferocity, who thunders onto the scene to claim the girl.

Interwoven through the plot is the presence of Erronius (Buster Keaton) who, searching for his lost children, unties the knotted situation.

FUN WITH DICK AND JANE

1977, 95 mins, ◇ ⦿ *Dir* Ted Kotcheff   US

★ **Stars** George Segal, Jane Fonda, Ed McMahon, Dick Gautier, Allan Miller, Hank Garcia

Fun with Dick and Jane is a great comedy idea [from a story by Gerald Gaiser] largely shot down by various bits of tastelessness, crudity and nastiness. Stars George Segal and Jane Fonda are an upper middle-class family which turns to armed robbery when hubby loses his aerospace job.

Fonda and Segal have all the basic comedy essentials necessary to fulfill the minimum demands of the story, and that seems to be the problem: they seem to have gotten no help from direction and/or writing in getting off the ground.

Ed McMahon is terrific as Segal's employer whose boozy bonhomie conceals the heart of a true Watergater. Making this essentially shallow and hypocritical character into a fascinating figure of corporate logrolling was a major challenge.

GAMBIT

1966, 107 mins, ◇ ⦿ *Dir* Ronald Neame   US

★ **Stars** Shirley MacLaine, Michael Caine, Herbert Lom, Roger C. Carmel, Arnold Moss, John Abbott

Shirley MacLaine and Michael Caine star in a first-rate suspense comedy, cleverly scripted, expertly directed and handsomely mounted.

Sidney Carroll's original story has been adapted into a zesty laugh-getter as MacLaine becomes Miss Malaprop in Caine's scheme to loot the art treasures of mid-East potentate Herbert Lom. An idealized swindle sequence lasting 27 min-

utes opens pic, after which the execution of the plan shifts all characterizations and sympathies.

Director Ronald Neame has obtained superior characterizations from all hands. MacLaine, playing a Eurasian gal, displays her deft comedy abilities after the opening segment, in which she is stone-faced and silent. Caine socks over a characterization which is at first tightlipped and cold, then turning warm with human and romantic frailty.

Lom is excellent as the potentate, so assured of his security devices that audience sympathy encourages the machinations of Caine and MacLaine.

GARBO TALKS

1984, 103 mins, ◇ ⦿ *Dir* Sidney Lumet   US

★ **Stars** Anne Bancroft, Ron Silver, Carrie Fisher, Catherine Hicks, Steven Hill, Hermione Gingold

Garbo Talks is a sweet and sour film clearly not for all tastes. Packed with New York in-jokes, not everyone will appreciate its aggressive charm. But beneath its cocky exterior, picture has a beat on some very human and universal truths.

Estelle Rolfe (Anne Bancroft) is a certifiable eccentric who has worshipped Garbo from afar since childhood, until the star has become woven into the fabric of her imagination. Her identification with Garbo has become a way for her to glamorize her day-to-day life.

Estelle is no ordinary housewife. Divorced from her husband (Steven Hill), she is continually arrested for defending any and all causes and fighting the everyday indignities of life in NY. If not for Bancroft's spirited performance, Estelle would deteriorate into a caricature.

THE GENERAL

1927, 77 mins, ⊗ ⊘ *Dir* Buster Keaton, Clyde Bruckman   US

★ **Stars** Buster Keaton, Marien Mack, Glen Cavender, Jim Farley, Frederick Vroom, Charles Smith

The General is far from fussy. Its principal comedy scene is built on that elementary bit, the chase, and you can't continue a fight for almost an hour and expect results. Especially is this so when the action is placed entirely in the hands of the star. It was his story, he directed, and he acted. The result is a flop.

The story is a burlesque of a Civil War meller. Buster Keaton has the role of a youthful engineer on the Watern and Atlantic RR, running through Georgia, when war is declared. He tries to enlist, but is turned down, as it is figured that he would be of greater value to the cause as an engineer. His girl, however, won't believe this, and tells him not to see her again until he is in a uniform. The girl is on a visit to her dad when 10 Union daredevils steal the train in the middle of Confederate territory and start off with it, intending to burn all bridges behind them, so that the line of communication and supplies for the enemy shall be cut. The girl is on the train, and Keaton, sore because his beloved engine has been stolen, gives chase in another locomotive.

There are some corking gags in the picture, but as they are all a part of the chase they are overshadowed.

GENEVIEVE

1953, 86 mins, ◇ ⦿ *Dir* Henry Cornelius   UK

★ *Stars* John Gregson, Dinah Sheridan, Kenneth More, Kay Kendall, Geoffrey Keen, Joyce Grenfell

The 'Genevieve' of the title is a vintage 1904 car which has been entered for the annual London-to-Brighton rally by its enthusiastic owner (John Gregson). His wife (Dinah Sheridan) hardly shares his enthusiasm but joins him on the run and there is constant good-natured bickering between them and their friendly rival (Kenneth More) and his girl-friend (Kay Kendall). But the rivalry becomes intense on the return journey, ending up with a wager as to which car will be the first over Westminster Bridge.

First-rate direction by Henry Cornelius keeps the camera focused almost entirely on the four principals, and rarely has a starring foursome been so consistently good. Dinah Sheridan's sophisticated performance is a good contrast to

Veteran cars in vintage comedy Genevieve, with John Gregson, Dinah Sheridan, Kenneth More and Kay Kendall.

John Gregson's more sullen interpretation. Kenneth More's exuberance is well-matched by Kay Kendall's effervescent portrayal.

GEORGY GIRL

1966, 100 mins, ⦸ *Dir* Silvio Narizzano   UK

★ *Stars* James Mason, Alan Bates, Lynn Redgrave, Charlotte Rampling, Rachel Kempson, Bill Owen

The role of a gawky ungainly plain Jane [in this adaptation of the novel by Margaret Forster] is a natural for Lynn Redgrave's talents, and she frequently overwhelms her co-stars by sheer force of personality.

She's sharing a slovenly apartment with an attractive, brittle and promiscuous girl friend (Charlotte Rampling). And whenever a lover is being entertained in the communal bedroom, Redgrave takes herself off to the home of her parents' wealthy employer. Girl friend becomes pregnant, opts for marriage instead of another abortion, but when mother-to-be is in hospital, husband (Alan Bates) realizes he chose the wrong girl.

James Mason, as the wealthy employer, attempts to adopt a father figure in relations to the girl, but is actually nothing more than a conventional old roue.

Redgrave has a pushover of a part, and never misses a trick to get that extra yock, whether it's her first passionate encounter with Alan Bates or her fielding of Mason's amorous overtures.

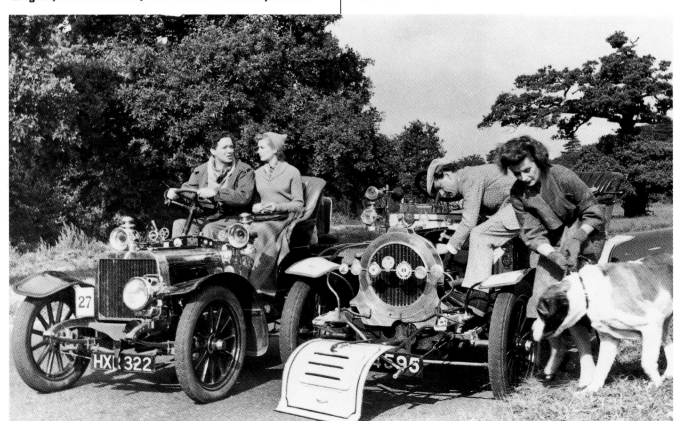

Ernie Hudson, Dan Aykroyd, Bill Murray and Harold Ramis battle the demons in Ghost Busters.

GHOST BUSTERS

1984, 107 mins, ◇ Ⓥ *Dir* Ivan Reitman   US

★ **Stars** Bill Murray, Dan Aykroyd, Sigourney Weaver, Harold Ramis, Rick Moranis, Annie Potts

Ghost Busters is a lavishly produced ($32 million) but only intermittently impressive all-star comedy lampoon of supernatural horror films.

Originally conceived as a John Belushi–Dan Aykroyd vehicle called *Ghostsmashers* before Belushi's death in 1982, *Ghost Busters* under producer-director Ivan Reitman makes a fundamental error: featuring a set of top comics but having them often work alone.

A Manhattan apartment building inhabited by beautiful Dana Barrett (Sigourney Weaver) and her nerd neighbor Louis Tully (Rick Moranis) becomes the gateway for demons from another dimension to invade the Earth.

To battle them come the Ghostbusters, a trio of scientists who have been kicked off campus and are now freelance ghost catchers for hire. Aykroyd is the gung-ho scientific type, Bill Murray is faking competency (he's had no higher education in parapsychology) and using the job to meet women, while Harold Ramis is the trio's technical expert.

Within the top-heavy cast, it's Murray's picture, as the popular comedian deadpans, ad libs and does an endearing array of physical schtick. Aykroyd, trying too hard, gets virtually no laughs at all. Ramis is merely along for the ride and Moranis is underutilized but quite effective when given screen time.

GHOSTBUSTERS II

1989, 102 mins, ◇ Ⓥ *Dir* Ivan Reitman   US

★ **Stars** Bill Murray, Dan Aykroyd, Sigourney Weaver, Harold Ramis, Rick Moranis, Peter MacNicol

Ghostbusters II is babyboomer silliness. Kids will find the oozing slime and ghastly, ghostly apparitions to their liking and adults will enjoy the preposterously clever dialog of this sequel to the earlier film, again written by Ramis and Aykroyd.

In *II*, the foe is a sea of slime, a pinkish, oozing substance that has odd, selective powers – all of them (humorously) evil. Its origins have something to do with a bad imitation Rembrandt painting, the lecherous art historian with an indecipherable foreign accent who's restoring it (Peter MacNicol), and all the bad and negative vibes generated by millions of cranky, stressed-out New Yorkers. The worse their attitude, the worse the slime' problem, which is very bad indeed.

The Ghostbusters, naturally, are the only guys suitable for the job.

Bill Murray gets the plum central role (or he forced it by seemingly ad libbing dozens of wisecracks) at the same time his character also manages to skip out on a lot of the dirty ghostbusting work, leaving it to his pals Dan Aykroyd, Harold Ramis and Ernie Hudson to save New York from slime attack.

While they are zapping Slimer, the main nasty creature from the original film, Murray's time is spent wooing back Sigourney Weaver, now a single mother.

It may be a first time, but Weaver gets to play a softie, a nice break for the actress and her admirers (even if shots with her cute imperiled baby are scene-stealers).

THE GIRL CAN'T HELP IT

1956, 96 mins, ◇ Ⓥ *Dir* Frank Tashlin   US

★ **Stars** Tom Ewell, Jayne Mansfield, Edmond O'Brien, Henry Jones, John Emery, Juanita Moore

The Girl Can't Help It is an hilarious comedy with a beat. On the surface, it appears that producer-director-scripter Frank Tashlin concentrated on creating fun for the juniors – a chore that he completes to a tee. However, the suspicion lurks that he also poked some fun at the dance beat craze. There are so many sight gags and physical bits of business, including Jayne Mansfield and a couple of milk bottles, that males of any age will get the entertainment message.

Mansfield doesn't disappoint as the sexpot who just wants to be a successful wife and mother, not a glamor queen. She's physically equipped for the role, and also is competent in sparking considerable of the fun. Nature was so much more bountiful with her than with Marilyn Monroe

that it seems Mansfield should have left MM with her voice. However, the vocal imitation could have been just another part of the fun-poking indulged in.

Edmond O'Brien, rarely seen in comedy, is completely delightful as the hammy ex-gangster who thinks his position demands that his girl be a star name. Tom Ewell scores mightily as the has-been agent who is haunted by the memory of Julie London, another girl he had pushed to reluctant stardom.

THE GODS MUST BE CRAZY

1984, 108 mins, ◇ Ⓥ *Dir* Jamie Uys   BOTSWANA

★ **Stars** Marius Weyers, Sandra Prinsloo, N!xau, Louw Verwey, Michael Thys, Jamie Uys

The Gods Must Be Crazy is a comic fable by one-man-band South African filmmaker Jamie Uys, who shot the picture in Botswana in 1979.

Uys' basic storyline has Xi (N!xua), a bushman who lives deep in the Kalahari desert, setting off on a trek to destroy a Coca Cola bottle which fell from a passing airplane and by virtue of its strange usefulness as a utensil (thought

Jayne Mansfield and Tom Ewell in **The Girl Can't Help It,** *a classic send-up of the early rock 'n' roll business.*

to be thrown by the gods from heaven) has caused great dissension within his tribe.

Xi plans to throw the unwanted artifact of modern civilization off the edge of the world and in his trek encounters modern people.

Film's main virtues are its striking, widescreen visuals of unusual locations, and the sheer educational value of its narration.

THE GODS MUST BE CRAZY 2

1989, 99 mins, ◇ Ⓥ   *Dir* Jamie Uys   BOTSWANA, US

★ **Stars** N!xau, Lena Farugia, Hans Strydom, Eiros, Nadies, Erick Bowen

Jamie Uys has concocted a genial sequel to his 1983 international sleeper hit *The Gods Must Be Crazy* that is better than its progenitor in most respects.

His tongue-clicking Kalahari Bushman hero, again played by a real McCoy named N!xau, is once more unwittingly embroiled in the lunacies of civilization.

First plotline has N!xau's two adorable offspring getting innocently borne away on the trailer truck of a pair of unsuspecting ivory poachers. N!xau follows the tracks and comes across two other odd couples from the nutty outside world.

There is a New York femme lawyer (Lena Faragia), who is stranded in the middle of the Kalahari with a handsome, phlegmatic game warden (Hans Strydom) when their ultra-light plane is downed in a sudden storm.

Then there are two hapless mercenaries, an African and a Cuban, who keep taking one another prisoner in a series of table-turning pursuits through the brush.

Uys orchestrates a desert farce of criss-crossing destinies with more assured skill and charming sight-gags, marred only by facile penchant for speeded-up slapstick motion.

THE GOODBYE GIRL

1977, 110 mins, ◇ Ⓥ   *Dir* Herbert Ross   US

★ **Stars** Richard Dreyfuss, Marsha Mason, Quinn Cummings, Paul Benedict, Barbara Rhoades, Theresa Merritt

Academy Award 1977: Best Picture (Nomination)

Richard Dreyfuss in offbeat romantic lead casting, and vibrant Marsha Mason head the cast as two lovers in spite of themselves.

Story peg finds Mason, once-divorced and now jilted, finding out that her ex-lover has sublet their NY pad to aspiring thesp Dreyfuss. Mason has two other problems: a precocious daughter, Quinn Cummings, and her own thirtyish age which will prevent a successful resumption of a dancing career necessary to make ends meet.

The Neil Simon script evolves a series of increasingly intimate and sensitive character encounters as the adults progress from mutual hostility to an enduring love.

Performances by Dreyfuss, Mason and Cummings are all great, and the many supporting bits are filled admirably.

GO WEST

1940, 79 mins, Ⓥ   *Dir* Edward Buzzell   US

★ **Stars** Groucho Marx, Harpo Marx, Chico Marx, John Carroll, Diana Lewis, Walter Woolf King

The three Marx Bros ride a merry trail of laughs and broad burlesque in a speedy adventure through the sagebrush country. Story is only a slight framework on which to parade the generally nonsensical antics of the trio. Attracted to the wide open spaces by tales of gold lining the street, Chico, Harpo, and Groucho get involved in ownership of a deed to property wanted by the railroad for its western extension, and the action flashes through typical dance hall, rumbling stagecoach and desert waste episodes – with a wild train ride for a climax to outwit the villains.

Material provided by tightly knit script is topnotch while direction by Edward Buzzell smacks over the gags and comedy situations for maximum laughs. The Marxes secured pre-production audience reaction through tour of key picture houses trying out various sequences, which undoubtedly aided in tightening the action and dialog.

Groucho, Chico and Harpo handle their assignments with zestful enthusiasm. There's a bill-changing routine in Grand Central Station, wild melee and clowning in the rolling stagecoach, a comedy safe-cracking episode, and the train chase for a finish that winds up with the upper car structures dismantled by the silent Harpo to provide fuel for the engine. It's all ridiculous, but tuned for fun.

THE GREAT DICTATOR

1940, 127 mins, Ⓥ   *Dir* Charles Chaplin   US

★ **Stars** Charles Chaplin, Paulette Goddard, Jack Oakie, Reginald Gardiner, Henry Daniell, Billy Gilbert

Academy Award 1940: Best Picture (Nomination)

Chaplin makes no bones about his utter contempt for dictators like Hitler and Mussolini in his production of *The Great Dictator*. He takes time out to make fun about it, but the preachment is strong, notably in the six-minute speech at the finish.

Chaplin speaks throughout the film, but wherever convenient depends as much as he can on pantomime. His panto has always talked plenty.

Chaplin plays a dual role, that of a meek little Jewish barber in Tomania and the great little dictator of that country, billed as Hynkel. It's when he is playing the dictator that the comedian's voice raises the value of the comedy content of the picture to great heights. He does various bits as a Hitler spouting at the mouth in which he engages in a lot of double talk in what amounts to a pig-Latin version of the

German tongue, with grunts thrown in here and there, plus a classical 'Democracy shtoonk'. On various occasions as Hitler he also speaks English. In these instances he talks with force, as contrasted by the mousey, half-scared way he speaks as the poor barber.

Somewhat of a shock is the complete transformation of the barber when he delivers the speech at the finish, a fiery and impassioned plea for freedom and democracy. It is a peculiar and somewhat disappointing climax with the picture ending on a serious rather than a comical note.

The vast majority of the action is built around Hynkel and the Jewish barber. Not so much is devoted to the dictator who is Napaloni (Mussolini). Jack Oakie plays the satirized Duce to the hilt and every minute with him is socko.

In making up the billing, Chaplin has displayed an unusually keen sense of humor. While Hynkel is the dictator of Tomania, Napaloni is the ruler of Bacteria. Tomania higherups include Garbitsch (Goebels) and Herring (Goering). These two are played effectively by Henry Daniell and Billy Gilbert.

Teenage trauma as gentle comedy, with John Gordon Sinclair and Dee Hepburn in **Gregory's Girl.**

THE GREAT ST. TRINIAN'S TRAIN ROBBERY

1966, 94 mins, ◇ ⓥ   *Dir* Frank Launder, Sidney Gilliat   UK

★ **Stars** Frankie Howerd, Reg Varney, Stratford Johns, Eric Barker, Dora Bryan, George Cole

Ronald Searle's little schoolgirl demons from St. Trinian's are berserk again on the screen in a yarn with a topical twist, the [1963] Great Train Robbery.

Having pulled off a $7 million train robbery, a hapless gang of crooks stash the loot in a deserted country mansion. But when they go back to collect they find the St. Trinian's school has taken over, and they are completely routed by the hockey sticks and rough stuff handed out by the little shemonsters. When the gang returns on parents' day for a second attempt at picking up the loot they run into further trouble and complications and eventually get involved in a great train chase which is quite the funniest part of the film, having a great deal in common with the old silent slapstick technique.

Among the many performances which contribute to the gaiety are those of Frankie Howerd as a crook posing as a French male hairdresser, Raymond Huntley as a Cabinet Minister with amorous eyes on the St. Trinian's headmistress (Dora Bryan), Richard Wattis in one of his typical harassed civil servant roles and Peter Gilmore as his confrere. George Cole crops up again as Flash Harry, the school bookie.

GREGORY'S GIRL

1982, 91 mins, ◇ ⓥ   *Dir* Bill Forsyth   UK

★ **Stars** John Gordon Sinclair, Dee Hepburn, Jake D'Arcy, Clare Grogan, Robert Buchanan, William Greenlees

Filmmaker Bill Forsyth, whose friendly, unmalicious approach recalls that of Rene Clair, is concerned with young students (in particular, a soccer team goalie, Gregory) seeking out the opposite sex. Much of the pic's peculiar fascination comes from tangential scenes, limning each character's odd obsession, be it food, girls, soccer, or just watching the traffic drive by.

Main narrative thread has Gregory becoming infatuated with the cute (and athletic) new girl on his soccer team, Dorothy (Dee Hepburn), while her schoolmates delightfully maneuver him into giving the out-going Susan (Clare Grogan) a tumble.

As Gregory, John Gordon Sinclair is adept at physical comedy. Hepburn is properly enigmatic as the young object of his desire, with ensemble approach giving Gregory's precocious 10-year-old sister played by Allison Forster a key femme role.

A GUIDE FOR THE MARRIED MAN

1967, 89 mins, ◇ ⓥ   *Dir* Gene Kelly   US

★ **Stars** Walter Matthau, Robert Morse, Inger Stevens, Sue Ane Langdon, Claire Kelly, Linda Harrison

Walter Matthau plays a married innocent, eager to stray under the tutelage of friend and neighbor Robert Morse. But this long-married hubby is so retarded in his immorality (it takes him 12 years to get the seven-year-itch) that, between his natural reluctance and mentor Morse's suggestions (interlarded with warnings against hastiness), he needs the entire film to have his mind made up.

Guide is packed with action, pulchritude, situations, and considerable (if not quite enough) laughs. Inger Stevens is beautiful as Matthau's wife, and so unbelievably perfect that it makes his reluctance most understandable.

Some of the guest talent have no more than one line (Jeffrey Hunter, Sam Jaffe), some are mimed (Wally Cox, Ben Blue) and others have several lines (Sid Caesar, Phil Silvers, Jack Benny, Hal March).

HAIRSPRAY

1988, 90 mins, ◇ Ⓥ *Dir* John Waters   US

★ *Stars* Sonny Bono, Ruth Brown, Divine, Colleen Fitzpatrick, Michael St Gerard, Debbie Harry

John Waters' appreciation for the tacky side of life is in full flower in *Hairspray*, a slight but often highly amusing diversion about integration, big girls' fashions and music-mad teens in 1962 Baltimore.

Ricki Lake, chubette daughter of Divine and Jerry Stiller, overcomes all to become queen of an afternoon teenage dance show, much to the consternation of stuck-up blond Colleen Fitzpatrick, whose parents are Debbie Harry and Sonny Bono.

Divine spits out some choice bon mots while denigrating her daughter's pastime, but finally rejoicing in her success, takes Lake off for a pricelessly funny visit to Hefty Hideaway, where full-figure girls can shop to their hearts' content.

Divine, so big he wears a tent-like garment big enough for three ordinary mortals to sleep in, is in otherwise fine form in a dual role. Harry has little to do but act bitchy and sport increasingly towering wigs, while Pia Zadora is virtually unrecognizable as a beatnik chick. All the kids in the predominantly teenage cast are tirelessly enthusiastic.

THE HAPPIEST DAYS OF YOUR LIFE

1950, 81 mins, *Dir* Frank Launder   UK

★ *Stars* Alastair Sim, Margaret Rutherford, Joyce Grenfell, Richard Wattis

Bright script and brisk direction conceal the stage origin. The story is given a wider canvas and isn't wanting in action. In fact, the pace never lets up and one hilarious farcical incident only ends to give place to another.

Setting of the film is a college for boys, to which, as a result of a slip at the Ministry of Education, a girl's school is evacuated. The story builds up to a boisterous climax in which the principals are trying to conceal the real situation from visitors to the college.

There is no shortage of laughs, but the joke is a little too protracted and wears thin before the end. It's an ideal vehicle for Alastair Sim as the harassed headmaster, while Margaret Rutherford admirably suggests the overpowering headmistress. Joyce Grenfell never fails to raise a chuckle as the over-anxious sports mistress and there are fine contributions from John Turnbull, Guy Middleton and Edward Rigby, with a trivial touch of romance added by John Bentley and Bernadette O'Farrell.

Black comedy at its darkest, Ruth Gordon and Bud Cort play the oddly humorous Harold and Maude.

HAROLD AND MAUDE

1971, 90 mins, ◇ Ⓥ *Dir* Hal Ashby   US

★ *Stars* Ruth Gordon, Bud Cort, Vivian Pickles, Cyril Cusack, Charles Tyner, Ellen Geer

Harold and Maude has all the fun and gaiety of a burning orphanage. Ruth Gordon heads the cast as an offensive eccentric who becomes a beacon in the life of a self-destructive rich boy, played by Bud Cort. Together they attend funerals and indulge in specious philosophizing.

Director Hal Ashby's second feature is marked by a few good gags, but marred by a greater preponderance of sophomoric, overdone and mocking humor.

Cort does well as the spoiled neurotic whose repeated suicide attempts barely ruffle the feathers of mother Vivian Pickles, whose urbane performance is outstanding. She solicits a computer dating service to provide three potential brides: Shari Summers and Judy Engles are frightened off by Cort's bizarre doings, but Ellen Geer is delightful as one who goes him one better.

One thing that can be said about Ashby – he begins the film in a gross and macabre manner, and never once deviates from the concept. That's style for you.

HARRY AND TONTO

1974, 115 mins, ◇ Ⓥ *Dir* Paul Mazursky   US

★ *Stars* Art Carney, Ellen Burstyn, Chief Dan George, Geraldine Fitzgerald, Larry Hagman, Arthur Hunnicutt

Harry and Tonto stars Art Carney and a trained cat, respectively, in a pleasant film about an old man who rejuvenates himself on a cross-country trek. Script is a series of good human comedy vignettes, with the large supporting cast of many familiar names in virtual cameo roles.

Carney is excellent as an old NY widower, evicted by force from a building being torn down. The rupture in his life triggers an odyssey, with pet cat named Tonto, to LA, with family stopovers at the Jersey home of son Phil Bruns, then to Chicago where Ellen Burstyn remains a warm antagonist, finally to LA where Larry Hagman emerges as a failure in life. En route, Carney picks up young hitchhiker Melanie Mayron, eventually paired off with grandson Joshua Mostel.

HARVEY

1950, 103 mins, *Dir* Henry Koster   US

★ *Stars* James Stewart, Josephine Hull, Peggy Dow, Charles Drake, Cecil Kellaway, Wallace Ford

Harvey, Mary Chase's Pulitzer Prize play, loses little of its whimsical comedy charm in the screen translation.

Three of the principals, James Stewart, Josephine Hull and Jesse White, were seasoned in the wacky characters by playing them on stage.

The exploits of Elwood P. Dowd, a man who successfully escaped from trying reality when his invisible six-foot rabbit pal Harvey came into his life, continually spring chuckles, often hilarity, as the footage unfolds. Stewart would seem the perfect casting for the character so well does he convey the idea that escape from life into a pleasant half-world existence has many points in its favor. Josephine Hull, the slightly balmy aunt who wants to have Elwood committed, is immense, socking the comedy for every bit of its worth.

THE HEARTBREAK KID

1972, 104 mins, ◇ Ⓥ *Dir* Elaine May   US

★ *Stars* Charles Grodin, Cybill Shepherd, Jeannie Berlin, Eddie Albert, Audra Lindley, William Prince

The Heartbreak Kid is the bright, amusing saga of a young NY bridegroom whose bride's maddening idiosyncrasies freak him and he leaves her at the end of a three-day Miami honeymoon to pursue and wed another doll. Scripted by Neil Simon from Bruce Jay Friedman's *Esquire* mag story [*A Change of Plan*], film has a sudden shut-off ending with no climax whatever.

Elaine May's deft direction catches all the possibilities of young romance and its tribulations in light strokes and cleverly accents characterization of the various principals. Most of the pace is as fast as Charles Grodin's speeding to his Florida honeymoon, and falling for a gorgeous blonde on the beach the first day there.

Grodin is slick and able as the fast-talking bridegroom whose patience is worn thin and he's a natural for the charms of another.

HEART CONDITION

1990, 95 mins, ◇ Ⓥ *Dir* James D. Parriott   US

★ *Stars* Bob Hoskins, Denzel Washington, Chloe Webb, Roger E. Mosley

From what seems like a far-fetched premise – a cop who gets a heart transplant ends up depending on his worst enemy's ticker – writer-director James D. Parriott spins a most engrossing and rewarding tale in an auspicious feature debut.

Bob Hoskins plays vice detective Moony, an intense, crazy, racist slob who briefly has a girl in his life – a hooker, Crystal (Chloe Webb). She disappears and gets involved with her black lawyer, Stone (Denzel Washington), a handsome self-possessed smooth operator who becomes the object of Moony's obsessive rage.

Moony, who lives on greaseburgers and booze, has a heart attack the same night Stone is killed in a car crash. Thanks to expedient transplant surgery he ends up a 'blood brother' to his enemy. To Mooney's horror, the sarcastic, clever Stone appears in ghostlike form visible only to him, and becomes his constant, unwanted companion.

Washington creates a most compelling character in Stone, finding the rhythm of the role with an assurance that never flags; Hoskins is gutsy and amusing, exhibiting bug-eyed discomfort when he's manicured and barbered in a Stone-style transformation.

HEATHERS

1989, 102 mins, ◇ Ⓥ *Dir* Michael Lehmann   US

★ *Stars* Winona Ryder, Christian Slater, Shannen Doherty, Lisanne Falk, Kim Walker

Heathers is a super-smart black comedy about high school politics and teenage suicide that showcases a host of promising young talents.

Daniel Waters' enormously clever screenplay blazes a trail of originality through the dead wood of the teen-comedy genre by focusing on the *Heathers*, the four prettiest and most popular girls at Westerburg High, three of whom are named Heather.

Setting the tone for the group is founder and queen bitch Heather No. 1, who has a devastating put-down or comeback for every occasion and could freeze even a heat-seeking missile in its tracks with her icy stare.

Heathers No. 2 and 3 get off their own zingers once in a while, while the fourth nubile beauty, Veronica (Winona Ryder), goes along for the ride but seems to have a mind of her own. She also has eyes for a rebellious-looking school newcomer named J.D. (Christian Slater).

Goaded by the seductive J.D., Veronica half-heartedly goes along with an attempt to murder Heather No. 1, who has become irritating beyond endurance.

Winona Ryder is utterly fetching and winning as an intelligent but seriously divided young lady. Oozing an

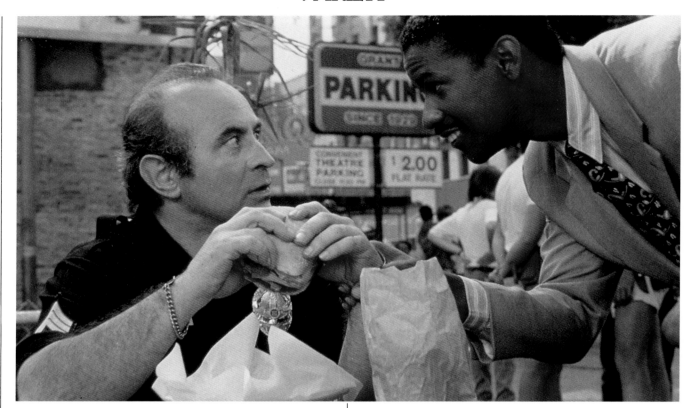

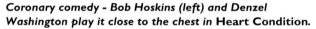

Coronary comedy - Bob Hoskins (left) and Denzel Washington play it close to the chest in **Heart Condition.**

insinuating sarcasm reminiscent of Jack Nicholson, Christian Slater has what it takes to make J.D. both alluring and dangerous. The three Heathers (Shannen Doherty, Lisanne Falk and Kim Walker) look like they've spent their lives practising putdowns.

HEAVEN CAN WAIT

1943, 112 mins, ◇ *Dir* Ernst Lubitsch   US

★ **Stars** Gene Tierney, Don Ameche, Charles Coburn, Marjorie Main, Laird Cregar, Louis Calhern

Academy Award 1943: Best Picture (Nomination)

Provided with generous slices of comedy, skilfully handled by producer-director Ernst Lubitsch, this is for most of the 112 minutes a smooth, appealing and highly commercial production. Lubitsch has endowed it with light, amusing sophistication and heart-warming nostalgia. He has handled Don Ameche and Gene Tierney, in (for them) difficult characterizations, dexterously.

The Laszlo Bus-Fekete play covers the complete span of a man's life, from precocious infancy to in this case, the sprightly senility of a 70-year-old playboy. It opens with the deceased (Ameche) asking Satan for a passport to hell, which is not being issued unless the applicant can justify his right to it.

This is followed by a recital of real and fancied misdeeds from the time the sinner discovers that, in order to get girls, a boy must have plenty of beetles, through the smartly fashioned hilarious drunk scene with a French maid at the age of 15, to the thefting of his cousin's fiancee, whom he marries.

Charles Coburn as the fond grandfather who takes a hand in his favorite grandson's romantic and domestic problems, walks away with the early sequences in a terrific comedy performance.

HEAVENS ABOVE!

1963, 118 mins, ⊘ *Dir* John Boulting   UK

★ **Stars** Peter Sellers, Bernard Miles, Eric Sykes, Irene Handl, Miriam Karlin, Isabel Jeans

A measure of the merit of *Heavens Above!* is that its theme could have been just as acceptably used as a straight drama. But the Boulting Brothers effectively employ their favorite weapon, the rapier of ridicule. The screenplay is full of choice jokes, but the humor is often uneven.

Story concerns the appointment, by a clerical error, of the Reverend John Smallwood (Peter Sellers) to the parish of Orbiston Parva, a prosperous neighborhood ruled by the Despard family, makers of Tranquilax, the three-in-one restorative (Sedative! Stimulant! Laxative!). He's a quiet, down-to-earth chap who happens to believe in the scriptures and lives by them.

From the moment he gives his first sermon all hell breaks out, so to speak. He shocks the district by making a Negro trashman his warden and takes a bunch of disreputable evicted gypsies into the vicarage. Soon he makes his first convert, Lady Despard.

Within this framework there are some very amusing verbal and visual jokes, and both are largely aided by some deft acting. Sellers gives a guileful portrayal of genuine simplicity. Bernard Miles, as an acquisitive butler; Eric Sykes, Irene Handl, Miriam Karlin and Roy Kinnear (leader of the gypsies); and Isabel Jeans, a regal Lady Despard, all contribute heftily.

Those who expect to see church steeples crumble under a blistering attack will be unlucky. But there is enough amusement to satisfy even those who want to duck the film's unmistakable and uncomfortable conclusion: 'That in this material world anyone who tries to lead a truly Christian life is weighing himself down with socko odds.'

HELLZAPOPPIN

1941, 92 mins, *Dir* H.C. Potter   US

★ **Stars** Ole Olsen, Chic Johnson, Martha Raye, Hugh Herbert, Mischa Auer

---

There's the thinnest thread of a romantic story, but it's incidental to Olsen and Johnson's [1938] stage formula for *Hellzapoppin.*

Vaudeville double act Olsen and Johnson crashed into the movies in a big way with Hellzapoppin.

The yarn itself can be summed up in a few words: the rich girl in love with the poor boy, who in turn doesn't want to cross his rich pal, favored by the girl's socially conscious parents. The poor boy stages a charity show for the girl, and his stagehand pals (O&J) think they can save him from the girl, by lousing it up.

One of the picture's saving graces is the originality of presentation of screwball comedy. The business of Olsen & Johnson talking from the screen to the comic film projectionist (Shemp Howard) is one such detail; ditto the slide bit telling a kid in the audience, 'Stinky go home', with Jane Frazee and Robert Paige interrupting a duet until Stinky finally leaves.

Don Raye and Gene DePauf have contributed several nice songs for this film. There are some lavish production numbers – Jules Levey (Mayfair), producer, was obviously unstinting.

HER HUSBAND'S AFFAIRS

1947, 84 mins, *Dir* S. Sylvan Simon   US

★ **Stars** Lucille Ball, Franchot Tone, Edward Everett Horton, Mikhail Rasumny, Gene Lockhart, Jonathan Hale

---

Her Husband's Affairs is well-premised fun that has a laugh a minute. As a comedy team, Lucille Ball and Franchot Tone excel. Tone is a slightly screwball advertising-slogan genius while Ball is his ever-loving wife who somehow always winds up with the credit for his spectacular stunts.

Director S. Sylvan Simon's pace is perfect and he welds zany situations into socko laughs. Motivation for much of the comedy comes from Tone's sponsorship of a screwball inventor and the products that he develops while searching for the perfect embalming fluid. Gentle fun is poked at advertising agencies and bigshot sponsors and public figures.

Mikhail Rasumny is the crazy inventor and wraps up the role for honors, Edward Everett Horton, Gene Lockhart, a business tycoon, Nana Bryant, his wife, and Jonathan Hale are among others who keep the laughs busy.

HIGH ANXIETY

1977, 94 mins, ◇ Ⓥ *Dir* Mel Brooks   US

★ *Stars* Mel Brooks, Madeline Kahn, Cloris Leachman, Harvey Korman, Ron Carey, Howard Morris

High Anxiety is a straight Hitchcockian sendup – homage applies as well – with highs and lows ranging from a brilliant restaging of the shower scene in *Psycho* to childish bathroom humor.

Besides playing the role of a Harvard professor and psychiatrist with a fear of heights who takes over the Psycho-Neurotic Institute for the Very, Very Nervous, Mel Brooks dons the producer, director and co-writer caps.

Even more than the games he can play with the Hitchcock story, Brooks seems to enjoy toying with the technical references – the tight closeups, shots of hands and feet, stairway sequences and manipulation of the interaction between music and visuals. Nearly all of these gags, and none of them require the background of a buff, score.

The shower scene from Psycho, with Mel Brooks taking the part of Janet Leigh, parodied in High Anxiety.

HIGH HOPES

1988, 112 mins, ◇ Ⓥ *Dir* Mike Leigh   UK

★ *Stars* Philip Davis, Ruth Sheen, Edna Dore, Philip Jackson, Heather Tobias

In the working-class London district of King's Cross, yuppies are moving into old houses, restoring them, and driving out the locals who've lived there for ages. Old Mrs Bender, a widow, lives in one house; her neighbors are the fearfully uppercrust Booth-Braines and they treat the old lady with ill-disguised contempt.

Mrs Bender's two children are an ill-assorted pair. Cyril, with long hair and beard, works as a courier, lives with his down-to-earth girlfriend Shirley, and despises the British establishment.

Daughter Valerie, on the other hand, is very much a would-be yuppie, who is married to a crass used-car dealer, and lives in a garishly over-decorated house. She is completely self-centered and totally insensitive to the needs of her elderly mother.

Around these characters, Leigh builds up a slight story intended to be a microcosm of today's London.

HIGH SPIRITS

1988, 97 mins, ◇ Ⓥ *Dir* Neil Jordan   UK, US

★ *Stars* Daryl Hannah, Peter O'Toole, Steve Guttenberg, Beverly D'Angelo, Liam Neeson, Ray McAnally

High Spirits is a piece of supernatural Irish whimsy with a few appealing dark underpinnings, but it still rises and falls

constantly on the basis of its moment-to-moment inspirations.

Elaborate physical production is set almost entirely at Castle Plunkett, a rundown Irish edifice that proprietor Peter O'Toole opens as a tourist hotel in order to meet the mortgage payments. With the American market in mind, O'Toole bills the place as a haunted castle, to this end having his staff dress up like ghouls of various persuasions.

It comes as little surprise that the castle turns out to be actually haunted. Steve Guttenberg, who is not getting along with wife Beverly D'Angelo, comes to meet ghost Daryl Hannah, who was killed on the premises years ago on her wedding night by Liam Neeson, who takes a fancy to D'Angelo.

HIS GIRL FRIDAY

1940, 92 mins, ⊙   *Dir* Howard Hawks   US

★ **Stars** Cary Grant, Rosalind Russell, Ralph Bellamy, Gene Lockhart, Helen Mack, John Qualen

No doubt aiming to dodge the stigma of having *His Girl Friday* termed a remake, Columbia blithely skips a pertinent point in the credits by merely stating 'From a play by Ben Hecht and Charles·MacArthur.' It's inescapable, however, that this is the former legit and pic smash *The Front Page*. The trappings are different – even to the extent of making reporter Hildy Johnson a femme – but it is still *Front Page*.

With more of the feminine-romance angle injected than was in the original, this new edition becomes more the modern-style sophisticated comedy than the hard, biting picture of newspapermen that Hecht and MacArthur painted in their stage play. Its remake in this revised form was a happy idea, especially since it still moves punchily, retains plenty of its laughs and almost all of its drama.

Casting is excellent, with Cary Grant and Rosalind Russell in the top roles. Grant is the sophisticated, hard-boiled, smart-alec managing editor who was portrayed by Adolphe Menjou in the earlier version. A newly-injected part, required by the switch in sex of Hildy, is taken by Ralph Bellamy.

Principal action of the story still takes place in a courthouse pressroom. All of the trappings are there, including the crew of newshawks who continue their penny-ante poker through everything and the practice of the sheriff's crew on the gallows for an execution in the morning. With the wider vista given the story, there is, in addition, the newspaper office.

Star-reporter Russell tells managing editor Grant, from whom she has just been divorced, that she is quitting his employ to marry another man. Grant neither wants to see her resign nor marry again, retaining hope of a rehitching. To prevent her escaping, he prevails upon her to cover one more story, that of a deluded radical charged with murder and whom the paper thinks is innocent. Escape of the convicted man, his virtual falling into Russell's lap as she sits

alone in the pressroom, and attempts by Grant and Russell to bottle up the story, are w.k., but still exciting.

HISTORY OF THE WORLD – PART I

1981, 92 mins, ◇   *Dir* Mel Brooks   US

★ *Stars* Mel Brooks, Dom DeLuise, Madeline Kahn, Cloris Leachman, Gregory Hines, Sid Caesar

Boisterous cinematic vaudeville show is comprised of five distinct sections: the *2001* parody *Dawn of Man*, *The Stone Age*, featuring Brooks' acid comment on the role of the art critic, and a brief 'Old Testament' bit, which together run 10 minutes; *The Roman Empire*, the best-sustained and, at 43 minutes, longest episode; *The Spanish Inquisition*, a splashy nine-minute production number; *The French Revolution*, a rather feeble 24-minute sketch; and *Coming Attractions* which, with end credits, runs six minutes and at least punches up the finale with the hilarious *Jews in Space* intergalactic musical action number.

Although Monty Python's *Life of Brian* went well beyond Brooks in the blasphemy department, many of the pic's most successful gags poke holes in religious pieties. When Brooks as Moses comes down from the mountain, he's carrying three tablets. Frightened by a lightning blast, he drops one of them and quickly switches to 10 commandments instead of 15.

The one interlude which really brings down the house has Brooks working as a waiter at the Last Supper and asking the assembled group. 'Are you all together or is it separate checks?'

As the old ad line said, there's something here to offend everybody, particularly the devout of all persuasions and homosexuals.

HOME ALONE

1990, 102 mins, ◇ ⓥ   *Dir* Chris Columbus   US

★ *Stars* Macauley Culkin, Joe Pesci, Daniel Stern, Catherine O'Hara, John Heard, John Candy

The family of poor little dumped-upon Kevin (Macauley Culkin) has rushed off to catch their holiday plane and accidentally left him behind. Now they're in Paris, frantically trying to reach him, and he's home alone, where a storm has knocked out the telephones, the neighbors are away for the holiday and the houses on the street are being systematically cleaned out by a team of burglars.

Generally perceived by his family as a helpless, hopeless little geek, Kevin is at first delighted to be rid of them, gorging on forbidden pleasures like junk food and violent videos, but when the bandits (Joe Pesci, Daniel Stern) begin circling his house, he realizes he's on his own to defend the place.

Kevin proves he's not such a loser by defending the fort with wits and daring and by the time Mom (Catherine O'Hara) comes rushing back from Europe, everything's in order.

In Home Alone, *Macauley Culkin proved a States-wide hit as a little boy having to cope on his own with burglars.*

A first-rate production in which every element contributes to the overall smartly realized tone, pic boasts wonderful casting, with Culkin a delight as funny, resilient Kevin, and O'Hara bringing a snappy, zesty energy to the role of mom. Pesci is aces in the role of slippery housebreaker Harry, who does a Two Stooges routine with lanky side-kick Stern.

HONEY, I SHRUNK THE KIDS

1989, 86 mins, ◇ ⓥ   *Dir* Joe Johnston   US

★ *Stars* Rick Moranis, Matt Frewer, Marcia Strassman, Kristine Sutherland, Thomas Brown

Borrowing two good end elements from two 1950s sci-fi pics, *The Incredible Shrinking Man* and *Them*, scripters pit two sets of unfriendly neighbor kids, mistakenly shrunk to only 1/4-inch high, against what ordinarily would be benign backyard fixtures, both alive and inanimate.

Their misfortune was to get caught in the beam of ne'er-do-well inventor Wayne Szalinski's (Rick Moranis)

Good mornings were never like this; drowning in the breakfast cereal in **Honey I Shrunk the Kids.**

molecule-reducing contraption while he's out giving a lecture to a group of skeptical scientists.

He sweeps them into the dustpan along with the other flotsam that goes out with the trash.

Now, they must make it back to the house among towering vegetation, humungous bugs and fierce water showers on a quest that would be nightmarish except that it seems mostly like a lot of fun.

Pic [story by Stuart Gordon, Brian Yuzna and Ed Naha] is in the best tradition of Disney and even better than that because it is not so juvenile that adults won't be thoroughly entertained.

THE HONEY POT

1967, 150 mins, ◇ ⓥ *Dir* Joseph L. Mankiewicz   UK

★ *Stars* Rex Harrison, Susan Hayward, Cliff Robertson, Capucine, Edie Adams, Maggie Smith

An elegant, sophisticated screen vehicle for more demanding tastes, previously billed as *Mr Fox of Venice* and *Anyone for Venice?* Vaguely drawing its inspiration from Ben Jonson's *Volpone*, film's updated plot centers around the fabulously rich Cecil Fox (Rex Harrison) who with the aid of a sometimes gigolo and secretary, William McFly

(Cliff Robertson), plays a joke of sorts on three one-time mistresses by feigning grave illness and gauging their reactions as they come flocking to his bedside.

There is the wisecracking hypochondriac, Mrs Sheridan (Susan Hayward), who was Fox's first love, accompanied by the attractive nurse, Sarah Watkins (Maggie Smith). There's Princess Dominique, a glacially beautiful jet-setter played by Capucine. And there's the ebullient Merle McGill (Edie Adams), a Hollywood star without a care in the world – except for a massive debt to Uncle Sam.

The dialog is often a delight in its hark-back to the days when the turn of a phrase and the tongue-in-cheek were a staple of better Hollywood product. The playing is all of a superior character.

HOPSCOTCH

1980, 104 mins, ◇ ⓥ *Dir* Ronald Neame   US

★ *Stars* Walter Matthau, Glenda Jackson, Ned Beatty, Sam Waterston, Herbert Lom

Hopscotch is a high-spirited caper comedy which, unfortunately, reaches its peak too soon.

Grizzled as usual, Walter Matthau plays CIA agent whose independent ways are too much for his finicky, double-dealing boss (Ned Beatty). So Matthau is put in charge of the files.

But he never shows up for the new assignment, deciding instead to hide out and write a book that will embarrass

not only the CIA but spies in every country, making himself a target for extinction from several directions.

Hiding out, Matthau takes up with Glenda Jackson. They are old flames and their initial moments together serve up the same good bantering chemistry that was evident in *House Calls*.

It's all for laughs as Matthau evades the hunters while dreaming up additional ways to make fools of them.

HORSE FEATHERS

1932, 70 mins, ⊛ *Dir* Norman Z. McLeod   US

★ **Stars** Groucho Marx, Chico Marx, Harpo Marx, Zeppo Marx, Thelma Todd, David Landau

The madcap Marxes, in one of their maddest screen frolics. The premise of Groucho Marx as the college prexy and his three aides and abettors putting Huxley College on the gridiron map promises much and delivers more.

Zeppo is his usual straight opposite Thelma Todd as the college widow. She's a luscious eyeful and swell foil for the Marxian boudoir manhandling, which is getting to be a trade-marked comedy routine.

On the matter of formula, the harp and piano numbers were repeated against the Marxes' personal wishes but by exhibitor demands to the studio. The piano is oke, but the harp reprise of 'Everyone Says I Love You' (by Bert Kalmar and Harry Ruby) substantiates the boys' opinion that it tends to slow up the comedy.

The plot, such as it is, is motivated around gambler David Landau's planting of two pros on the Darwin team which meets Huxley. Groucho visits the speak where the Darwin ringers have been engaged and mistakes dog-catcher Harpo and bootlegging iceman Chico as gridiron material.

HOW TO GET AHEAD IN ADVERTISING

1989, 95 mins, ◇ ⊛ *Dir* Bruce Robinson   UK

★ **Stars** Richard E. Grant, Rachel Ward, Richard Wilson, Jacqueline Tong, John Shrapnel

As a hotshot go-getter in the British equivalent of Madison Avenue, Richard E. Grant is having a problem coming up with an original campaign for a pimple cream and the pressure is on from the client and his boss (wonderfully droll Richard Wilson).

As dutiful wives do, Rachel Ward tries to assure him that something in his genius will come forward, but he's floundering.

When a small boil breaks out on his own neck, Grant realizes the stress has become too much for him and it's time to quit the business. However, it's too late. The boil begins to grow – and starts to talk, giving form to all that's vile and venal in his nature.

The picture would be genuinely hilarious were the subject matter not so overworked.

HOW TO MARRY A MILLIONAIRE

1953, 95 mins, ◇ ⊛ *Dir* Jean Negulesco   US

★ **Stars** Betty Grable, Marilyn Monroe, Lauren Bacall, David Wayne, Rory Calhoun, Cameron Mitchell

The script draws for partial source material on two plays, Zoe Akins' *The Greeks Had a Word for It* and *Loco* by Dale Eunson and Katherine Albert. Nunnally Johnson has blended the legiter ingredients with his own material for snappy comedy effect.

The plot has three girls pooling physical and monetary resources for a millionaire man hunt and as the predatory sex game unfolds the chuckles are constant. Each winds up with a man.

One is David Wayne, a fugitive from Uncle Sam's Internal Revenue agents whose apartment the girls have leased as a base for the chase. He gets Marilyn Monroe.

Another is Cameron Mitchell, a young tycoon who dresses like a lowly wage slave. He winds up with Lauren Bacall. Third is Rory Calhoun, a poor but honest forest ranger who gains Betty Grable as a fire-watching companion. None is what the femme trio expected to get when the hunt started.

Certain for audience favor is Monroe's blonde with astigmatism who goes through life bumping into things, including men, because she thinks glasses would detract. Also captivating is Grable's Loco, a friendly, cuddly blonde who turns situations to advantage until the great outdoors overwhelms her. As the brains of the trio, Bacall's Schatze is a wise-cracking, hard-shelled gal who gives up millions for love and gets both.

A real standout among the other players is William Powell as the elderly Texas rancher who woos, wins and then gives up Bacall.

HOW TO MURDER YOUR WIFE

1965, 118 mins, ◇ ⊛ *Dir* Richard Quine   US

★ **Stars** Jack Lemmon, Virna Lisi, Terry-Thomas, Eddie Mayehoff, Claire Trevor, Sidney Blackmer

George Axelrod's plot deals with the antics of a bachelor cartoonist, played by Jack Lemmon, who has a policy of acting out the escapades of his newsprint sleuth hero to test their credibility before actually committing them to paper. So it is that, awakening one morning to find himself married to an Italian dish who had popped out of a cake at a party the night before and after trying to make a go of this unwanted wedlock, he simulates the 'murder' of said spouse one evening by dumping a dummy likeness of her into a building construction site.

When Lemmon's wife, played by Virna Lisi, spots the cartoonist's sketches of his 'crime' on his work table she panics and flees. The strip appears in the papers and, unable to explain his wife's whereabouts, Lemmon is arrested for murder and brought to trial.

All of this has moments of fine comic style but, overall, emerges as prefabricated as Lemmon's comic strip character. The comedian's efforts are considerable and consistent but finesse and desire aren't enough to overcome the fact that Axelrod's script doesn't make the most of its potentially antic situations.

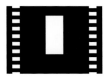

I'M NO ANGEL

1933, 87 mins, *Dir* Wesley Ruggles   US

★ *Stars* Mae West, Cary Grant, Edward Arnold, Ralf Harolde, Russell Hopton, Gregory Ratoff

It's fairly obvious that the same plot mechanics and situations [from suggestions by Lowell Brentano and a treatment by Harlan Thompson] without Mae West wouldn't be a motion picture at all. But that's no criticism. It's all West, plus a good directing job by Wesley Ruggles and first-rate studio production quality in all departments.

Laughs are all derived from the West innuendos and the general good-natured bawdiness of the heroine, whose progress from a carnival mugg-taker to a deluxe millionaire-annexer is marked by a succession of gentlemen friends, mostly temporary and usually suckers.

When reaching affluence the carnival gal is serviced by four colored maids in an ultra-penthouse and garbed in the flashy manner of an Oriental potentate's pampered pet.

Every now and again West bursts into a song, generally just a chorus or a strain. They're of the Frankie and Johnny genre, but primarily she plays a lion tamer, not a songstress.

THE IMPORTANCE OF BEING EARNEST

1952, 95 mins, ◇ ⓥ *Dir* Anthony Asquith   UK

★ *Stars* Michael Redgrave, Edith Evans, Michael Denison, Dorothy Tutin, Margaret Rutherford, Joan Greenwood

All the charm and glossy humor of Oscar Wilde's classic comedy emerges faithfully in this British production. Apart from a few minor cuts, director Anthony Asquith has taken few liberties with the original. His skilful direction extracts all the polish of Wilde's brilliant dialog.

Michael Redgrave brings a wealth of sincerity to the role of the earnest young man, without knowledge of his origin, whose invention of a fictitious brother leads to romantic complications. Michael Denison plays the debonair Algernon Moncrieff in a gay lighthearted style, and makes his characterization the pivot for much of the comedy.

The two romantic femme roles are adroitly played by Joan Greenwood and Dorothy Tutin.

IMPROPER CHANNELS

1981, 91 mins, ◇ *Dir* Eric Till   CANADA

★ *Stars* Alan Arkin, Mariette Hartley, Sarah Stevens, Monica Parker

Alan Arkin puts his hapless schnook characterization to good use in *Improper Channels*. It's a screwball comedy that starts slowly, shifts into overdrive, peters out a bit halfway through and then gets its second wind for a fast-paced, down-with-the-computer finish.

He's an architect, separated from his writer spouse (Mariette Hartley) and precocious five-year-old daughter (Sarah Stevens). And one thing leads to another; the daughter is injured slightly in his camper and when taken to hospital she is thought to have been beaten by her father.

A domineering social worker (Monica Parker) has a computer expert call up all available information on Arkin and the daughter is bundled off by court order to an orphanage. Arkin and Hartley attempt to get her back.

Eric Till's direction is surefire most of the time, though he's let down by a script that wants to do too much. Pic was shot under the title of 'Proper Channels' and was changed for reasons not explained.

INSPECTOR CLOUSEAU

1968, 105 mins, ◇ *Dir* Bud Yorkin   UK

★ *Stars* Alan Arkin, Frank Finlay, Delia Boccardo, Patrick Cargill, Beryl Reid, Barry Foster

Inspector Clouseau, the gauche and Gallic gumshoe, gets a healthy revitalization via Alan Arkin in the title role and director Bud Yorkin. Film is a lively, entertaining and episodic story of bank robbers. Good scripting, better acting and topnotch direction get the most out of the material.

Clouseau is assigned to Scotland Yard to help solve a major bank heist. Story develops to a simultaneous robbery of about a dozen Swiss banks, by a ring whose members wear face masks patterned after Clouseau.

Story develops leisurely, which could have worked to overall disadvantage were it not for the excellent work of Arkin and Yorkin keeping plot adrenalin flowing. Instead, enough momentum is sustained to hold amused interest.

ISHTAR

1987, 107 mins, ◇ ⓥ *Dir* Elaine May   US

★ *Stars* Warren Beatty, Dustin Hoffman, Isabelle Adjani, Charles Grodin, Jack Weston, Tess Harper

Here's how the story goes: Warren Beatty and Dustin Hoffman are struggling and mightily untalented songwriters-

singers in New York. They hook up with talent agent Jack Weston (who delivers a fine character performance) and wind up getting booked into the Chez Casablanca in Morocco. Yes, there's the obvious parallels to the Hope-Crosby *Road* films.

Arrival in Africa finds Beatty-Hoffman stopping in the mythical kingdom of Ishtar, where swirl of events leads them into vortex of Middle East political turmoil, with Isabelle Adjani functioning as a left-wing rebel trying to overthrow the US-backed Emir of Ishtar.

Enter Charles Grodin, who upstages all involved via his savagely comical portrayal of a CIA agent. He provides the connecting link as a series of zigzag plot points unfold because of an important map.

Desert sequences provide some of the film's high points as Beatty and Hoffman finally develop some genuine rapport under adverse conditions. There are also a few hilarious scenes as vultures circle an exhausted Hoffman and later as he's thrust into role as a translator for gunrunners and their Arab buyers.

IT HAPPENED ONE NIGHT

1934, 105 mins, *Dir* Frank Capra   US

★ **Stars** Clark Gable, Claudette Colbert, Walter Connolly, Roscoe Karns, Jameson Thomas, Alan Hale

Academy Award 1934: Best Picture

The story [by Samuel Hopkins Adams] has that intangible quality of charm which arises from a smooth blending of the various ingredients. It starts off to be another long-distance bus story, but they get out of the bus before it palls.

Plot is a simple one. The headstrong but very charming daughter of a millionaire marries a suitor of whom her father does not approve. She quarrels with her father on the yacht off Miami, and the girl goes over the rail. She seeks to

An early Gable romantic comedy, **It Happened One Night** *established the star in relaxed vein with Claudette Colbert*

make her way to New York, with the old man raising the hue and cry. Clark Gable who has just been fired from his Florida correspondent's job, is on the same bus.

But the author would have been nowhere without the deft direction of Frank Capra and the spirited and good-humored acting of the stars and practically most of their support. Walter Connolly is the only other player to get much of a show, but there are a dozen with bit parts well played.

Claudette Colbert makes hers a very delightful assignment and Gable swings along at sustained speed. Both play as though they really liked their characters, and therein lies much of the charm.

IT'S A MAD MAD MAD MAD WORLD

1963, 190 mins, ◇ ⊚ *Dir* Stanley Kramer   US

★ **Stars** Spencer Tracy, Milton Berle, Sid Caesar, Mickey Rooney, Ethel Merman, Phil Silvers

It's a mad, mad, mad, mad picture. Being a picture of extravagant proportions, even its few flaws are king-sized, but the plusses outweigh by far the minuses. It is a throwback to the wild, wacky and wondrous time of the silent screen comedy, a kind of Keystone Kop Kaper with modern conveniences.

The plot is disarmingly simple. A group of people are given a clue by a dying man (Jimmy Durante) as to the whereabouts of a huge sum of money he has stolen and buried. Unable to come to a compromise in apportionment of the anticipated loot, each sets out for the roughly specified site of the buried cash, breaking his back to beat the others there. All are unaware that they are under secret surveillance by state police authorities, who are allowing them simply to lead the way to the money.

Nothing is done in moderation in this picture. All the stops are out. Nobody goes around what they can go over, under, through or into. Yet, as noted, the film is not without its flaws and oversights. Too often it tries to throw a wild haymaker where a simple left jab would be more apt to locate the desired target. Certain pratfalls and sequences are unneccesarily overdone to the point where they begin to grow tedious and reduce the impact of the whole.

An array of top-ranking comics has been rounded up by director Stanley Kramer, making this one of the most unorthodox and memorable casts on screen record. The comic competition is so keen that it is impossible to single out any one participant as outstanding.

IT'S A WONDERFUL WORLD

1939, 84 mins, *Dir* W.S Van Dyke   US

★ **Stars** Claudette Colbert, James Stewart, Guy Kibbee, Frances Drake, Nat Pendleton, Edgar Kennedy

Metro saturates the screwball comedy type of picture with some pretty broad burlesque in *It's a Wonderful World*.

Milton Berle and Terry-Thomas in **It's a Mad, Mad, Mad, Mad World,** *slapstick screen comedy on an epic scale.*

Claudette Colbert is a zany poetess in continual conflict and love with James Stewart. Story [an original by Ben Hecht and Herman J. Mankiewicz] is thinly laid foundation to provide the wacky and slapsticky situations and rapid-fire laugh dialog.

Stewart, a novice private detective, is assigned to watch millionaire Ernest Truex. Latter goes on a bender, and winds up convicted of a murder. Stewart is implicated, and escapes from the train en route to prison determined to solve the murder mystery and save his client. Kidnapping Colbert and requisitioning her car, Stewart runs through series of disguises – a Boy Scout leader, chauffeur, and actor.

W.S. Van Dyke presents the yarn with good humor and a let's-have-fun attitude.

IT SHOULD HAPPEN TO YOU

1954, 86 mins, ⚇ *Dir* George Cukor   US

★ **Stars** Judy Holliday, Peter Lawford, Jack Lemmon, Michael O'Shea, Vaughn Taylor, Connie Gilchrist

Judy Holliday is reunited with director George Cukor and scripter Garson Kanin, a trio that clicked big with *Born*

Yesterday, and the laugh range is from soft titters to loud guffaws as Cukor's smartly timed direction sends the players through hilarious situations. Plot is about a small town girl who comes to the big city to make a name for herself. Fresh angles belt the risibilities while dialog is adult, almost racy at times.

As the Gladys Glover of the plot, Holliday has a romp for herself, and she gets major assists in the comedy from Peter Lawford and Jack Lemmon, making his major screen bow.

Gladys has a different angle to flashing her name in the best places. With her meager savings she rents a signboard on Columbus Circle and has her name emblazoned thereon. This quest for fame sets off a lot of repercussions. She becomes a television celebrity and is pursued romantically by Lawford. Also in the amatory chase is Lemmon, who has a hard time keeping his romance with the new celebrity on even keel.

I WAS A MALE WAR BRIDE

1949, 105 mins, *Dir* Howard Hawks   US

★ **Stars** Cary Grant, Ann Sheridan, Marion Marshall, Randy Stuart

Title describes the story perfectly. Cary Grant is a French army officer who, after the war, marries Ann Sheridan, playing a WAC officer. From then on it's a tale of Grant's attempts to get back to the US with his wife by joining a contingent of war brides.

Picture's chief failing, if it can be called that in view of the frothy components, is that the entire production crew, from scripters to director Howard Hawks and the cast, were apparently so intent on getting the maximum in yocks that they overlooked the necessary characterizations.

Story was filmed for the most part in Germany, until illness of the stars and several of the supporting players forced their return to Hollywood, where the remaining interiors were lensed. Illness, however, did not hamper the cast's cavortings.

JABBERWOCKY

1977, 100 mins, ◇ Ⓥ *Dir* Terry Gilliam   UK

★ **Stars** Michael Palin, Max Wall, Deborah Fallender, John Le Mesurier, Annette Badland, Warren Mitchell

A Monty Python splinter faction bears responsibility for *Jabberwocky*, a medieval farce based on a Lewis Carroll poem. Film is long on jabber but short on yocks.

Ex-Pythonite Terry Gilliam directed and co-scripted. Michael Palin is well-cast as a bumpkin who threads his way through jousting knights, grubby peasants, 'drag' nuns, and damsels both fair and plump to become the inadvertent hero who slays the vile monster menacing Max Wall's cartoon kingdom. The monster, who doesn't appear till the final minutes, is a work of inspired dark imagination.

Film goes for gags instead of sustained satire, including several typically English lavatorial jokes also some repulsively bloody ones.

Some of the slapstick works okay but at a very intermittent pace in a mish-mash scenario.

THE JERK

1979, 104 mins, ◇ *Dir* Carl Reiner   US

★ **Stars** Steve Martin, Bernadette Peters, Catlin Adams, Mabel King, Richard Ward

Pic is an artless, non-stop barrage of off-the-wall situations, funny and unfunny jokes, generally effective and sometimes hilarious sight gags and bawdy non sequiturs.

The premise of *The Jerk* can be found in one of Steve Martin's more famous routines. Upon receiving the stunning news that he's the adopted, not natural, son of black parents Martin leaves home with his dog to make his way in the world. Opening sequences with the family are among the best.

The Jerk sees typical Steve Martin set pieces laced with knowing side glances at contemporary American life.

Martin's odyssey through contemporary America sees him taking odd jobs, such as a gas station attendant for proprietor Jackie Mason and as the driver of an amusement park train, and taking up with women.

But lunacy is never strayed from very far, as Martin strikes it rich as the inventor of a ridiculous nose support device for eyeglasses. Hilarity ebbs during his decline and fall.

JOE VERSUS THE VOLCANO

1990, 102 mins, ◇ Ⓥ *Dir* John Patrick Shanley   US

★ **Stars** Tom Hanks, Meg Ryan, Lloyd Bridges, Robert Stack, Abe Vigoda, Ossie Davis

Joe Versus the Volcano is an overproduced, disappointing shaggy dog comedy: A nebbish is bamboozled by unscrupulous types to trade his meaningless existence for a grand adventure that's linked to a suicide pact.

Pic starts promisingly with Tom Hanks going to work in the ad department of the grungy American Panascope surgical supplies factory. Meg Ryan as DeDe (in the first of her three gimmicky roles) sports dark hair in an amusingly ditzy

Carol Kane impression as his mousey co-worker. As an in-joke, the real Carol Kane pops up also in black wig later in the film, uncredited.

Hanks is a hypochondriac and his doctor, guest star Robert Stack, diagnoses a 'brain cloud', giving the hapless guy only six months to live. Coincidentally, eccentric super-conductors tycoon Lloyd Bridges pops in to offer Hanks to 'live like a king' for 20 days before heading for a remote Polynesian island to 'die like a man', i.e. jump into an active volcano to appease the fire god.

Hanks indulges himself in some rather unfunny solo bits. Ryan has fun in her three personas, but they're simply revue sketches.

KALEIDOSCOPE

1966, 102 mins, ◇ *Dir* Jack Smight   UK

★ *Stars* Warren Beatty, Susannah York, Clive Revill, Eric Porter, Murray Melvin, George Sewell

---

Kaleidoscope is an entertaining comedy suspenser about an engaging sharpie who tampers with playing card designs so he can rack up big casino winnings. The production has some eyecatching mod clothing styles, inventive direction and other values which sustain the simple story line.

The original screenplay turns on the exploits of Warren Beatty as he etches hidden markings on cards, wins big at various Continental casinos and, via an affair with Susannah York, comes under o.o. of her dad, Scotland Yard inspector Clive Revill.

The relaxed progress of the story becomes, under Jack Smight's direction, more dynamic through his use of Christopher Challis' mobile camera. Subsidiary events and characterizations – York's dress shop, her estrangement from Revill, latter's mechanical toy hobby, Porter's deliberate viciousness, climactic card game, etc – keep the pace moving.

THE KENTUCKY FRIED MOVIE

1977, 90 mins, ◇ ⓥ *Dir* John Landis   US

★ *Stars* Donald Sutherland, George Lazenby, Henry Gibson, Bill Bixby, Tony Dow

---

The Kentucky Fried Movie boasts excellent production values and some genuine wit, though a few of the sketches are tasteless.

Some of the appeal here is purely juvenile – the dubious kick of hearing 'TV performers' use foul language and seeing them perform off-color activities – but there is also a more substantial undertone in using satire of TV and films as a means of satirizing American cultural values.

Though each viewer will have his favourites, the standout segs certainly include *Zinc Oxide*, a terrific physical comedy routine spoofing an educational film, *Cleopatra Schwartz*, parody of a Pam Grier action film, but with a black Amazon woman married to a rabbi.

THE KID FROM BROOKLYN

1946, 114 mins, ◇ ⓥ *Dir* Norman Z. McLeod   US

★ *Stars* Danny Kaye, Virginia Mayo, Vera-Ellen, Steve Cochran, Eve Arden, Lionel Stander

---

Based on the old Harold Lloyd starrer, *The Milky Way* (originally legit play by Lynn Root and Harry Clark), the film is aimed straight at the bellylaughs and emerges as a lush mixture of comedy, music and gals, highlighted by beautiful Technicolor and ultra-rich production mountings.

Danny Kaye is spotted in almost three-fourths of the picture's sequences, but the audience will be clamoring for more at the final fadeout. Zany comic clicks with his unique mugging, song stylizing and antics, but still packs in plenty of the wistful appeal.

With a top cast and screenplay to work with, director Norman Z. McLeod gets the most out of each situation. Story has Kaye as a mild-mannered milkman who gets involved with a prizefight gang when he accidentally knocks out the current middleweight champ. With the champ's publicity shot to pieces, his manager decides to capitalize on the situation by building Kaye into a contender and then cleaning up on the title bout.

Kaye's supporting cast does uniformly fine work, keeping their sights trained on the comedy throughout. Virginia Mayo, as the love interest, serves as a beautiful foil for Kaye's madcap antics and sings two ballads in acceptable fashion. Vera-Ellen gets in ably on the comedy and does some spectacular terpsichore in two equally spectacular production numbers.

KIND HEARTS AND CORONETS

1949, 106 mins, ⓥ *Dir* Robert Hamer   UK

★ *Stars* Dennis Price, Alec Guinness, Valerie Hobson, Joan Greenwood, Miles Malleson

---

Story of the far-removed heir to the Dukedom of Chalfont who disposes of all the obstacles to his accession to the title and subsequently finds himself tried for a murder of which he is innocent may appear to be somewhat banal. But translation to a screen comedy has been effected with a mature wit.

Opening shot shows the arrival of the executioner at the prison announcing that this is his grand finale. Then the story is told in a constant flashback, recounting the methodical manner in which the one-time draper's boy works his way up to the dukedom. In this role Dennis Price is in top form, giving a quiet, dignified and polished portrayal.

Alec Guinness in the marathon eight roles he tackles in the British classic **Kind Hearts and Coronets.**

Greatest individual acting triumph, however, is scored by Alec Guinness who plays in turn all the members of the ancestral family.

KING RALPH

1991, 97 mins, ◇ Ⓥ   *Dir* David S. Ward   US

★ *Stars* John Goodman, Peter O'Toole, John Hurt, Camille Coduri, Richard Griffiths, Leslie Phillips

Crowned with John Goodman's lovable loutishness and a regally droll performance by Peter O'Toole, *King Ralph* doesn't carry much weight in the story department, though the wispy premise is handled with a blend of sprightly comedy and sappy romance.

Britain's entire royal family dies in a pre-credit sequence, resulting in a boorish American nightclub entertainer – the product of a dalliance between a prince and the American's paternal grandmother – becoming king.

After that, it's a basic fish-out-of-water tale, with King Ralph (Goodman) adjusting to the perks and constraints of nobility, aided by a group of harried advisers including his mentor Willingham (O'Toole) and officious bureaucratic Phipps (Richard Griffiths).

John Hurt plays a British lord seeking to bring the new king down so his own family can regain the throne. He facilitates a liaison between the king and a buxom lower-class British girl (Camille Coduri) in order to force his resignation.

Lensing was done on UK locations and at London's Pinewood Studios.

K-9

1989, 102 mins, ◇ Ⓥ   *Dir* Rod Daniel   US

★ *Stars* James Belushi, Mel Harris, Kevin Tighe, Ed O'Neill, Jerry Lee

The mismatched-buddy cop picture has literally and perhaps inevitably gone to the dogs, and the only notable thing about *K-9* is that it managed to dig up the idiotic premise first.

Since the black-white pairing in *48HRS.*, there have been numerous cop film teamings. *K-9* has all the trappings of its precedessors: a flimsy plot dealing with the cop (Belushi) trying to break a drug case, an unwanted partner (Jerry Lee, a gifted German shepherd) being foisted on him and a grudging respect that develops between the two during the course of a series of shootouts, brawls and sight gags.

There are a few amazing moments (the dog's rescue of Belushi in a bar). In between lingers lots of standard action-pic fare, plenty of toothless jokes and some downright mangy dialog.

KOTCH

1971, 113 mins, ◇ ⊛ *Dir* Jack Lemmon   US

★ *Stars* Walter Matthau, Deborah Winters, Felicia Farr, Charles Aidman, Ellen Geer

Kotch is a great film in several ways: Jack Lemmon's outstanding directorial debut; Walter Matthau's terrific performance as an unwanted elderly parent who befriends a pregnant teenager; John Paxton's superior adaptation of Katharine Topkins' novel and a topnotch supporting cast. This heart-warming, human comedy will leave audiences fully nourished, whereas they should be left a bit starved for more.

Paxton's script fully develops many interactions between Matthau and the other players. There's Charles Aidman, smash as his loving son, slightly embarrassed at Dad's apparent dotage; Felicia Farr, Aidman's wife who wants Pop out of the house; and Deborah Winters, as the couple's baby-sitter made pregnant by Darrell Larson, then shipped off in disgrace by her brother.

The film's somewhat too leisurely pace often sacrifices primary plot movement to brilliantly-filmed digression-vignette. Basically the story has Matthau and Winters sharing a desert house together. She learns a lot about life from him, and he has the opportunity to act both as a loving father and a friend.

THE LADY EVE

1941, 90 mins, ⊛ *Dir* Preston Sturges   US

★ *Stars* Henry Fonda, Barbara Stanwyck, Charles Coburn, Eugene Pallette, William Demarest, Eric Blore

Third writer-director effort of Preston Sturges [from a story by Monckton Hoffe] is laugh entertainment of top proportions with its combo of slick situations, spontaneous dialog and a few slapstick falls tossed in for good measure.

Basically, story is the age-old tale of Eve snagging Adam, but dressed up with continually infectious fun and good humor. Barbara Stanwyck is girl-lure of trio of confi-

More often cast in dramatic roles, **The Lady Eve** *provided a successful comedy vehicle for both Fonda and Stanwyck.*

dence operators. She's determined, quick-witted, resourceful and personable. Henry Fonda is a serious young millionaire, somewhat sappy, deadpan and slow-thinking, returning from a year's snake-hunting expedition up the Amazon. He's a cinch pushover for girl's advances on the boat – but pair fall in love, while girl flags Charles Coburn's attempts to coldeck the victim at cards.

Sturges provides numerous sparkling situations in his direction and keeps picture moving at a merry pace. Stanwyck is excellent in the comedienne portrayal, while Fonda carries his assignment in good fashion. Coburn is a finished actor as the con man.

THE LADYKILLERS

1955, 96 mins, ◇ ⊚ *Dir* Alexander Mackendrick   UK

★ *Stars* Alec Guinness, Cecil Parker, Herbert Lom, Peter Sellers, Katie Johnson, Danny Green

This is an amusing piece of hokum, being a parody of American gangsterdom interwoven with whimsy and

exaggeration that makes it more of a macabre farce. Alec Guinness sinks his personality almost to the level of anonymity. Basic idea of thieves making a frail old lady an unwitting accomplice in their schemes is carried out in ludicrous and often tense situations.

A bunch of crooks planning a currency haul call on their leader, who has temporarily boarded with a genteel widow near a big London rail terminal. They pass as musicians gathering for rehearsals, but wouldn't deceive a baby.

Guinness tends to overact the sinister leader while Cecil Parker strikes just the right note as a conman posing as an army officer. Herbert Lom broods gloomily as the most ruthless of the plotters, with Peter Sellers contrasting well as the dumb muscle man. Danny Green completes the quintet.

THE LAST MARRIED COUPLE IN AMERICA

1980, 103 mins, ◇ ⊙   *Dir* Gilbert Cates   US

★ *Stars* George Segal, Natalie Wood, Richard Benjamin, Dom DeLuise

The Last Married Couple In America is basically a 1950s comedy with cursing. John Herman Shaner's script offers not a single new idea about divorce in suburbia and doesn't even develop the cliches well.

Gilbert Cates' direction consists largely of letting his stars reenact favorite roles of the past. So Wood plays the nice pretty lady who wants a happy, faithful marriage to George Segal, who plays the nice, handsome husband befuddled by the world around him.

Richard Benjamin is again the neurotic modern male and Dom DeLuise the likable, nutty fat guy, while Valerie Harper is essentially Rhoda running rampant, tresses turned blonde from the sheer excitement of it all.

L.A. STORY

1991, 95 mins, ◇ ⊙   *Dir* Mick Jackson   US

★ *Stars* Steve Martin, Victoria Tennant, Richard E. Grant, Marilu Henner, Sarah Jessica Parker, Susan Forristal

Goofy and sweet, *L.A. Story* constitutes Steve Martin's satiric valentine to his hometown and a pretty funny comedy in the bargain.

Martin is in typically nutty form as an LA TV meteorologist who doesn't hesitate to take the weekends off since the weather isn't bound to change. What he can't predict, however, is the lightning bolt that hits him in the form of Brit journalist Victoria Tennant, who arrives to dish up the latest English assessment of America's new melting pot.

Martin's relationship with his snooty longtime g.f. Marilu Henner is essentially over and, convinced that nothing can ever happen with his dreamgirl, he stumblingly takes up with ditzy shopgirl Sarah Jessica Parker.

Even after Martin and Tennant have gotten together and he has declared the grandest of romantic intentions, the

future looks impossible, as she has promised her ex (Richard E. Grant) to attempt a reconciliation.

Despite the frantic style, the feeling behind Martin's view of life and love in LA comes through, helped by the seductively adoring treatment of Tennant (who actually is Martin's wife).

THE LAST REMAKE OF BEAU GESTE

1977, 84 mins, ◇ ⊙   *Dir* Marty Feldman   US

★ *Stars* Ann-Margret, Marty Feldman, Michael York, Peter Ustinov, James Earl Jones, Trevor Howard

Marty Feldman's directorial debut on *The Last Remake of Beau Geste* emerges as an often hilarious, if uneven, spoof of Foreign Legion adventure films. An excellent cast, top to bottom, gets the most out of the stronger scenes, and carries the weaker ones.

Feldman stars [in a story by him and Sam Bobrick] as the ugly duckling brother of Michael York (as Beau Geste), both adopted sons of Trevor Howard, an aging lech whose marriage to swinger Ann-Margret causes York to join the Foreign Legion and Feldman to serve time for alleged theft of a family gem.

Feldman joins up with York in the desert, where sadistic Peter Ustinov and bumbling Roy Kinnear together run the garrison for urbane Henry Gibson, in the character of the Legion general.

THE LAVENDER HILL MOB

1951, 81 mins, ⊙   *Dir* Charles Crichton   UK

★ *Stars* Alec Guinness, Stanley Holloway, Sidney James, Alfie Bass, Marjorie Fielding, Ronald Adam

With *The Lavender Hill Mob*, Ealing clicks with another comedy winner.

Story is notable for allowing Alec Guinness to play another of his w.k. character roles. This time, he is the timid escort of bullion from the refineries to the vaults. For 20 years he has been within sight of a fortune, but smuggling gold bars out of the country is a tough proposition. Eventually, with three accomplices, he plans the perfect crime. Bullion worth over £1 million is made into souvenir models of the Eiffel Tower and shipped to France.

One of the comedy highspots of the film is a scene at a police exhibition where Guinness and his principal accomplice (Stanley Holloway) first become suspect. They break out of the cordon, steal a police car, and then radio phony messages through headquarters. This sequence and the other action scenes are crisply handled, with a light touch.

Guinness, as usual, shines as the trusted escort, and is at his best as the mastermind plotting the intricate details of the crime. Holloway is an excellent aide, while the two professional crooks in the gang (Sidney James and Alfie Bass) complete the quartet with an abundance of cockney humor.

LIFE OF BRIAN

1979, 93 mins, ◇ Ⓥ *Dir* Terry Jones   UK

★ **Stars** Terry Jones, Michael Palin, John Cleese, Eric Idle, Spike Milligan, George Harrison

Monty Python's *Life Of Brian*, utterly irreverent tale of a reluctant messiah whose impact proved somewhat less pervasive than that of his contemporary Jesus Christ, is just as wacky and imaginative as their earlier film outings. Film was shot using stunning Tunisian locales.

As an adult in Roman-occupied Palestine, Brian's life parallels that of Jesus, as he becomes involved in the terrorist Peoples Front of Judea, works as a vendor at the Colosseum, paints anti-Roman graffiti on palace walls, unwittingly wins a following as a messiah and is ultimately condemned to the cross by a foppish Pontius Pilate.

Tone of the film is set by such scenes as a version of the sermon on the mount in which spectators shout out that they can't hear what's being said and start fighting amongst themselves.

Sacrilege or satire, Monty Python's Life Of Brian took screen comedy into a previously taboo area.

LIFE STINKS

1991, 95 mins, ◇ Ⓥ *Dir* Mel Brooks   US

★ **Stars** Mel Brooks, Lesley Ann Warren, Jeffrey Tambor, Stuart Pankin, Howard Morris, Rudy De Luca

Mel Brooks' *Life Stinks* is a fitfully funny vaudeville caricature about life on Skid Row. Premise of a rich man who chooses to live among the poor for a spell feels sorely undeveloped, and suffers from the usual gross effects and exaggerations.

Pic gets off to a good start with Brooks' callous billionaire Goddard Bolt informing his circle of yes-men of his plans to build a colossal futuristic development on the site of Los Angeles' worst slums, the plight of its residents be damned.

Tycoon Jeffrey Tambor bets his rival that he can't last a month living out in the neighborhood he intends to buy.

In a series of vignettes that play like blackout routines, Bolt, renamed Pepto by a local denizen, tries various survival tactics, such as dancing for donations. After being robbed of his shoes, he encounters baglady Lesley Ann Warren, a wildly gesticulating man-hater who slowly comes to admit Pepto is the only person she can stand.

Some effective bug-eyed, free-wheeling comedy is scattered throughout, much of it descending to the Three Stooges level of sophistication. But distressingly little is done with the vast possibilities offered by the setting and the characters populating it.

THE LITTLE SHOP OF HORRORS

1961, 70 mins, Ⓥ *Dir* Roger Corman   US

★ **Stars** Jonathan Haze, Jackie Joseph, Mel Welles, Myrtle Vail, Leola Wendorff, Jack Nicholson

Reportedly only two shooting days and $22,500 went into the making of this picture, but limited fiscal resources didn't deter Roger Corman and his game, resourceful little Filmgroup from whipping up a serviceable parody of a typical screen horror number.

Little Shop of Horrors is kind of one big sick joke, but it's essentially harmless and good-natured. The plot concerns a young, goofy florist's assistant who creates a talking, blood-sucking, man-eating plant, then feeds it several customers from skid row before sacrificing himself to the horticultural gods.

There is a fellow who visits the Skid Row flower shop to munch on purchased bouquets ('I like to eat in these little out-of-the-way places'). There is also the Yiddish proprietor, distressed by his botanical attraction ('we not only got a talking plant, we got one dot makes smart cracks'), but content to let it devour as the shop flourishes. And there are assorted quacks, alcoholics, masochists [Jack Nicholson, as a dental patient], sadists and even a pair of private-eyes who couldn't solve the case of the disappearing fly in a hothouse for Venus Fly-Traps.

The acting is pleasantly preposterous. Mel Welles, as the proprietor, and Jonathan Haze, as the budding Luther Burbank, are particularly capable, and Jackie Joseph is decorative as the latter's girl. Horticulturalists and vegetarians will love this film.

LOCAL HERO

1983, 111 mins, ◇ Ⓥ *Dir* Bill Forsyth   UK

★ *Stars* Burt Lancaster, Peter Riegert, Fulton MacKay, Denis Lawson, Norman Chancer, Peter Capaldi

While modest in intent and gentle in feel, *Local Hero* is loaded with wry, offbeat humor.

Basic story has Peter Riegert, rising young executive in an enormous Houston oil firm, sent to Scotland to clinch a deal to buy up an entire village, where the company intends to construct a new oil refinery. Far from being resistant to the idea of having their surroundings ruined by rapacious, profit-minded Yankees, local Scots can hardly wait to sign away their town, so strong is the smell of money in the air.

Back in Houston, oil magnate Burt Lancaster keeps up to date on the deal's progress with occasional phone calls to Riegert, but is more concerned with his prodding, sadistic psychiatrist and his obsessive hobby of astronomy, which seems to dictate everything he does.

Riegert's underplaying initially seems a bit inexpressive, but ultimately pays off in a droll performance. As his Scottish buddy, the gangling Peter Capaldi is vastly amusing, and Denis Lawson is very good as the community's chief spokesman.

THE LONELY GUY

1984, 90 mins, ◇ Ⓥ *Dir* Arthur Hiller   US

★ *Stars* Steve Martin, Charles Grodin, Judith Ivey, Steven Lawrence, Robyn Douglass, Merv Griffin

Derived from a comic tome by Bruce Jay Friedman, premise has Steve Martin bounced by sexpot girlfriend Robyn Douglass and thereby banished to the world of Lonely Guys. He meets and commiserates with fellow LG Charles Grodin, who gets Martin to buy a fern with him and throws a party attended only by Martin and a bunch of life-sized cardboard cutouts of celebs like Dolly Parton and Tom Selleck.

Finally, Martin meets cute blonde Judith Ivey, who, having been previously married to six Lonely Guys, instantly falls for him.

Martin's trademark wacky humor is fitfully in evidence, but seems much more repressed than usual in order to fit into the relatively realistic world of single working people.

Peter Riegert and Christopher Rozycki in Local Hero, the story of the impact of oil money on a small Scots village.

Look Who's Talking: *successful product of a late-Eighties trend that moved from teen-comedy to tot-comedy.*

LOOK WHO'S TALKING

1989, 90 mins, ◇ ⓥ *Dir* Amy Heckerling   US

★ *Stars* John Travolta, Kirstie Alley, Olympia Dukakis, George Segal, Abe Vigoda, Bruce Willis

Like a standup comic pouring "flopsweat," this ill-conceived comedy about an infant whose thoughts are given voice by actor Bruce Willis palpitates with desperation. One need look no further for underscoring the film's ineptitude than its title. "Look Who's Voice-Overing" would be a far more appropriate moniker, as Willis isn't heard by the film's other characters.

The camera simply homes in on one of the four strikingly dissimilar babies who play the leading role and Willis lets fly with asides to match their "cute" expressions.

Kirstie Alley does the best she can as the child's mother – an accountant whose married boyfriend (George Segal) gets her pregnant. Convinced he'll leave his wife for her and the child, she spurns the attentions of the sweet, earnest young cab driver (John Travolta) who helped her at the hospital when she was going into labor.

There's no way to generate suspense from a plot whose outcome can be guessed simply by reading the casting credits.

John Travolta continues to exude the casual charm that once gave his name box office potency, but it's wasted in a vehicle unworthy of him – or anyone else connected to it, for that matter.

LOOK WHO'S TALKING TOO

1990, 81 mins, ◇ ⓥ *Dir* Amy Heckerling   US

★ *Stars* John Travolta, Kirstie Alley, Olympia Dukakis, Elias Koteas, Twink Caplan, Neal Israel

This vulgar sequel to 1989's longest-running sleeper hit looks like a rush job. Joined by her husband Neal Israel (who also appears as star Kirstie Alley's mean boss) in the scripting, filmmaker Amy Heckerling overemphasizes toilet humor and expletives to make *Look Who's Talking Too* appealing mainly to adolescents rather than an across-the-board family audience.

Unwed mom Alley and cabbie John Travolta are married for the sequel, with her cute son Mikey metamorphosed here into Lorne Sussman, still voiceovered as precocious by Bruce Willis. First mutual arrival is undeniably cute Megan Milner, unfortunately voiced-over by Roseanne Barr. The comedienne gets a couple of laughs but is generally dull, leaving Willis to again carry the load in the gag department with well-read quips.

Film's plotline revolves around the bickering of Alley and Travolta whose jobs (accountant and would-be airline pilot) and personalities clash, as well as the rites of passage of the two kids. New characters, notably Alley's obnoxious

brother Elias Koteas, are added to ill effect. Mel Brooks is enlisted to voice-over Mr Toilet Man, a fantasy bathroom bowl come to life, spitting blue water and anxious to bite off Mikey's private bits.

LOOSE CONNECTIONS

1983, 99 mins, ◇ Ⓥ *Dir* Richard Eyre   UK

★ *Stars* Stephen Rea, Lindsay Duncan, Jan Niklas, Carole Harrison, Gary Olsen, Frances Low

Richard Eyre's second theatrical feature is an exceedingly amiable comic battle of the sexes.

Sally (Lindsay Duncan), together with two girlfriends, has built a jeep in which to drive from London to a feminist conference in Munich, but at the last moment she is left on her own. She takes a newspaper ad for a fellow driver, seeking a female non-smoking vegetarian, who speaks German and knows something about car engines. The only applicant is Harry (Stephen Rea), who claims to fill all the requirements except sex, and furthermore claims he's gay. Needless to say, Harry's a liar.

The trip to Munich is one comic disaster after another. But the odd couple are drawn to each other, and the inevitable happens.

Both roles are played to perfection. It's not a film of hearty laughs, but of continual quiet chuckles.

LORD LOVE A DUCK

1966, 105 mins, *Dir* George Axelrod   US

★ *Stars* Roddy McDowall, Tuesday Weld, Lola Albright, Martin West, Ruth Gordon, Harvey Korman

Some may call George Axelrod's *Lord Love a Duck* satire, others way-out comedy, still others brilliant, while there may be some who ask, what's it all about?

Whatever the reaction, there is no question that the film [based on Al Hire's novel] is packed with laughs, often of the truest anatomical kind, and there is a veneer of sophistication which keeps showing despite the most outlandish goings-on. Some of the comedy is inspirational, a gagman's dream come true, and there is bite in some of Axelrod's social commentary beneath the wonderful nonsense.

The characters are everything here, each developed brightly along zany lines, topped by Roddy McDowall as a Svengali-type high school student leader who pulls the strings on the destiny of Tuesday Weld, an ingenuish-type sexpot whose philosophy is wrapped up in her words 'Everybody's got to love me'.

McDowall is in good form as the mastermind of the school, and he has a strong contender for interest in blonde Weld in a characterization warm and appealing. Scoring almost spectacularly is Lola Albright as Weld's mother, a cocktail bar 'bunny' who commits suicide when she thinks she's ruined her daughter's chances for marriage.

LOST IN AMERICA

1985, 91 mins, ◇ Ⓥ *Dir* Albert Brooks   US

★ *Stars* Albert Brooks, Julie Hagerty, Garry Marshall, Art Frankel, Michael Greene, Tom Tarpey

Film opens on Albert Brooks and wife Julie Hagerty in bed on eve of their move to a $450,000 house and also what Brooks presumes will be his promotion to a senior exec slot in a big ad agency. Brooks is a nervous mess, made worse when vaguely bored Hagerty tells him their life has become 'too responsible, too controlled.'

Her suppressed wish for a more dashing life comes startlingly true the next day when a confident Brooks glides into his boss' LA office only to hear that his expected senior v.p. stripes are going to someone else and he's being transferred to New York.

Brooks quits his job and convinces his wife to quit her personnel job. The pair will liquidate their assets, buy a Winnebago, and head across America.

Brooks, who directed and co-wrote with Monica Johnson, is irrepressible but always very human.

LOVE AND DEATH

1975, 85 mins, ◇ *Dir* Woody Allen   US

★ *Stars* Woody Allen, Diane Keaton

Woody Allen and Diane Keaton invade the land and spirit of Anton Chekhov. *Love and Death* is another mile-a-minute visual-verbal whirl by the two comedy talents, this time through Czarist Russia in the days of the Napoleonic Wars.

Allen's script traces his bumbling adventures with distant cousin Keaton, latter outstanding as a prim lady of both philosophical and sexual bent. Between malaprop battlefield heroics and metaphysical deliberations, Allen eventually combines with Keaton in an assassination attempt on Napoleon himself. It is impossible to catalog the comedic blueprint; suffice to say it is another zany product of the terrific synergism of the two stars.

About 54 supporting players have roles which range from a few feet to a few frames. Joffe's location production was shot in France and Hungary, where some gorgeous physical values serve as backdrop to the kooky antics.

LOVE AT FIRST BITE

1979, 96 mins, ◇ Ⓥ *Dir* Stan Dragoti   US

★ *Stars* George Hamilton, Susan Saint James, Richard Benjamin, Dick Shawn, Arte Johnson

'What would happen if Dracula was victimized by life in modern New York City?

It's a fun notion and George Hamilton makes it work. In the first place, he's funny just to watch. Veteran make-up artist William Tuttle, who created Lugosi's Dracula look in 1934, retains the grey, drained visage while adding a nutty quality that Hamilton accents with the arch of an eyebrow.

Story evicts Dracula from his Transylvania castle and takes him in pursuit of Susan Saint James, a fashion model he loves from an old photo. In the care of his bumbling manservant, slightly overplayed by Arte Johnson, Hamilton's coffin is naturally misrouted by the airline, winding up in a black funeral home.

Director Stan Dragoti keeps the chuckles coming, spaced by a few good guffaws.

LUCKY JIM

1957, 95 mins, ⊘   *Dir* John Boulting   UK

★ *Stars* Ian Carmichael, Terry-Thomas, Hugh Griffith, Sharon Acker, Clive Morton, Kenneth Griffith

Kingsley Amis's novel has been built up into a farcical comedy which, though slim enough in idea, provides plenty of opportunity for smiles, giggles and belly laughs. John Boulting directs with a lively tempo and even though the comedy situations loom up with inevitable precision, they are still irresistible.

The lightweight story spotlights Ian Carmichael as a junior history lecturer at a British university in the sticks who becomes disastrously involved in such serious college goings-on as a ceremonial lecture on 'Merrie England' and a

Lucky Jim *featuring Ian Carmichael (left) as a hapless junior lecturer at a British university.*

procession to honor the new university chancellor. There are also some minor shenanigans such as a riotous car chase, a slaphappy fist fight, a tipsy entry into a wrong bedroom containing a girl he is trying to shake off and a number of other happy-go-lucky situations.

The screenplay veers from facetiousness to downright slapstick but never lets up on its irresistible attack on the funnybone. Carmichael is a deft light-comedy performer who proves that he also can take hold of a character and make him believable.

THE 'MAGGIE'

1954, 93 mins,   *Dir* Alexander Mackendrick   UK

★ *Stars* Paul Douglas, Alex Mackenzie, James Copeland, Abe Barker, Tommy Kearins, Hubert Gregg

One of the small coastal colliers which ply in Scottish waters provides the main setting for this Ealing comedy. The story of a hustling American businessman who gets involved with a leisurely-minded but crafty skipper gives the film an Anglo-US flavor.

The yarn has been subtly written as a piece of gentle and casual humor. The pace is always leisurely, and the background of Scottish lakes and mountains provides an appropriate backcloth to the story.

The skipper of the *Maggie* is a crafty old sailor, short of cash to make his little coaster seaworthy. By a little smart

practice he gets a contract to transport a valuable cargo but when a hustling American executive realizes what has happened, he planes from London to Scotland to get his goods transferred to another vessel.

There is virtually an all-male cast with only minor bits for a few femme players. Paul Douglas, playing the American executive, provides the perfect contrast between the old world and the new. His is a reliable performance which avoids the pitfall of overacting.

MANHATTAN

1979, 96 mins, ⓥ   *Dir* Woody Allen   US

★ *Stars* Woody Allen, Diane Keaton, Michael Murphy, Mariel Hemingway, Meryl Streep

Woody Allen uses New York City for the familiar story of the successful but neurotic urban over-achievers whose relationships always seem to end prematurely. The film is just as much about how wonderful a place the city is to live in as it is about the elusive search for love.

Allen has, in black and white, captured the inner beauty that lurks behind the outer layer of dirt and grime in Manhattan.

The core of the story revolves around Allen as Isaac Davis, an unfulfilled television writer and his best friends, Yale and Emily, an upper-middle class, educated Manhattan couple. Isaac has lately taken up with Tracy (Mariel Hemingway) a gorgeous 17-year-old, but the age difference is becoming too much of an obstacle for him.

That's especially the case when he meets Yale's girlfriend, Mary, a fast-talking, pseudo-intellectual, expertly played by Diane Keaton, to whom Isaac is instantly attracted.

THE MAN IN THE WHITE SUIT

1951, 97 mins, ⓥ   *Dir* Alexander Mackendrick   UK

★ *Stars* Alec Guinness, Joan Greenwood, Cecil Parker, Michael Gough, Ernest Thesiger, Vida Hope

The plot is a variation of an old theme, but it comes out with a nice fresh coat of paint. A young research scientist invents a cloth that is everlasting and dirt resisting. The textile industry sees the danger signal and tries to buy him out, but he outwits them.

Particular tribute must be paid to the sound effects department. The bubbly sound of liquids passing through specially prepared contraptions in the lab is one of the most effective running gags seen in a British film.

Alec Guinness, as usual, turns in a polished performance. His interpretation of the little research worker is warm, understanding and always sympathetic. Joan Greenwood is nicely provocative as the mill-owner's daughter who encourages him with his work, while Cecil Parker contributes another effective character study as her father. Michael Gough and Ernest Thesiger represent the textile bosses who see disaster.

Vida Hope makes a fine showing as one of the strike leaders who fears unemployment returning to the mills.

THE MAN WITH TWO BRAINS

1983, 93 mins, ◇ ⓥ   *Dir* Carl Reiner   US

★ *Stars* Steven Martin, Kathleen Turner, David Warner, Paul Benedict, Richard Brestoff, James Cromwell

The Man with Two Brains is a fitfully amusing return by Steve Martin to the broad brand of lunacy that made his first feature, *The Jerk* [1979], so successful.

Plot is a frayed crazy quilt barely held together as if by clothespins. Ace neurosurgeon Martin almost kills beauteous Kathleen Turner in an auto accident, only to save her via his patented screwtop brain surgery technique. Turner proves to be a master at withholding her sexual favors from her frustrated husband, who decides to take her on a honeymoon to Vienna in an attempt to thaw her out.

While there, Martin visits the lab of colleague David Warner and meets the love of his life, a charming woman and marvelous conversationalist who also happens to be a disembodied brain suspended in a jar, her body having been the victim of a crazed elevator killer.

Much humor, of course, stems from the befuddled Martin groveling at the feet of the knockout Turner he comes to call a 'scum queen', but too much of the film seems devoted to frantic overkill to compensate for general lack of bellylaughs and topnotch inspiration.

Martin delivers all that's expected of him as a performer, and Turner is a sizzling foil for his comic and pent-up sexual energy.

MARRIED TO THE MOB

1988, 103 mins, ◇ ⓥ   *Dir* Jonathan Demme   US

★ *Stars* Michelle Pfeiffer, Matthew Modine, Dean Stockwell, Mercedes Ruehl, Alec Baldwin

Fresh, colorful and inventive, *Married to the Mob* is another offbeat entertainment from director Jonathan Demme.

Storyline's basic trajectory has unhappy suburban housewife Michelle Pfeiffer taking the opportunity presented by the sudden death of her husband, who happens to have been a middle-level gangster, to escape the limitations of her past and forge a new life for herself and her son in New York City.

Opening with a hit on a commuter train and following with some murderous bedroom shenanigans, film establishes itself as a suburban gangster comedy. Demme and his enthusiastic actors take evident delight in sending up the gauche excesses of these particular nouveau riches, as the men strut about in their pinstripes and polyester and the women spend their time at the salon getting their hair teased.

The enormous cast is a total delight, starting with Pfeiffer, with hair dyed dark, a New York accent and a con-

Mathew Modine and Michelle Pfeiffer manage to forget the Mafia for a moment in **Married to the Mob.**

tinuously nervous edge. Matthew Modine proves winning as the seemingly inept FBI functionary who grows into his job, and Dean Stockwell is a hoot as the unflappable gangland boss, slime under silk and a fedora.

M★A★S★H

1970, 116 mins, ◇ Ⓥ *Dir* Robert Altman   US

★ Stars Elliott Gould, Donald Sutherland, Tom Skerritt, Sally Kellerman, Jo Ann Pflug, Rene Auberjonois

Academy Award 1970: Best Picture (Nomination)

A Mobile Army Surgical Hospital (M★A★S★H) two minutes from bloody battles on the 38th Parallel of Korea, is an improbable setting for a comedy, even a stomach-churning, gory, often tasteless, but frequently funny black comedy.

Elliott Gould, Donald Sutherland and Tom Skerritt head an extremely effective, low-keyed cast of players whose skilful subtlety eventually rescue an indecisive union of script and technique.

Gould is the totally unmilitary but arrogantly competent, supercool young battlefield surgeon, a reluctant draftee whose credo is let's get the job done and knock off all this Army muck.

The sardonic, cynical comments of the doctors and nurses patching and stitching battle-mangled bodies and casually amputating limbs before sending their anonymous patients out may be distasteful to some. It has the sharp look of reality when professionals become calloused from working 12 hours at a stretch to keep up with the stream of casualties from the battlefield.

MEATBALLS

1979, 92 mins, ◇ Ⓥ *Dir* Ivan Reitman   CANADA

★ Stars Bill Murray, Harvey Atkin, Kate Lynch, Russ Banham, Kristine DeBell

It's difficult to come up with a more cliche situation for a summer pic than a summer camp, where all the characters and plot turns are readily imaginable. That makes director Ivan Reitman's accomplishment all the more noteworthy.

Bill Murray limns a head counselor in charge of a group of misfit counselors-in-training. The usual types predominate:

Robert Altman's black comedy **M★A★S★H** *was the blueprint for the highly successfully TV series.*

the myopic klutz, the obese kid who wins the pig-out contest, the smooth-talking lothario, and a bevy of comely lasses.

Scripters have managed to gloss over the stereotypes and come up with a smooth-running narrative that makes the camp hijinks part of an overall human mosaic. No one is unduly belittled or mocked, and *Meatballs* is without the usual grossness and cynicism of many contempo comedy pix.

MIDNIGHT RUN

1988, 122 mins, ◇ Ⓥ *Dir* Martin Brest   US

★ *Stars* Robert De Niro, Charles Grodin, Yaphet Kotto, John Ashton, Dennis Farina

Midnight Run shows that Robert De Niro can be as wonderful in a comic role as he is in a serious one. Pair him, a gruff ex-cop and bounty hunter, with straight man Charles Grodin, his captive, and the result is one of the most entertaining, best executed, original road pictures *ever*.

It's De Niro's boyish charm that works for him every time and here especially as the scruffy bounty hunter ready to do his last job in a low-life occupation. He's to nab a philanthropically minded accountant hiding out in Gotham (Grodin) who embezzled $15 million from a heroin dealer/Las Vegas mobster and return him to Los Angeles in time to collect a $100,000 fee by midnight Friday.

Kidnapping Grodin is the easy part; getting him back to the west coast turns out to be anything but easy. The two

John Ashton, Charles Grodin and Robert De Niro playing it for laughs in the chaser-caper Midnight Run.

guys, who can't stand each other, are stuck together for the duration of a journey neither particularly wants to be on.

Midnight Run is more than a string of well-done gags peppered by verbal sparring between a reluctant twosome; it is a terrifically developed script full of inventive, humorous twists made even funnier by wonderfully realized secondary characters.

A MIDSUMMER NIGHT'S SEX COMEDY

1982, 88 mins, ◇ Ⓥ *Dir* Woody Allen   US

★ *Stars* Woody Allen, Mia Farrow, Jose Ferrer, Julie Hagerty, Tony Roberts, Mary Steenburgen

Woody Allen's *A Midsummer Night's Sex Comedy* is a pleasant disappointment, pleasant because he gets all the laughs he goes for in a visually charming, sweetly paced picture, a disappointment because he doesn't go for more.

The time is the turn of the century, the place a lovely old farmhouse in upstate New York. Here, Wall St stockbroker Allen spends his spare time inventing odd devices and trying to bed his own wife (Mary Steenburgen) who has turned cold.

Arriving for a visit and also a wedding 84 are Steenburgen's cousin Jose Ferrer, a stuffy, pedantic scholar, and his bride to be (Mia Farrow), a former near-nympho who's decided to settle down with Ferrer's intellect.

Also arriving are Allen's best friend, who else but Tony Roberts, an amorous physician and his current short-term fling (Julie Hagerty), a nurse dedicated to the study of anatomy and all its possibilities.

With this daffy assortment and Allen's gift for laughlines, the picture can't avoid being fun, even at a rather leisurely pace in keeping with its times.

THE MILLIONAIRESS

1960, 90 mins, ◇ *Dir* Anthony Asquith   UK

★ *Stars* Sophia Loren, Peter Sellers, Alastair Sim, Vittorio De Sica, Dennis Price, Alfie Bass

This stylized pic has Sophia Loren at her most radiant, wearing a series of stunning Balmain gowns. George Bernard Shaw's Shavianisms on morality, riches and human relationship retain much of their edge, though nudged into a practical screenplay by Wolf Mankowitz.

Anthony Asquith's direction often is slow, but he breaks up the pic with enough hilarious situation to keep the film from getting tedious. A major fault is that the cutting of the film, which is mainly episodic, is often needlessly jerky and indecisive. But against this, there is handsome artwork and the relish with which Jack Hildyard has brought his camera to work on them.

Briefly, the yarn concerns a beautiful, spoiled young heiress who has all the money in the world but can't find love. Her eccentric deceased old man has stipulated that she mustn't marry unless the man of her choice can turn $1,400 into $42,000 within three months. She cheats. Her first marriage flops, she contemplates suicide and then sets her cap for a dedicated, destitute Indian doctor runing a poor man's clinic. He's attracted to her, but scared of her money and power.

Loren is a constant stimulation. She catches many moods. Whether she's wooing the doctor brazenly, confiding in a psychiatrist, trying to commit suicide, upbraiding her lawyer or just pouting she is fascinating. Sellers plays the doctor straight, apart from an offbeat accent, but he still manages to bring in some typical Sellers comedy touches which help to make it a fascinating character study. He even injects a few emotional throwaways which are fine.

THE MIRACLE OF MORGAN'S CREEK

1944, 101 mins, ⊗ *Dir* Preston Sturges   US

★ **Stars** Eddie Bracken, Betty Hutton, Diana Lynn, William Demarest

Morgan's Creek is the name of the town where the action takes place and the miracle, as director Preston Sturges terms it, is the birth to Eddie Bracken and Betty Hutton of a set of sextuplets.

Done in the satirical Sturges vein, and directed with that same touch, the story makes much of characterization and somewhat wacky comedy, plus some slapstick, with excellent photography figuring throughout. The Sturges manner of handling crowds and various miscellaneous characters who are almost nothing more than flashes in the picture, such as the smalltown attorney and the justice of the peace, contribute enormously to the enjoyment derived.

However, some of the comedy situations lack punch, and the picture is slow to get rolling, but ultimately picks up smart pace and winds up quite strongly on the birth of the sextuplets with the retiring Bracken and Hutton as national heroes.

Bracken is a smalltown bank clerk who yearns to get into uniform and is madly in love with Hutton. Getting out on an all-night party with soldiers, the latter wakes up to remember that she married a serviceman, but can't remember the name, what the spouse looked like, or anything except that they didn't give their right names.

Bracken does a nice job. Hutton and he make a desirable team. Among the supporting cast, largest assignment is that given William Demarest, smalltown cop father of Hutton, who has his troubles with his daughters, the other being attractive Diana Lynn.

THE MONEY PIT

1986, 91 mins, ◇ ⊗ *Dir* Richard Benjamin   US

★ **Stars** Shelley Long, Tom Hanks, Alexander Godunov, Maureen Stapleton, Joe Mantegna

The Money Pit is simply the pits. Shortly after the starring couple has bought a beautiful old house which quickly

shows itself to be at the point of total disrepair, Tom Hanks says to Shelley Long, 'It's a lemon, honey, let's face it'. There is really very little else to be said about this gruesomely unfunny comedy.

Unofficial remake of the 1948 Cary Grant–Myrna Loy starrer *Mr Blandings Builds His Dream House* begins unpromisingly and slides irrevocably downward in to its own pit from there.

Most of the scenes in this demolition derby begin with something or other caving in or falling apart, an event which is invariably followed by the two leads yelling and screaming at each other for minutes on end.

MONTY PYTHON AND THE HOLY GRAIL

1975, 89 mins, ◇ ⊗ *Dir* Terry Gilliam, Terry Jones   UK

★ **Stars** Graham Chapman, John Cleese, Terry Gilliam, Eric Idle, Terry Jones, Michael Palin

Monty Python's Flying Circus, the British comedy group which gained fame via BBC-TV, send-up Arthurian legend, performed in whimsical fashion with Graham Chapman an effective straight man as King Arthur.

Story deals with Arthur's quest for the Holy Grail and his battles along the way with various villains and is basically an excuse for set pieces, some amusing, others overdone.

Running gags include lack of horses for Arthur and his men, and a lackey clicking cocoanuts together to make suitable hoof noises as the men trot along. The extravagantly gruesome fight scenes, including one which ends with a man having all four limbs severed, will get laughs from some and make others squirm.

THE NAKED GUN

1988, 85 mins, ◇ ⊗ *Dir* David Zucker   US

★ **Stars** Leslie Nielsen, George Kennedy, Priscilla Presley, Ricardo Montalban, O.J. Simpson

Naked Gun is crass, broad, irreverent, wacky fun – and absolutely hilarious from beginning to end.

Subtitled *From the Files of Police Squad!*, based on ill-fated too-hip-for-TV series a few seasons earlier, comedy from the crazed Jerry Zucker, Jim Abrahams, David Zucker yock factory is chockablock with sight gags.

Leslie Nielsen is the clumsy detective reprising his TV role and George Kennedy his straight sidekick who wreaks havoc in the streets of Los Angeles trying to connect shipping magnate and socialite Ricardo Montalban with heroin smuggling.

Graham Chapman and Terry Jones looking heroic in the round table spoofer **Monty Python and the Holy Grail.**

Scintilla of a plot weaves in an inspired bit of nonsense with Queen Elizabeth II lookalike Jeannette Charles as the target for assassination at a California Angels' baseball games, where she stands up and does the wave like any other foolish-looking fan, plus a May–December romance between Nielsen and vapid-acting Priscilla Presley whose exchanges of alternatingly drippy or suggestive dialog would make great material for a soap parody.

Leslie Nielsen and Priscilla Presley in **The Naked Gun,** *a send-up of the* **Dragnet** *cop genre of the Fifties.*

NASTY HABITS

1976, 98 mins, ◇ Ⓥ *Dir* Michael Lindsay-Hogg   UK

★ **Stars** Glenda Jackson, Melina Mercouri, Geraldine Page, Sandy Dennis, Anne Jackson, Anne Meara

A witty, intelligent screenplay [from Muriel Spark's novella *The Abbess of Crewe*] leaves no doubts that this is the Watergate circus transposed to a convent, complete with Machiavellian intrigues and power plays, sexual hanky panky, visiting plumbers, hypocritical television chats, national and international political play, roving ambassadors, and so on.

Told straight, it's all about the battle for power in a Philly convent once the aged abbess dies, an all-stops-out dirty scrap which pits establishment against young lib 'outsiders' who want a change.

Glenda Jackson is superb, making her role as the scheming climber unerringly her own. Only one actress nearly bests her: Edith Evans in a memorable cameo, the actress' last stint in a distinguished legit/pic career.

NATIONAL LAMPOON'S ANIMAL HOUSE

1978, 109 mins, ◇ ⓥ *Dir* John Landis   US

★ **Stars** John Belushi, Tom Matheson, John Vernon, Verna Bloom, Thomas Hulce, Donald Sutherland

Steady readers of the *National Lampoon* may find *National Lampoon's Animal House* a somewhat soft-pedalled, punches-pulled parody of college campus life circa 1962. However, there's enough bite and bawdiness to provide lots of smiles and several broad guffaws.

Writers have concocted a pre-Vietnam college confrontation between a scruffy fraternity and high-elegant campus society. Interspersed in the new faces are the more familiar John Vernon, projecting well his meany charisma here as a corrupt dean; Verna Bloom, Vernon's swinging wife; Cesare Danova, the Mafioso-type mayor of the college town; Donald Sutherland as the super-hip young professor in the days when squares were still saying 'hep'.

Of no small and subtle artistic help is the score by Elmer Bernstein which blithely wafts 'Gaudeamus Igitur' themes amidst the tumult of beer 'orgies', neo-Nazi ROTC drills, cafeteria food fights and a climactic disruption of a traditional Homecoming street parade.

Among the younger players, John Belushi and Tim Matheson are very good as leaders of the unruly fraternity, while James Daughton and Mark Metcalf are prominent as the snotty fratmen, all of whom, quite deliberately, look like Nixon White House aides.

NATIONAL LAMPOON'S EUROPEAN VACATION

1985, 94 mins, ◇ ⓥ *Dir* Amy Heckerling   US

★ **Stars** Chevy Chase, Beverly D'Angelo, Jason Lively, Dana Hill, Eric Idle, Victor Lanoux

Most imaginative stroke is the passport-stamped credit sequence that opens this sequel to the 1983 *National Lampoon's Vacation*. Story of a frenetic, chaotic tour of the Old World, with Chevy Chase and Beverley D'Angelo reprising their role as determined vacationers, is graceless and only intermittently lit up by lunacy and satire.

As the family of characters cartwheel through London, Paris, Italy and Germany – with the French deliciously taking it on the chin for their arrogance and rudeness – director Amy Heckerling gets carried away with physical humor while letting her American tourists grow tiresome and predictable. The film unfolds like a series of travel brochures.

Uneven screenplay by John Hughes and Robert Klare never sails, and it's left to Chase to fire up the film. His character is actually rather sympathetic – if boorish – in his insistence on turning every Continental moment into a delight (scanning Paris, he shouts 'I want to write, I want to paint, I got a romantic urge!'), and there's an inspired bit of business when Chase does a "Sound of Music"-Julie Andrews take off on a German mountaintop.

NATIONAL LAMPOON'S VACATION

1983, 96 mins, ◇ ⓥ *Dir* Harold Ramis   US

★ **Stars** Chevy Chase, Beverly D'Angelo, Anthony Michael Hall, Imogene Coca, Randy Quaid, John Candy

National Lampoon's Vacation is an enjoyable trip through familiar comedy landscapes.

Chevy Chase is perfectly mated with Beverly D'Angelo as an average Chicago suburban couple setting out to spend their annual two-week furlough. Determined to drive, Chase wants to take the two kids to 'Walley World' in California. She would rather fly.

Despite home-computer planning, this trip is naturally going to be a disaster from the moment Chase goes to pick up the new car. No matter how bad this journey gets – and it gets pretty disastrous – Chases perseveres in treating each day as a delight, with D'Angelo's patient cooperation. His son, beautifully played by Anthony Michael Hall, is a help, too.

Vacation peaks early with the family's visit to Cousin Eddie's rundown farm, rundown by the relatives residing there. As the uncouth cousin, Randy Quaid very nearly steals the picture.

Credit goes to director Harold Ramis for populating the film with a host of well-known comedic performers in passing parts.

THE NAVIGATOR

1924, 60 mins, ⊗ *Dir* Donald Crisp, Buster Keaton   US

★ **Stars** Buster Keaton, Kathryn McGuire, Frederick Vroom

Keaton's comedy is spotty. That is to say it's both commonplace and novel, with the latter sufficient to make the picture a laugh getter.

The Navigator is novel in that it has Keaton in a deep-sea diving outfit with the camera catching him under water for comedy insertions. There's a possibility of doubling during some of the film's action, but close-ups are registered underwater that reveal Keaton, personally, behind the glass within the helmet.

There's an abundance of funny business in connection with Keaton's going overboard to fix a propeller shaft and a thrill has been inserted through the comedian getting mixed up with a devil fish.

The actual story carries little weight. It has Keaton as a wealthy young man being matrimonially rejected by the girl. Having secured passage to Hawaii, he unknowingly boards a deserted steamship selected to be destroyed by foreign and warring factions. The girl's father, owner of the vessel, visits the dock, is set upon by the rogues who are bent on casting the liner adrift, and when the girl goes to her parent's rescue she is also caught on board with no chance of a return to land. The entire action practically takes place on the deserted ship, with the girl (Kathryn McGuire) and Keaton the only figures.

NEVER GIVE A SUCKER AN EVEN BREAK

1941, 70 mins, 🖰 *Dir* Edward Cline   US

★ *Stars* W.C. Fields, Gloria Jean, Margaret Dumont

W.C. Fields parades his droll satire and broad comedy in this takeoff on eccentricities of filmmaking – from personal writings of the original story by Fields under nom de plume of Otis Criblecoblis. It's a hodge-podge of razzle-dazzle episodes, tied together in disjointed fashion but with sufficient laugh content for the comedian's fans.

Story focuses attention on Fields and his presentation of an imaginative script for his next picture at Esoteric Studios. In series of cutbacks depicting wild-eyed action as read by producer Franklin Pangborn, Fields horse-plays in a plane, dives out to land on a mountain plateau safely, and finally leaves the studio to embark on a crashing auto chase.

Fields is Fields throughout. He wrote the yarn for himself, and knew how to handle the assignment. Picture is studded with Fieldsian satire and cracks – many funny and several that slipped by the blue-pencil squad. Byplay and reference to hard liquor is prominent throughout.

A NEW LEAF

1971, 102 mins, ◇ 🖰 *Dir* Elaine May   US

★ *Stars* Walter Matthau, Elaine May, Jack Weston, George Rose, William Redfield, James Coco

Walter Matthau is both broad and satirically sensitive and Elaine May has gotten off some sharp and amusing dialog in her screenplay. It's sophisticated and funny, adroitly put

Elaine May plays a rich spinster and Walter Matthau, a hard-up bachelor, her suitor in A New Leaf.

together for the most part. May complained in a court action that final cuts were not hers and she would prefer not to have identity as the director.

Matthau is the marriage-aloof middle-ager who's running out of his inheritance because of high living and who has to come upon a rich wife to sustain himself. Rich wife turns out to be unglamorous May. The director and cosmetician have made May about as sexy as an Alsophiplia Grahamicus, which is a new leaf she has cultivated in her role as botanist. A new leaf is also something that Matthau turns over because after he weds May he decides, rather than kill her, to take care of her like the fine character he hadn't been in the past.

William Redfield fits in as the exasperated lawyer who has difficulty in conveying to Matthau that one doesn't drive a Ferrari and live in a luxurious town house when one is broke. James Coco is Uncle Harry, to whom Henry goes for a loan, which is provided on condition that Henry pay it back in six weeks or pay 10 times the principal.

A NIGHT AT THE OPERA

1935, 93 mins, ⊘ *Dir* Sam Wood   US

★ *Stars* Groucho Marx, Harpo Marx, Chico Marx, Margaret Dumont, Siegfried Rumann, Allan Jones

Story [by James K. McGuinness] is a rather serious grand opera satire in which the comics conspire to get a pair of Italian singers a break over here. For their foils the Marxes have Walter King and Siegfried Rumann as heavies, Robert Emmett O'Connor as a pursuing flatfoot, and Margaret Dumont to absorb the regulation brand of Groucho insults.

Although King also doubles on the vocals, Kitty Carlisle and Allan Jones do most of the singing as the film's love interest.

Groucho and Chico in a contract-tearing bit, the Marxes with O'Connor in a bed-switching idea, and a chase finale in the opera house are other dynamite comedy sequences, along with a corking build-up by Groucho while riding to his room on a trunk. The backstage finish, with Harpo doing a Tarzan on the fly ropes, contains more action than the Marxes usually go in for, but it relieves the strictly verbal comedy and provides a sock exit.

1941

1979, 118 mins, ◇ ⊘ *Dir* Steven Spielberg   US

★ *Stars* Dan Aykroyd, Ned Beatty, John Belushi, Toshiro Mifune, Nancy Allen, Robert Stack

Billed as a comedy spectacle, Steven Spielberg's *1941* is long on spectacle, but short on comedy. The Universal-Columbia Pictures co-production is an exceedingly entertaining, fast-moving revision of 1940s war hysteria in Los Angeles.

Pic [from a story by Robert Zemeckis, Bob Gale and John Milius] is so overloaded with visual humor of a rather monstrous nature that feeling emerges, once you've seen 10 explosions, you've seen them all.

Main comic appeal resides in whatever audience enjoyment will result from seeing Hollywood Boulevard trashed (in miniature scale), paint factories bulldozed, houses toppled into the sea, and a giant ferris wheel rolling to a watery demise.

9 TO 5

1980, 110 mins, ◇ ⓥ *Dir* Colin Higgins   US

★ *Stars* Jane Fonda, Lily Tomlin, Dolly Parton, Dabney Coleman, Sterling Hayden

Anyone who has ever worked in an office will be able to identify with the antics in *9 to 5*. Although it can probably be argued that Patricia Resnick and director Colin Higgins' script [from a story by Resnick] at times borders on the inane, the bottom line is that this picture is a lot of fun.

Story concerns a group of office workers (Lily Tomlin the all-knowing manager who trained the boss but can't get promoted, Jane Fonda, the befuddled newcomer and Dolly Parton the alluring personal secretary) who band together to seek revenge on the man who is making their professional lives miserable.

Tomlin comes off best in certainly the film's most appealing role as the smart yet under-appreciated glue in the office cement.

Parton makes a delightful screen debut here, in a role tailored to her already well-defined country girl personality. Surprisingly, Fonda, initiator of the project, emerges as the weakest.

NINOTCHKA

1939, 111 mins, ⓥ *Dir* Ernst Lubitsch   US

★ *Stars* Greta Garbo, Melvyn Douglas, Bela Lugosi, Sig Rumann, Felix Bressart, Ina Claire

Academy Award 1939: Best Picture (Nomination)

Selection of Ernst Lubitsch to pilot Garbo in her first light performance in pictures proves a bull's-eye.

The punchy and humorous jabs directed at the Russian political system and representatives, and the contrast of bolshevik receptiveness to capitalistic luxuries and customs, are displayed in farcical vein, but there still remains the serious intent of comparisons between the political systems in the background.

Three Russian trade representatives arrive in Paris to dispose of royal jewels 'legally confiscated'. Playboy Melvyn Douglas is intent on cutting himself in for part of the jewel sale. Tying up the gems in lawsuit for former owner, Ina Claire, Douglas is confronted by special envoy Garbo who arrives to speed the transactions. Douglas gets romantic, while Garbo treats love as a biological problem.

Poking political fun at East and West, Ninotchka starred Greta Garbo, in her comedy debut, and Melvyn Douglas.

NOT WITH MY WIFE, YOU DON'T!

1966, 118 mins, ◇ *Dir* Norman Panama   US

★ *Stars* Tony Curtis, Virna Lisi, George C. Scott, Carroll O'Connor, Richard Eastham, Eddie Ryder

Not With My Wife, You Don't! is an outstanding romantic comedy about a US Air Force marriage threatened by jealousy as an old beau of the wife returns to the scene. Zesty scripting, fine performances, solid direction and strong production values sustain hilarity throughout.

Story sets up Tony Curtis and George C. Scott as old Korean conflict buddies whose rivalry for Virna Lisi is renewed when Scott discovers that Curtis won her by subterfuge. The amusing premise is thoroughly held together via an unending string of top comedy situations, including domestic squabbles, flashback, and an outstanding takeoff on foreign pix.

Curtis is excellent as the husband whose duties as aide to Air Force General Carroll O'Connor create the domestic vacuum into which Scott moves with the time-tested instincts of a proven, and non-marrying, satyr.

NUNS ON THE RUN

1990, 90 mins, ◇ Ⓥ *Dir* Jonathan Lynn   UK

★ *Stars* Eric Idle, Robbie Coltrane, Camille Coduri, Janet Suzman, Doris Hare, Tom Hickey

Like Jack Lemmon and Tony Curtis in the Billy Wilder classic *Some Like It Hot*, Eric Idle and Robbie Coltrane are motivated by fear for their lives to dress in women's garb. New pic has rival British and Chinese gangs trying to recover two suitcases full of illicit cash.

Idle and Coltrane make a wonderful pair of dumbbells, both in and out of their habits. Both are oddly believable as nuns, even while writer/director Jonathan Lynn mines all the expected comic benefits of drag humor.

Idle and Coltrane are a lookout and a getaway driver for believable nasty London crime lord Robert Patterson. Their desire to escape their surroundings and the lure of easy cash backfire ominously, and they take refuge in a convent school run by Janet Suzman.

The constant double entendres are done with wit and the slapstick is mostly agreeable and efficiently directed, although the sight gags about Camille Coduri's extreme myopia are pushed a little far on occasion. Coduri otherwise is sweet and endearing in the Marilyn Monroe part.

THE NUTTY PROFESSOR

1963, 107 mins, ◇ Ⓥ *Dir* Jerry Lewis   US

★ *Stars* Jerry Lewis, Stella Stevens, Del Moore, Kathleen Freeman, Howard Morris

The Nutty Professor is not one of Jerry Lewis' better films. Although attractively mounted and performed with flair by a talented cast, the production is only fitfully funny. Too often, unfortunately, the film bogs down in pointless, irrelevant or repetitious business, nullifying the flavor of the occasionally choice comic capers and palsying the tempo and continuity of the story.

The star is cast as a meek, homely, accident-prone chemistry prof who concocts a potion that transforms him into a handsome, cocky, obnoxiously vain 'cool cat' type. But the transfiguration is of the Jekyll-Hyde variety in that it wears off, restoring Lewis to the original mold, invariably at critical, embarrassing moments.

Another standard characteristic of the Lewis film is its similarity to an animated cartoon, especially noticeable on this occasion in that the professor played by Lewis is a kind of live-action version of the nearsighted Mr Magoo.

Musical theme of the picture is the beautiful refrain 'Stella by Starlight'. By starlight or any other light, Stella is beautiful – Stella Stevens, that is, who portrays the professor's student admirer. Stevens is not only gorgeous, she is a very gifted actress. This was an exceptionally tough assignment, requiring of her almost exclusively silent reaction takes, and Stevens has managed almost invariably to pro-

duce the correct responsive expression. On her, even the incorrect one would look good.

THE ODD COUPLE

1968, 105 mins, ◇ Ⓥ *Dir* Gene Saks   US

★ *Stars* Jack Lemmon, Walter Matthau, John Fiedler, Herbert Edelman, David Sheiner, Larry Haines

The Odd Couple, Neil Simon's smash legit comedy, has been turned into an excellent film starring Jack Lemmon and Walter Matthau. Simon's somewhat expanded screenplay retains the broad, as well as the poignant, laughs inherent in the rooming together of two men whose marriages are on the rocks.

The teaming of Lemmon and Matthau here has provided each with an outstanding comedy partner. As the hypochondriac, domesticated and about-to-be-divorced Felix, Lemmon is excellent. Matthau also hits the bullseye in a superior characterization.

Carrying over from the legit version with Matthau are Monica Evans and Carole Shelley, the two English girls from upstairs, and John Fiedler, one of the poker game group which, until Lemmon moved in, revelled in cigarette butts, clumsy sandwiches, and other signs of disarray.

New to the plot is opening scene of Lemmon bumbling in suicide attempts in a Times Square flophouse. By the time he arrives at Matthau's apartment, his amusing misadventures have caused a wrenched back and neck. Staggered main titles help prolong this good intro.

OH, GOD!

1977, 97 mins, ◇ Ⓥ *Dir* Carl Reiner   US

★ *Stars* George Burns, John Denver, Teri Garr, Donald Pleasence, Ralph Bellamy, William Daniels

Oh, God! is a hilarious film which benefits from the brilliant teaming of George Burns, as the Almighty in human form, and John Denver, sensational in his screen debut as a supermarket assistant manager who finds himself a suburban Moses.

Carl Reiner's controlled and easy direction of a superb screenplay and a strong cast makes the Jerry Weintraub production a warm and human comedy.

An Avery Corman novel is the basis for Larry Gelbart's adaptation which makes its humanistic points while taking gentle pokes at organized Establishment religions, in particular the kind of fund-raising fundamentalism epitomized by Paul Sorvino. Teri Garr is excellent as Denver's perplexed but loyal wife.

Matthau and Lemmon going to the dogs as **The Odd Couple***, ill-paired refugees from marriage break-ups.*

ONLY WHEN I LARF

1968, 103 mins, ◇ *Dir* Basil Dearden   UK

★ **Stars** Richard Attenborough, David Hemmings, Alexandra Stewart, Nicholas Pennell, Melissa Stribling

Only When I Larf is a pleasant little joke, based on a Len Deighton novel and rather less complicated than some of his other work, with sound, unfussy direction and witty, observed thesping.

Filmed in London, New York and Beirut, it has Richard Attenborough, David Hemmings and Alexandra Stewart as a con-trio. Situation arises whereby Attenborough and Hemmings fall out and seek to doublecross each other.

Mood is admirably set with the gang pulling off a slickly-planned con trick in a New York office. Talk is minimal, though the sript opens up into a more gabby talk-fest later, but dialog is usually pointed and crisp.

Attenborough plays an ex-brigadier and takes on various guises. His brigadier is a masterly piece of observation and the whole film has Attenborough at his considerable comedy best. Hemmings is equally effective as the discontented young whiz-kid lieutenant and Stewart, with little to do, manages to look both efficient and sexy.

OTLEY

1969, 90 mins, ◇ *Dir* Dick Clement   UK

★ **Stars** Tom Courtenay, Romy Schneider, Alan Badel, James Villiers, Leonard Rossiter

Otley seeks to break away from over-done Ian Fleming-like spy tales [of the period]. It focuses on exploits of bumbling 'everyman type' thrust into the espionage game.

Storyline is pegged around Tom Courtenay unfortuitously present at an acquaintance's London flat, when the latter is bumped off. It soon evolves that the recently deceased was a defector from a gang of state-secret smugglers, and now all parties concerned think that Courtenay somehow knew as much as his late friend.

Because of this, he is first kidnapped and beaten up by Romy Schneider and her cohorts, then after bumbling his way out of their clutches, he is caught by the opposing side and bounced about by them.

In seeking to avoid overheroics as well as the pitfalls of parody, the film has an uneasy lack of a point of view and fails to focus viewer's attention on any particular character or plotline philosophy.

THE OWL AND THE PUSSYCAT

1970, 98 mins, ◇ ⓥ *Dir* Herbert Ross   US

★ *Stars* Barbra Streisand, George Segal, Robert Klein, Allen Garfield, Roz Kelly, Jacques Sandulescu

A zany, laugh-filled story of two modern NY kooks who find love at the end of trail of hilarious incidents.

Bill Manhoff's 1954 play, adapted here by Buck Henry, has been altered in that, as originally cast, one of the principals was white, the other black (on Broadway, Alan Alda and Diana Sands). Here it's two Bronx-Brooklyn Caucasian types, with Barbra Streisand giving it a Jewish Jean Arthur treatment and George Segal as an amiable, low-key foil.

The story is basically that of the out-of-work quasi-model and the struggling writer who cut up and down apartment corridors and in public to the astonishment of all others.

Streisand is a casual hooker, who first confronts Segal after he has finked on her activities to building superintendent Jacques Sandulescu. Their harangues then shift to apartment of buddy Robert Klein who decides it is better to leave with gal Evelyn Lang than lie awake listening.

One of her old scores turns out to be Jack Manning, Segal's intended father-in-law, but that plot turn blows up his affair and leads into the excellent climax we have been waiting for.

THE PALEFACE

1948, 91 mins, ◇ ⓥ *Dir* Norman Z. McLeod   US

★ *Stars* Bob Hope, Jane Russell, Robert Armstrong

The Paleface is a smart-aleck travesty on the west, told with considerable humor and bright gags. Bob Hope has been turned loose on a good script.

Hope isn't all the film has to sell. There's Jane Russell as Calamity Jane, that rough, tough gal of the open west whose work as a government agent causes Hope's troubles, but whose guns save him from harm and give him his hero reputation. She makes an able sparring partner for the Hope antics, and is a sharp eyeful in Technicolor.

'Buttons and Bows' is top tune of the score's three pop numbers. Jay Livingston and Ray Evans cleffed and Hope renders as a plaintive love chant to Russell.

Script poses an amusing story idea – Hope as a correspondence school dentist touring the west in a covered wagon. He's having his troubles, but they're nothing compared to the grief that catches up with him when Calamity Jane seduces him into marriage so she can break up a gang smuggling rifles to the Indians.

THE PALM BEACH STORY

1942, 96 mins, ⓥ *Dir* Preston Sturges   US

★ *Stars* Claudette Colbert, Joel McCrea, Mary Astor, Rudy Vallee, William Demarest, Sig Arno

This Preston Sturges production is packed with delightful absurdities. Claudette Colbert comes through with one of her best light comedy interpretations. She's strikingly youthful and alluring as the slightly screwball wife of five years standing, who, after seeing husband Joel McCrea out of debt, suddenly decides to seek a divorce, adventure and a bankroll for the husband she leaves behind.

Tongue-in-cheek spoofing of the idle rich attains hilarious proportions in scenes where Rudy Vallee, as John D. Hackensacker the Third, proposes to the errant wife and later woos her by singing to her to the accompaniment of a privately hired symphony orch big enough to fill the Radio City Music Hall pit.

McCrea plays it straight, for the most part, as the husband intent on winning his wife back.

PARENTHOOD

1989, 124 mins, ◇ ⓥ *Dir* Ron Howard   US

★ *Stars* Steve Martin, Mary Steenburgen, Dianne Wiest, Jason Robards, Rick Moranis, Tom Hulce

An ambitious, keenly observed, and often very funny look at one of life's most daunting passages, *Parenthood*'s masterstroke is that it covers the range of the family experience, offering the points of view of everyone in an extended and wildly diverse middle-class family.

At its centre is over-anxious dad Steve Martin, who'll try anything to alleviate his eight-year-old's emotional problems, and Mary Steenburgen, his equally conscientious but better-adjusted wife.

Rick Moranis is the yuppie extreme, an excellence-fixated nerd who forces math, languages, Kafka and karate on his three-year-old girl, to the distress of his milder wife (Harley Kozak).

Dianne Wiest is a divorcee and working mother whose rebellious teens (Martha Plimpton and Leaf Phoenix) dump their anger in her lap.

Jason Robards is the acidic patriarch of the family whose neglectful fathering made his eldest son (Martin) grow

Steve Martin entertains his son's friends in **Parenthood,** *a study of the baby-boom generation and their children.*

up with an obsession to do better. The old man is forced to take another shot at fatherhood late in life when his ne'er-do-well, 27-year-old son (Tom Hulce) moves back in.

THE PARTY

1968, 98 mins, ◇ Ⓥ *Dir* Blake Edwards   US

★ *Stars* Peter Sellers, Claudine Longet, Marge Champion, Steve Franken, Fay McKenzie

All the charm of two-reel comedy, as well as all the resulting tedium when the concept is distended to 10 reels, is evident in *The Party.*

The one-joke script, told in laudable, if unsuccessful, attempt to emulate silent pix technique, is dotted with comedy ranging from drawing-room repartee to literally, bathroom vulgarity.

Peter Sellers is a disaster-prone foreign thesp, who, in an amusing eight-minute prolog to titles, fouls up an important Bengal Lancer-type film location. His outraged producer (Gavin MacLeod) blackballs him to studio chief J. Edward McKinley, but, in a mixup, Sellers gets invited to a party at McKinley's home.

Production designer Fernando Carrere has done an outstanding job in creating, on the one set used, a super-gauge house of sliding floors, pools, centralized controls and bizarre trappings.

Besides Sellers, most prominent thesps are Claudine Longet, the romantic interest, and Steve Franken as a tipsy butler. Eventually it all becomes a big yawn.

PASSPORT TO PIMLICO

1949, 84 mins, Ⓥ *Dir* Henry Cornelius   UK

★ *Stars* Stanley Holloway, Barbara Murray, Raymond Huntley, Paul Dupuis, Jane Hylton, Hermione Baddeley

Sustained, lightweight comedy scoring a continual succession of laughs.

Story describes what happens when a wartime unexploded bomb in a London street goes off and reveals ancient documents and treasure which make the territory part of the duchy of Burgundy. Ration cards are joyfully torn up and customs barriers are put up by British.

The theme is related with a genuine sense of satire and clean, honest humor. The principal characters are in the hands of experienced players with Stanley Holloway leading the new government, Raymond Huntley the bank manager turned Chancellor of the Exchequer, Hermione Baddeley as the shopkeeper and Sydney Tafler as the local bookmaker.

Post-war escapism in an austere England, **Passport to Pimlico** *is a classic comedy of its time.*

PAT AND MIKE

1952, 94 mins, ⚉ *Dir* George Cukor   US

★ *Stars* Spencer Tracy, Katharine Hepburn, Aldo Ray, William Ching, Sammy White, George Mathews

The smooth-working team of Spencer Tracy and Katharine Hepburn spark the fun in *Pat and Mike*. Hepburn is quite believable as a femme athlete taken under the wing of promoter Tracy. The actress, as a college athletic instructor engaged to eager-beaver prof William Ching, enters an amateur golf tournament to prove to herself and to fiance Ching that she is good. Deed attracts the attention of Tracy, who quick-talks her into signing a pro contract for a number of sports.

Film settles down to a series of laugh sequences of training, exhibitions and cross-country tours in which Hepburn proves to be a star.

Tracy is given some choice lines in the script and makes much of them in an easy, throwaway style that lifts the comedy punch.

PEE-WEE'S BIG ADVENTURE

1985, 90 mins, ◇ ⚉ *Dir* Tim Burton   US

★ *Stars* Paul Reubens, Elizabeth Daily, Mark Holton, Diane Salinger, Judd Omen, Jon Harris

Children should love the film and adults will be dismayed by the light brushstrokes with which Paul Reubens (one of three credited screenwriters, but star-billed under his stage name, Pee-wee Herman) suggests touches of Buster Keaton and Eddie Cantor.

Pee-wee wakes up in a children's bedroom full of incredible toys, slides down a fire station-like brass pole, materializing in his trademark tight suit with white shoes and red bow-tie, proceeds to make a breakfast a la Rube Goldberg, and winds up in a front yard that looks like a children's farm.

It's a delicious bit, with Reubens making noises like a child, walking something like Chaplin, and remarkably drawing for adult viewers the joys and frustrations of being a kid. Rest of narrative deals with Pee-wee's unstoppable pursuit of his prized lost bicycle, a rambling kidvid-like spoof.

THE PERILS OF PAULINE

1947, 93 mins, ◇ ⚉ *Dir* George Marshall   US

★ *Stars* Betty Hutton, John Lund, Constance Collier, William Demarest

Betty Hutton is tiptop in the title role, giving distinction to antics of early day picturemaking and four bright tunes. It's

a funfest for the actress and she makes the most of it. Pointing up many solid laughs are sequences depicting old open-air stages on which all variety of entertainment was ground out side by side in utter confusion. George Marshall draws heavily on his long picture experience to make it all authentic and garners himself a top credit for surefire direction.

Screenplay purports to show how Pearl White, early-day serial queen, got her start in silent films. Scripters carry her from a New York sweatshop to a traveling stock company and then into pictures with credible writing. Romance angle is the only apparent hoke factor in script but it, too, blends well with overall high entertainment level.

John Lund co-stars as a ham stock actor who is loved by the cliffhanger queen. Choice performances are delivered by Constance Collier, as the character actress, and William Demarest, as the silent director.

PERSONAL SERVICES

1987, 105 mins, ◇ ⚉ *Dir* Terry Jones   UK

★ *Stars* Julie Walters, Alec McCowan, Shirley Stelfox, Danny Schiller, Tim Woodward, Victoria Hardcastle

For a pic about sex, *Personal Services* is remarkably unerotic. It deals with society's two-faced attitude to sex-for-sale in a humorous but essentially sad way, and is excellently acted and directed. Film is based on a real madam who became a household name as a result of a trial in 1986.

Pic tells the story of the transition of Christine Painter (a dominating performance by Julie Walters) from waitress to madam of Britain's most pleasant brothel, where the perversions are served up with a cooked breakfast and a cup of tea to follow. She looks after the aged and infirm along with eminent clients, none of whom has a kink her girls can't cater to.

Julie Walters plays Christine as a charmingly vulgar yet benign madam, whose brothel-keeping career seemingly comes to an end when the police raid her London house during a Christmas party. At her trial she recognizes the judge as one of her regular clients.

Alex McCowan is excellent as her friend and business partner, a former pilot who proudly boasts of a World War II record of 207 missions over enemy territory in 'bra and panties'.

THE PHILADELPHIA STORY

1940, 112 mins, ⚉ *Dir* George Cukor   US

★ *Stars* Cary Grant, Katharine Hepburn, James Stewart, Ruth Hussey, John Howard, Roland Young

Academy Award 1940: Best Picture (Nomination)

It's Katharine Hepburn's picture, but with as fetching a lineup of thesp talent as is to be found, she's got to fight every clever line of dialog all of the way to hold her lead. Pushing hard is little Virginia Weidler, the kid sister, who has as twinkly an eye with a fast quip as a blinker light. Ruth Hussey is another from whom director George Cukor has milked maximum results to get a neat blend of sympathy-winning softness under a python-tongued smart-aleckness. As for Cary Grant, James Stewart and Roland Young, there's little to be said that their reputation hasn't established. John Howard, John Halliday and Mary Nash, in lesser roles, more than adequately fill in what Philip Barry must have dreamt of when he wrote the 1939 play.

The perfect conception of all flighty but characterful Main Line socialite gals rolled into one, Hepburn has just the right amount of beauty, just the right amount of disarray in wearing clothes, just the right amount of culture in her voice – it's no one but Hepburn.

Story is localed in the very social and comparatively new (for Philly, 1860) Main Line sector in the suburbs of Quakertown. Hepburn, divorced from Grant, a bit of rather useless uppercrust like herself, is about to marry a stuffed-bosom man of the people (Howard). Grant, to keep Henry Daniell, publisher of the mags *Dime* and *Spy* (*Time* and *Life*, get it?) from running a scandalous piece about Hepburn's father (Halliday), agrees to get a reporter and photog into the Hepburn household preceding and during the wedding. Stewart and Hussey are assigned and Grant, whose position as ex-husband is rather unique in the mansion, manages to get them in under a pretext. Everyone, nevertheless, knows why Stewart and Hussey are there and the repartee is swift.

When the acid tongues are turned on at beginning and end of the film it's a laugh-provoker from way down. When the discussion gets deep and serious, however, on the extent of Hepburn's stone-like character, the verbiage is necessarily highly abstract and the film slows to a toddle.

PILLOW TALK

1959, 105 mins, ◇ Ⓥ *Dir* Michael Gordon   US

★ *Stars* Rock Hudson, Doris Day, Tony Randall, Thelma Ritter, Nick Adams

Pillow Talk is a sleekly sophisticated production that deals chiefly with s-e-x. The principals seem to spend considerable time in bed or talking about what goes on in bed, but the beds they occupy are always occupied singly. There's more talk than action natch.

The plot (slight) of the amusing screenplay by Stanley Shapiro and Maurice Richlin, from a story by Clarence Greene and Russell Rouse, is based on the notion that a telephone shortage puts Doris Day and Rock Hudson on a party line. Both have been cast somewhat against type. Hudson, usually the lovable, overgrown boy, is here a sophisticated man about town. Day, discarding her casual hair-style, displays a brace of smart Jean Louis gowns, and delivers crisply.

There is a good deal of cinema trickery in Pillow Talk. There are split screens; spoken thoughts by the main characters; and even introduction of background music orchestration for a laugh. It all registers strongly.

Peter Sellers and Capucine in his debut **Pink Panther** *role as the bumbling Inspector Clouseau.*

THE PINK PANTHER

1964, 115 mins, ◇ Ⓥ *Dir* Blake Edwards   US

★ *Stars* David Niven, Peter Sellers, Robert Wagner, Capucine, Claudia Cardinale, Brenda DeBanzie

This is filmmaking as a branch of the candy trade, and the pack is so enticing that few will worry about the jerky machinations of the plot.

Quite apart from the general air of bubbling elegance, the pic is intensely funny. The yocks are almost entirely the responsibility of Peter Sellers, who is perfectly suited as a clumsy cop who can hardly move a foot without smashing a vase or open a door without hitting himself on the head.

The Panther is a priceless jewel owned by the Indian Princess Dala (Claudia Cardinale), vacationing in the Swiss ski resort of Cortina. The other principals are introduced in their various habitats, before they converge on the princess and her jewel.

Sellers' razor-sharp timing is superlative, and he makes the most of his ample opportunities. His doting concern for criminal wife (Capucine), his blundering ineptitude with material objects, and his dogged pursuit of the crook all coalesce to a sharp performance, with satirical overtones.

David Niven produces his familiar brand of debonair ease. Robert Wagner has a somewhat undernourished role. Capucine, sometimes awkward and over-intense as if she were straining for yocks, is nevertheless a good Simone Clouseau.

THE PINK PANTHER STRIKES AGAIN

1976, 103 mins, ◇ Ⓥ *Dir* Blake Edwards   UK

★ *Stars* Peter Sellers, Herbert Lom, Colin Blakely, Leonard Rossiter, Lesley-Anne Down, Burt Kwouk

The Pink Panther Strikes Again is a hilarious film about the further misadventures of Peter Sellers as Inspector Clouseau.

Herbert Lom, Clouseau's nemesis in the police bureau, has had his character expanded into a Professor Moriarty-type fiend, which works just fine.

This time around, Lom is introduced nearly cured of his nervous collapse. But Sellers has assumed Lom's old chief inspector job, and when Lom escapes, Sellers is assigned to the case. Lom kidnaps scientist Richard Vernon who has a disappearing ray device; pitch is that Lom threatens world destruction unless Sellers is handed over to him for extermination.

Action proceeds smartly through plot-advancing action scenes, interleaved with excellent non-dialog sequences featuring Sellers and underscored superbly by Henry Mancini.

PLANES, TRAINS & AUTOMOBILES

1987, 93 mins, ◇ Ⓥ *Dir* John Hughes   US

★ **Stars** Steve Martin, John Candy, Laila Robbins, Michael McKean, Kevin Bacon

John Hughes has come up with an effective nightmare-as-comedy in *Planes, Trains & Automobiles*. Disaster-prone duo of Steve Martin and John Candy repeatedly recall a contemporary Laurel & Hardy as they agonizingly try to make their way from New York to Chicago by various modes of transport.

Man versus technology has been one of the staples of screen comedy since the earliest silent days, and Hughes makes the most of the format here packing as many of the frustrations of modern life as he can into this calamitous travelog of roadside America.

An ultimate situation comedy, tale throws together Martin, an ad exec, and Candy, a shower curtain ring salesman, as they head home from Manhattan to their respective homes in Chicago two days before Thanksgiving.

The problems start before they even get out of midtown. From there, it's a series of ghastly motel rooms, crowded anonymous restaurants, a sinister cab ride, an abortive train trip, an even worse excursion by rented car, some hitchhiking by truck, and, finally, a hop on the 'El' before sitting down to turkey.

PLAY IT AGAIN, SAM

1972, 84 mins, ◇ Ⓥ *Dir* Herbert Ross   US

★ **Stars** Woody Allen, Diane Keaton, Tony Roberts, Jerry Lacy, Susan Anspach, Jennifer Salt

Woody Allen's 1969 legit comedy-starrer, *Play It Again, Sam*, has become on the screen 84 minutes of fragile fun. Allen and other key players from the stage version encore to good results. The placid direction of Herbert Ross keeps Allen in the spotlight for some good laughs, several chuckles and many smiles.

Allen's adaptation showcases his self-deprecating, and sometimes erratic, comedy personality. Ditched by wife

Susan Anspach, who cannot stand his vicarious living of old Humphrey Bogart films, Allen is consoled by Diane Keaton and Tony Roberts, to the point that Keaton begins to fall for Allen. The interlude ends with a recreation of the final scene from Warners' *Cassablanca*. Jerry Lacy is most effective as the Bogart phantom who drops in from time to time.

PLAZA SUITE

1971, 114 mins, ◇ Ⓥ *Dir* Arthur Hiller   US

★ **Stars** Walter Matthau, Maureen Stapleton, Barbara Harris, Lee Grant

Neil Simon's excellent adaptation of his 1968 Broadway hit stars Walter Matthau in three strong characterizations of comedy-in-depth, teamed separately with Maureen Stapleton, Lee Grant and Barbara Harris.

Film opens with a 44-minute sketch featuring Stapleton as a nervous suburban wife who has taken her bridal suite at NY's Plaza Hotel while the paint dries at home. Hubby Matthau is a cool, jaded mate whose affair with secretary Louise Sorel is intuitively divined by the wife. Segment is the most dramatic, though filled with nervous comedy.

Middle episode is 33 minutes of lecherous farce, as Hollywood producer Matthau puts the make on Harris, a flame of 15 years past. She has become a reluctant matron of Tenafly, NJ. Some of the best laughs of the whole piece occur here.

Final 37 minutes involve father-of-the-bride Matthau, trying to coax frightened daughter Jenny Sullivan out of a locked hotel bathroom and into marriage to Thomas Carey. Grant is the harried mother. The comedy emphasis here is generally slapstick: rain-drenched clothes; torn tails and stockings; broken furniture.

Each of the femme stars is given much screen time and the result not only is excellent spotlighting of their own talents, but also an adroit restraint on Matthau's presence.

POLICE ACADEMY

1984, 95 mins, ◇ Ⓥ *Dir* Hugh Wilson   US

★ **Stars** Steve Guttenberg, G.W. Bailey, George Gaynes, Michael Winslow, Kim Cattrall, Bubba Smith

Police Academy at its core is a harmless, innocent poke at authority that does find a fresh background in a police academy. Women in the film, such as Kim Cattrall as an Ivy League-type and Leslie Easterbrook as a busty sergeant, have almost nothing to do. Marion Ramsey as a timid-voiced trainee is fine in the film's most vivid female part.

Co-writer Hugh Wilson, makes his feature film debut as director, and his scenes are short and fragmentary. He gets a fresh comic performance from Michael Winslow as a walking human sound effects system (the film's most appealing turn).

Through it all, Steve Guttenberg is a likable rogue in a role that's too unflappable to set off any sparks.

POLYESTER

1981, 94 mins, ◇ *Dir* John Waters   US

★ *Stars* Divine, Tab Hunter

Baltimore-based underground filmmaker John Waters, famous for his midnight circuit hits like *Pink Flamingos*, surfaces in the pro ranks with *Polyester*, a fitfully amusing comedy of not so ordinary people. Waters' fabled shock tactics are toned down here.

Transvestite thesp Divine never steps out of character essaying the role of a housewife stuck with horrid children (Mary Garlington and Ken King) an unsympathetic husband (David Samson) and a truly evil mother (Joni Ruth White). As the episodic situation comedy unfolds, camp followers may enjoy Divine's eyerolling reactions but to the uninitiated most scenes play as overacted melodrama.

After a couple of silent teaser shots, Tab Hunter finally enters the picture after a full hour has elapsed. He is unable to fit into Waters' world, straining to overact and pull faces as the rest of the troupe and even extras do.

With nudity and explicit sex and violence absent, *Polyester* strains for a marketing gimmick by introducing 'Odorama.' After a cute scientist-in-lab prolog explaining the process, cheap gimmick turns out to be a scratch and sniff card handed out to the viewer, keyed manually to numbers flashed on the screen periodically during the film. It's a far cry from the fumes in the theatre gimmicks of Walter Reade's 1959 AromaRama and Mike Todd Jrs 1960 Smell-O-Vision.

PORKY'S

1981, 94 mins, ◇ *Dir* Bob Clark   CANADA

★ *Stars* Dan Monahan, Mark Herrier, Wyatt Knight, Roger Wilson, Cyril O'Reilly, Tony Ganlos

If, by chance, *Porky's* should prove to be Melvin Simon's swan song in the film industry, it will either be perceived as a thunderously rude exit or a titanic raspberry uttered to audiences everywhere.

Virtually every scene and dialog exchange constitutes a new definition of lewdness. Locker room humor reaches new heights (depths), and script reads as if writer-director Clark had kept a diary of filthy pranks and one-liners since junior high school and collected them all here for posterity.

Film cannot be faulted for lack of a driving force – simply, all these young Florida boys are itching to score and most of their time is spent in pursuit of said goal.

Title refers to a redneck establishment out in the Everglades known for its available women. After being embarrassingly turned away on their first visit, the boys return to wreak havoc on the joint, proving once and for all that violence will result when the sex drive is repressed.

Ultimately, one either yields totally to the stupefying sophomorism of the film – in which case it can be painlessly enjoyed – or the viewer will be repulsed from frame one.

PORKY'S II THE NEXT DAY

1983, 95 mins, ◇ Ⓥ *Dir* Bob Clark   US

★ *Stars* Dan Monahan, Wyatt Knight, Mark Herrier, Roger Wilson, Cyril O'Reilly, Tony Ganios

Plot follows in the grand tradition of many early rock 'n' roll quickies, in which self-righteous upholders of comic morality attempted to stomp out the threat posed by the new primitive music. Replacing Chuck Mitchell's Porky as the heavy here is Bill Wiley's bigoted Rev. Bubba Flavel, who makes a crusade out of shutting down the school's Shakespeare festival due to the lewdness he finds strewn throughout the Bard's work.

Enlisted in his cause is the ample girls' gym teacher Miss Balbricker and the local contingent of the Ku Klux Klan, who are each the victims of two of the film's three 'big scenes'. Everyone who saw it remembers 'that scene' from the original. Here, some of the boys get back at Balbricker by sending a snake up into her toilet.

Director Bob Clark has not allowed success lead him astray into the dreaded realm of good taste.

PRIVATE BENJAMIN

1980, 109 mins, ◇ Ⓥ *Dir* Howard Zieff   US

★ *Stars* Goldie Hawn, Eileen Brennan, Armand Assante, Sam Wanamaker, Harry Dean Stanton, Robert Webber

Goldie Hawn's venture in producing her own film is actually a double feature – one is a frequently funny tale of an innocent who is conned into joining the US Army and her adventures therein; the other deals with the same innocent's personality problems as a Jewish princess with only an intermittent chuckle to help out.

The trouble may be with the use of too many screenwriters who have been told to always keep their star's image uppermost in their scribblings. But she's not so gifted that she can carry a heavy load of indifferent material on her own two little shoulders, without considerable sagging.

Another script problem is that the supporting characters are, even when they start out sympathetically, turned into unlikable types.

A PRIVATE FUNCTION

1984, 93 mins, ◇ Ⓥ *Dir* Malcolm Mowbray   UK

★ *Stars* Michael Palin, Maggie Smith, Liz Smith, Denholm Elliott, Richard Griffiths, John Normington

Pic is set in 1947, at a time of national rejoicing over a royal wedding and hardship caused by food rationing. Plot evolves out of a plan hatched by a group of town notables

Michael Palin, Maggie Smith and Betty the Pig hamming it up in a scene from A Private Function.

the changing of the final locale from a Paris apartment to a Swiss chalet. Both Norma Shearer and Robert Montgomery capably handle themselves as the divorced couple who again run away together the night of their honeymoons with their newly-acquired better halves. Both having tempestuous natures, their love making and quarreling is equally violent and the warfare is apt to start any time.

As the somewhat neurotic man in the case, Montgomery plays deftly and well. So does Shearer, but the medium of the screen has lost many of the laugh lines which did much to sustain the play. However, Franklin establishes and maintains a good pace after a rather slow start.

THE PRODUCERS

1968, 100 mins, ◇ ⓥ *Dir* Mel Brooks   US

★ **Stars** Zero Mostel, Gene Wilder, Kenneth Mars, Estelle Winwood, Dick Shawn, Christopher Hewitt

Mel Brooks has turned a funny idea into a slapstick film, thanks to the performers, particularly Zero Mostel.

Playing a Broadway producer of flops who survives (barely) by suckering little old ladies, he teams with an emotionally retarded accountant portrayed by Gene Wilder in a scheme to produce a flop. By selling 25,000% of production, they figure to be rich when it flops. For the twist, the musical comedy *Springtime for Hitler*, penned by a shell-shocked Nazi, is a smash. Certainly the Third Reich production number is hilarious.

The film is unmatched in the scenes featuring Mostel and Wilder alone together, and several episodes with other actors are truly rare. When the producers approach the most atrocious director on Broadway, they find Christopher Hewitt in drag exchanging catty comments with his secretary (Andreas Voutsinas).

Estelle Winwood is a winner as a salacious little old lady, and Kenneth Mars has his moments as the Nazi scripter. A very entertaining film.

Gene Wilder and Zero Mostel look on in disbelief as their tacky musical wows the audience in The Producers.

to fatten up a secret pig for festive devouring on the wedding night.

Private Function's central characters are a husband and wife team played by Maggie Smith and Michael Palin. She's a bullying wife anxious to reach the social highspots in the Yorkshire village where he works as a foot doctor. Their domestic crises are made more complex and amusing by the presence of a greedy mother (Liz Smith) who lives in terror of being put away.

Director Malcolm Mowbray neatly orchestrates the resulting drama, and points up the class antagonisms at play.

PRIVATE LIVES

1931, 82 mins, *Dir* Sidney Franklin   US

★ **Stars** Norma Shearer, Robert Montgomery, Reginald Denny, Una Merkel, Jean Hersholt

Sidney Franklin has followed the Noel Coward play closely with the addition of a number of interpolated scenes and

PYGMALION

1938, 96 mins, Ⓥ *Dir* Anthony Asquith, Leslie Howard   UK

★ *Stars* Wendy Hiller, Leslie Howard, Wilfred Lawson, Marie Lohr, Scott Sunderland, Jean Cadell

Academy Award 1938: Best Picture (Nomination)

Smartly produced, this makes an excellent job of transcribing George Bernard Shaw, retaining all the key lines and giving freshness to the theme. The speed of the first half contrives to show up the anti-climax, the play subsequently petering out in a flood of clever talk. But it's still a Cinderella story, which is one of the most reliable subjects for drama.

Leslie Howard's performance is excellent in its comedy. It's vital and at times dominating. Wendy Hiller carries off a difficult part faultlessly. She never loses sight of the fact that this is a guttersnipe on whom culture has been imposed; the ambassador's reception, where she moves like a sleepwalker, is eloquent of this, and even in the final argument the cockney is always peeping through the veneer.

Wilfred Lawson's Doolittle is only a shadow of the part G.B.S. wrote, but his moral philosophies could obviously not have been put on the screen in toto without gumming up the action. As it is he presents a thoroughly enjoyable old reprobate.

QUICK CHANGE

1990, 88 mins, ◇ Ⓥ *Dir* Howard Franklin, Bill Murray   US

★ *Stars* Bill Murray, Geena Davis, Randy Quaid, Jason Robards, Bob Elliott

Bill Murray delivers a smart, sardonic and very funny valentine to the rotten Apple in *Quick Change*. Pic became Murray's directing debut (he shares the chores with screenwriter Howard Franklin) after he and Franklin became too attached to the project to bring anyone else in. Material, based on Jay Cronley's book, is neither ambitious nor particularly memorable, but it's brought off with a sly flair that makes it most enjoyable.

Murray plays a fed-up New Yorker who enlists his girlfriend (Geena Davis) and lifelong pal (Randy Quaid) in a bank heist so they can get outta town. Hold-up, which nets $1 million and a very nice watch, sets off a carnival of police and crowd reaction in the New York streets, but none of it flaps the dynamite-rigged Murray.

With Jason Robards as a crusty police inspector who's as crazily sharp as *Twin Peaks* agent Cooper, pic offers some crazy little setpieces in a manic game of chase. Pic is so thick with gritty, tired, scuzzy NY atmosphere viewer wants to scrape it off the skin.

Only in the final reel do things feel broadly contrived, concurrent with pic's move from NY locations to a Florida soundstage for airport shooting.

RADIO DAYS

1987, 85 mins, ◇ Ⓥ *Dir* Woody Allen   US

★ *Stars* Mia Farrow, Seth Green, Julie Kavner, Josh Mostel, Michael Tucker, Dianne Wiest

Although lacking the bite and depth of his best work, *Radio Days* is one of Woody Allen's most purely entertaining pictures. It's a visual monolog of bits and pieces from the glory days of radio and the people who were tuned in.

Rockaway Beach, a thin strip of land on the outskirts of New York City is where young Joe (Seth Green) and his family live in not-so splendid harmony and for entertainment and escape listen to the radio. Set at the start of World War II, it's a world of aunts and uncles all living on top of each other and the magical events and people, real and imagined, that forever shape one's young imagination.

Radio Days is not simply about nostalgia, but the quality of memory and how what one remembers informs one's present life.

Dianne Wiest is delicious as an aunt who is desperate to find a husband but somehow keeps meeting Mr Wrong. The robust Masked Avenger is, in real life, the diminutive Wallace Shawn. Mia Farrow is a none-too-bright cigaret girl with a yen for stardom who magically transforms her life.

RAISING ARIZONA

1987, 94 mins, ◇ Ⓥ *Dir* Joel Coen   US

★ *Stars* Nicolas Cage, Holly Hunter, Trey Wilson, John Goodman, William Forsythe

Pic is the Coen Brothers' twisted view of family rearing in the American heartlands and full of quirky humor and off-the-wall situations as their debut effort, *Blood Simple*. The film captures the surrealism of everyday life. Characters are so strange here that they seem to have stepped out of late-night television, tabloid newspapers, talk radio and a vivid imagination.

Nicolas Cage and Holly Hunter are the off-center couple at the center of the doings. Cage is a well-meaning petty crook with a fondness for knocking off convenience stores.

Nicolas Cage steals a baby for his wife rather than adopt in off-the-wall comedy Raising Arizona.

Hunter is the cop who checks him into prison so often that a romance develops.

They soon learn marriage is 'no Ozzie and Harriet Show' and when she learns she can't have kids or adopt them, they do the next logical thing – steal one.

Loosely structured around a voice-over narration by Cage, *Raising Arizona* is as leisurely and disconnected as *Blood Simple* was taut and economical. While film is filled with many splendid touches and plenty of yocks, it often doesn't hold together as a coherent story.

While Cage and Hunter are fine as the couple at sea in the desert, pic sports at least one outstanding performance from John Goodman as the con brother who wants a family too.

REAL GENIUS

1985, 104 mins, ◇ Ⓥ *Dir* Martha Coolidge   US

★ *Stars* Val Kilmer, Gabe Jarret, Michelle Meyrink, William Atherton, Jonathan Gries, Patti D'Arbanville

Real Genius is *Police Academy* with brains. Setting the proceedings at a think tank for young prodigies seems a curious choice as most of the humor of the film comes out of character rather than place. Val Kilmer, punning his way through his senior year at Pacific Tech, is hardly convincing as a world-class intellect.

Plot about creating a portable laser system for the Air Force under the tutelage of campus creep Professor Hathaway (William Atherton) has the authority of an old

Abbott and Costello film. Theme about the exploitation of these youthful minds is lost in a sea of sight gags.

What lifts the production above the run-of-the-mill is swift direction by Martha Coolidge, who has a firm grasp over the manic material.

THE RETURN OF THE PINK PANTHER

1975, 115 mins, ◇ Ⓥ *Dir* Blake Edwards   UK

★ *Stars* Peter Sellers, Christopher Plummer, Catherine Schell, Herbert Lom, Peter Arne, Gregoire Aslan

The Return of the Pink Panther establishes Peter Sellers once again as the bane of the existence of chief detective Herbert Lom, who is forced to reinstate Sellers when the Pink Panther diamond is stolen from its native museum by a mysterious burglar.

Suspicion falls on Christopher Plummer, ostensibly retired phantom jewel thief who decides he must catch the real culprit to save himself. Catherine Schell plays Plummer's wife, who turns out to be a decoy in more ways than one.

Sellers' work takes him into contact with Peter Arne and Gregoire Aslan, native police under pressure from general Peter Jeffrey to find the gem: with befuddled concierge Victor Spinetti and perplexed bellboy Mike Grady, both at a posh Swiss resort hotel; and periodically with his valet Cato, played by Burt Kwouk.

All hands seem to be having a ball, especially Schell, whose unabashed amusement at Clouseau's seduction attempts often matches an audience's hilarity.

REUBEN, REUBEN

1983, 101 mins, ◇ Ⓥ *Dir* Robert Ellis Miller   US

★ *Stars* Tom Conti, Kelly McGillis, Roberts Blossom, Cynthia Harris, E. Katherine Kerr, Joel Fabiani

About a leching, alcoholic Scottish poet making the New England campus circuit, *Reuben, Reuben* is exceptionally literate, with lines that carom with wit from the superb adaptation by Julius J. Epstein of a 1964 Peter De Vries novel. Epstein, with De Vries' blessing, merged three separate stories in the novel into the character of the rascal poet on the slide.

Helmsman Robert Ellis Miller draws solid performances from debuting actress Kelly McGillis, whose chic blonde Vassar looks interestingly contrast, in this case, with her character's farmyard roots. She becomes the all-consuming obsession of Tom Conti as he lurches from one bottle and bed to another. Two of his sexual conquests on the poet's college town circuit are nicely and avariciously played by Cynthia Harris and E. Katherine Kerr.

But the film is a tour de force act for Conti (in his first US-made film) and he captures the vulnerability of a man whose plunge into darkness suggests the emotional time most closely associated with 4 a.m.

REVENGE OF THE PINK PANTHER

1978, 98 mins, ◇ Ⓥ   *Dir* Blake Edwards   US

★ *Stars* Peter Sellers, Herbert Lom, Dyan Cannon, Robert Webber, Burt Kwouk, Paul Stewart

Revenge of the Pink Panther isn't the best of the continuing film series, but Blake Edwards and Peter Sellers on a slow day are still well ahead of most other comedic filmmakers.

This time out, Sellers tracks down an international drug ring. Herbert Lom also encores as Sellers' nemesis and Dyan Cannon is delightful as the resourceful discarded mistress of dope smuggler industrialist Robert Webber.

The screenplay, from an Edwards story, is a paradoxical embarrassment of riches: Sellers, faithful servant Burt Kwouk, Lom, Cannon, etc, each alone and also in various combinations, are too much for a simple story line. The result is that the plot roams all over the map, trying to cover all the bases but in totality adding up to less than the parts.

RICHARD PRYOR . . . HERE AND NOW

1983, 94 mins, ◇ Ⓥ   *Dir* Richard Pryor   US

★ *Stars* Richard Pryor

As a concert film, *Richard Pryor . . . Here and Now* should attract and please those who appreciate him as a standup comic. But beyond the ample laughs, there is a beautiful monolog that's so painfully acute it would entrance even those who never laugh at his other stuff.

His third concert film, *Here and Now* is a mixture of the ones done before and after the fire that almost killed him. Drug-free and still grateful for a second chance, Pryor remains much more mellow, but less self-examining and contemplative than in *Live on Sunset Strip* (1982).

Some of the hostility and bite have returned, though well under control. On top of the laughs, he also displays a deepening sympathy for those doomed by substances.

RISKY BUSINESS

1983, 96 mins, ◇ Ⓥ   *Dir* Paul Brickman   US

★ *Stars* Tom Cruise, Rebecca De Mornay, Curtis Armstrong, Bronson Pinchot, Raphael Sbarge, Joe Pantoliano

Risky Business is like a promising first novel, with all the pros and cons that come with that territory.

High schooler Tom Cruise could literally be a next-door neighbor to Timothy Hutton in *Ordinary People* on Chicago's affluent suburban North Shore. That changes virtually overnight, however, when he meets sharp-looking hooker Rebecca De Mornay. On the lam from her slimy pimp, she shacks up in Cruise's splendid home while his

It's a **Risky Business** *as budding yuppy Tom Cruise markets wholesome hooker Rebecca De Mornay.*

parents are out of town and, since he's anxious to prove himself as a Future Enterpriser in one of his school's more blatantly greed-oriented programs, convinces him to make the house into a bordello for one night.

Ultimately, pic seems to endorse the bottom line, going for the big buck. In fact, not only is Cruise rewarded financially for setting up the best little whorehouse in Glencoe, but it gets him into Princeton to boot. Writer-director Paul Brickman can therefore be accused of trying to have it both ways, but there's no denying the stylishness and talent of his direction.

RITA, SUE AND BOB TOO

1987, 95 mins, ◇ Ⓥ   *Dir* Alan Clarke   UK

★ *Stars* Michelle Holmes, Siobhan Finneran, George Costigan, Lesley Sharp, Willie Ross, Patti Nicholls

Rita, Sue and Bob Too is a sad-funny comedy about sex and life in the Yorkshire city of Bradford.

Rita and Sue are two schoolgirls who sometimes babysit for a well-off couple, Bob and Michelle. In the film's opening sequence, the odious yet somehow charming Bob, a real-estate agent, gives the girls a lift home, but stops off first on the moors above the city and without preliminaries, proposes sex with them. The girls are agreeable, with Sue taking the first turn on the reclining seat in Bob's Rover.

Immediately screenwriter Andrea Dunbar [who adapted the film from her own plays *The Arbor* and *Rita, Sue and Bob Too*] injects a completely convincing mixture of raunchy comedy and sadness.

Rita and Sue, splendidly played by Siobhan Finneran and Michelle Holmes, are pathetic figures as they trip along in their tight miniskirts, but they're lively and funny. George Costigan makes Bob a charming character, despite his ingrained seediness.

ROAD TO BALI

1952, 91 mins, ◇ ▽ *Dir* Hal Walker   US

★ *Stars* Bob Hope, Bing Crosby, Dorothy Lamour, Murvyn Vye, Peter Coe, Leon Askin

Bing Crosby, Bob Hope and Dorothy Lamour are back again in another of Paramount's highway sagas, with nonsensical amusement its only destination. Five songs are wrapped up in the Harry Tugend production, teeing off with Crosby and Hope doing "Chicago Style".

Needing a job, Crosby and Hope hire out to Murvyn Vye, a South Seas island prince, as divers, sail for Vye's homeland and meet Princess Lamour, which is excuse enough for her to sing 'Moonflowers', later reprised as the finale tune.

There's no story to speak of in the script [from a story by Frank Butler and Harry Tugend] but the framework is there on which to hang a succession of amusing quips and physical comedy dealing with romantic rivalry and chuckle competition between the two male stars. It also permits some surprise guest star appearances, such as the finale walkon of Jane Russell; Humphrey Bogart pulling the African Queen through Africa; Martin & Lewis and Bob Crosby; all of whom serve no other purpose than to get a laugh.

THE ROAD TO HONG KONG

1962, 91 mins, *Dir* Norman Panama   UK

★ *Stars* Bing Crosby, Bob Hope, Joan Collins, Dorothy Lamour, Robert Morley, Felix Aylmer

The seventh *Road* comedy, after a lapse of seven years, takes the boys on a haphazard trip to a planet called Plutonius, though this only happens as a climax to some hilarious adventures in Ceylon and Hong Kong.

It's almost useless to outline the plot. But it involves Crosby and Hope as a couple of flop vaudevillians who turn con men. Somewhere along the line, Hope loses his memory and that, in a mysterious manner, leads them to involvement with a mysterious spy (Joan Collins) a secret formula and a whacky bunch of thugs called the Third Echelon, led by Robert Morley.

The script is spiced with a number of private jokes (golf, Hope's nose, Crosby's dough, reference to gags from previous *Road* films) but not enough to be irritating. Major disappointment is Joan Collins, who though an okay looker, never seems quite abreast of the comedians. Lamour plays herself as a vaude artist who rescues the Crosby-Hope team from one of their jams.

As guest artists, Frank Sinatra and Dean Martin help to round off the film. David Niven appears for no good reason, while the best interlude is that of Peter Sellers. He plays a native medico, examining Hope for amnesia and it is a brilliantly funny cameo.

ROAD TO MOROCCO

1942, 83 mins, ▽ *Dir* David Butler   US

★ *Stars* Bing Crosby, Bob Hope, Dorothy Lamour, Anthony Quinn, Vladimir Sokoloff, Dona Drake

Morocco is a bubbling spontaneous entertainment without a semblance of sanity; an uproarious patchquilt of gags, old situations and a blitz-like laugh pace that never lets up for a moment. It's Bing Crosby and Bob Hope at their best, with Dorothy Lamour, as usual, the pivotal point for their romantic pitch.

The story's absurdities, all of which are predicated on Crosby and Hope as shipwrecked stowaways cast ashore on the coast of North Africa, at no time weave a pattern of restraint. It's just a madcap holiday for the fun-makers.

The scripters, along with everyone else associated with the production, must surely have realized, of course, that the yarn couldn't be played straight. The result is some unorthodox filmmaking that finds both male stars making dialogistic asides that kid, for instance, some of the film's 'weaknesses' or, in other cases, poke fun at various objects that aren't even remotely associated with the picture.

ROAD TO RIO

1947, 100 mins, ▽ *Dir* Norman Z. McLeod   US

★ *Stars* Bing Crosby, Bob Hope, Dorothy Lamour, Gale Sondergaard

There are no talking animals in this to prep uproarish see-hear gags, but a capable substitute is a trumpet that blows musical bubbles. Stunt pays off as one of a number of top, hard-punching laugh-getters. Norman Z. McLeod's direction blends the music and comedy into fast action and sock chuckles that will please followers of the series.

Bing Crosby and Bob Hope repeat their slaphappy characters in the Edmund Beloin–Jack Rose plot. Opening establishes the boys, as usual, in trouble and broke. When they set a circus on fire, pair escape by taking refuge on a ship heading for Rio. It doesn't take them long to discover a damsel in distress (Dorothy Lamour) and action centers around their efforts to save her from a wicked aunt and a forced marriage.

ROAD TO SINGAPORE

1940, 84 mins, *Dir* Victor Schertzinger   US

★ *Stars* Bing Crosby, Bob Hope, Dorothy Lamour, Charles Coburn, Anthony Quinn, Jerry Colonna

Initial teaming of Bing Crosby and Bob Hope in *Road to Singapore* provides foundation for continuous round of good substantial comedy of rapid-fire order, swinging along

Bing Crosby, Dorothy Lamour and Bob Hope in Road to Morocco, the third of the Road films.

at a zippy pace. Contrast is provided in Crosby's leisurely presentation of situations and dialog, in comparison to the lightning-like thrusts and parries of Hope. Neat blending of the two brands accentuates the comedy values for laugh purposes.

Story is a light framework on which to drape the situations for Crosby and Hope, with Dorothy Lamour providing decorative character of a native gal in sarong-like trappings. Crosby is the adventurous son of a shipping magnate, who refuses to sit behind a desk. He walks out on both father and a socialite fiancee to ship to the South Seas with sailor-buddy Hope. Lamour moves in with the pair, and from there on it's a happy mixture of both making passes for the native beauty, while they struggle to raise the necessary coin to live in comfort on the island. Crosby eventually gets the girl, but not until the trio romps through some zany adventures.

ROAD TO UTOPIA

1945, 90 mins, ⊘ *Dir* Hal Walker   US

★ *Stars* Bing Crosby, Bob Hope, Dorothy Lamour, Robert Benchley, Hillary Brooke, Douglass Dumbrille

Bob Benchley is cut into an upper corner of various shots making wisecracks, first being that 'this is how not to make a picture'. Others are in the same groove, while additional off-the-path gags include Bob Hope and Dorothy Lamour in a kissing scene, topped by Hope's aside to the audience: 'As far as I'm concerned the picture is over right now'. Another is a guy walking across a scene asking Bing Crosby and Hope where Stage 8 is.

Action is laid in the Klondike of the gold rush days. On their way there, scrubbing decks because they'd lost their money, Crosby and Hope come upon a map leading to a rich gold mine. It had been stolen from Lamour's father by two of the toughest badmen of Alaska. Lamour goes to the Klondike in search of them.

Technically picture leaves nothing to be desired. Paul Jones, producer, and Hal Walker, who directed, make a fine combination in steering and in the production value provided. Performances by supporting cast are all good.

ROAD TO ZANZIBAR

1941, 89 mins, *Dir* Victor Schertzinger   US

★ *Stars* Bing Crosby, Bob Hope, Dorothy Lamour, Una Merkel, Jean Marsh, Eric Blore

Zanzibar is Paramount's second coupling of Bing Crosby, Bob Hope and Dorothy Lamour. Although picture has sufficient comedy situations and dialog between its male stars, it lacks the compactness and spontaneity of its predecessor.

The story framework is pretty flimsy foundation for hanging the series of comedy and thrill situations concocted for the pair. It's a fluffy and inconsequential tale, with Crosby–Hope combo, doing valiant work to keep up interest.

Pair are stranded in South Africa, with Crosby the creator of freak sideshow acts for Hope to perform. With his saved passage money back to the US, Crosby buys a diamond mine,

which is quickly sold by Hope for profit. Then pair start out on strange Safari with Lamour and Una Merkel, pair of Brooklyn entertainers, pursuing a millionaire hunter.

Comedy episodes generally lack sparkle and tempo, and musical numbers are also below par for a Crosby picture.

THE RUSSIANS ARE COMING! THE RUSSIANS ARE COMING!

1966, 124 mins, ◇ Ⓥ *Dir* Norman Jewison   US

★ *Stars* Carl Reiner, Eva Marie Saint, Alan Arkin, Brian Keith, Jonathan Winters, Theodore Bikel

Academy Award 1966: Best Picture (Nomination)

The Russians Are Coming! The Russians Are Coming! is an outstanding cold-war comedy depicting the havoc created on a mythical Massachusetts island by the crew of a grounded Russian sub.

Nathaniel Benchley's novel *The Off-Islanders* got its title from New England slang for summer residents, herein top-featured Carl Reiner, wife Eva Marie Saint, and their kids, Sheldon Golomb and Cindy Putnam.

Basically, story concerns aftermath of an accidental grounding of the Russian sub by overly curious skipper Theodore Bikel, who sends Alan Arkin ashore in charge of a landing party to get a towing boat. The wild antics which follow center around sheriff Brian Keith, sole resident who manages to keep cool except when arguing with Paul Ford, firebrand civil defense chief (self appointed) who arms himself to repel the 'invasion' with a sword and an American Legion cap.

Arkin, in his film bow, is absolutely outstanding as the courtly Russian who kisses a lady's hand at the same time as he draws a gun.

English music hall vet Tessie O'Shea, also in film debut, is very good as the island's telephone operator who contributes to the spread of the 'invasion' rumors, and her scenes with Reiner, in which they are lashed together and attempt to escape, is a comedy highlight.

RUTHLESS PEOPLE

1986, 93 mins, ◇ Ⓥ *Dir* Jim Abrahams, David Zucker, Jerry Zucker   US

★ *Stars* Danny DeVito, Bette Midler, Judge Reinhold, Helen Slater, Anita Morris, Bill Pullman

Ruthless People is a hilariously venal comedy about a kidnapped veritable harridan whose rich husband won't pay for her return.

In short, impoverished couple Judge Reinhold and Helen Slater kidnap Bel-Air princess Bette Midler because her mercenary husband, played by Danny DeVito, has ripped off Slater's design for spandex miniskirts.

***Bette Midler bargains with her kidnappers, Judge Reinhold and Helen Slater, in* Ruthless People.**

There is much, much more to it than that, as screenwriter Dale Launer cleverly builds twist upon complication to a point where practically everyone in the cast is writhing in frustration and mystification as they wonder whether their latest opportunistic scheme is going to work.

Midler, when first glimpsed, is an absolute fright who looks like a cross between Cyndi Lauper and Divine. After terrorizing her kidnappers, she embarks upon an energetic self-improvement program, and not surprisingly emerges with the upper hand.

SCENES FROM A MALL

1991, 87 mins, ◇ Ⓥ *Dir* Paul Mazursky   US

★ *Stars* Bette Midler, Woody Allen, Bill Irwin, Daren Firestone, Rebecca Nickels, Paul Mazursky

Paul Mazursky's 14th film as director is a cozy, insular middle-aged marital comedy that's about as deep and rewarding as a day of mall-cruising.

Talents of Bette Midler and Woody Allen seem misspent in roles as cuddly but squabbling spouses. Pic's title, a takeoff on Ingmar Bergman's *Scenes from a Marriage*, should be consumers' first clue as to what's in store.

Midler and Allen are a Hollywood Hills-dwelling twin-career couple of the 1990s. He's a successful sports lawyer; she's a psychologist who's written a high-concept book on how to renew a marriage. They pack their kids off for a ski weekend and head for the Beverly Center mall to spend their 16th anniversary indulging their every whim.

Allen drops the bombshell that he's just ended a six-month affair with a 25-year-old. Midler confesses to an ongoing affair with a Czechoslovakian colleague, played by Mazursky. These emotional storms never achieve any veracity. They seem like just another indulgence on the part of the pampered, secure spouses.

Pic shot exteriors at the Beverly Center and moved to a mall in Stamford, Conn, for two weeks of interior filming. For the remainder, a huge, two-story replica mall was constructed at Kaufman Astoria Studios, NY, and 2,600 New York extras were outfitted in LA garb.

SCENES FROM THE CLASS STRUGGLE IN BEVERLY HILLS

1989, 102 mins, ◇ ⊘ *Dir* Paul Bartel   US

★ **Stars** Jacqueline Bisset, Ray Sharkey, Robert Beltran, Mary Woronov, Ed Begley Jr, Wallace Shawn

Scenes from the Class Struggle in Beverly Hills is a lewd delight. In top form here, director Paul Bartel brings a breezy, sophisticated touch to this utterley outrageous sex farce and thereby renders charming even the most scabrous moments in Bruce Wagner's very naughty screenplay [from a story by him and Bartel].

Script is structured in the manner of a classical French farce, and features more seductions and coitus interuptus than a season of soap operas. Hoity-toity divorcee Mary Woronov is having her house fumigated and so, with her sensitive son, checks in for the weekend next door at the home of former sitcom star Jacqueline Bisset, whose husband has just kicked the bucket.

Joining the menagerie of the filthy rich are Woronov's pretentious playwright brother Ed Begley Jr, his brand-new sassy black wife Arnetia Walker, Woronov's crazed ex-husband Wallace Shawn, Bisset's precocious daughter Rebecca Schaeffer, 'thinologist' Bartel and, in a surprisingly real apparition, Bisset's late hubby, Paul Mazursky.

Droll tone is set at the outset by the quaintly 1950s titles and Stanley Myers' witty score, and the comic champagne is kept bubbly with only the most momentary of missteps.

SCHOOL FOR SCOUNDRELS

1960, 94 mins, ⊘ *Dir* Robert Hamer   UK

★ **Stars** Ian Carmichael, Terry-Thomas, Alastair Sim, Janette Scott, Dennis Price, Peter Jones

The gentle art of getting and remaining 'one up' on the next fellow, so painstaking chronicled by British humorist Stephen Potter in his series of books, is engagingly translated to the screen in this delicate English comedy. Those familiar with Potter's spoofs (*Lifemanship, Gamesmanship, Oneupmanship*) will get the biggest boot out of *School for Scoundrels*.

Although it is virtually impossible to capture Potter's many intimate ironies, the scenarists have successfully caught the essence of the author's maxim – 'How to Win Without Actually Cheating!' (as the film is subtitled).

Alastair Sim personifies the master lifeman down to the minutest detail – a brilliant performance. Ian Carmichael is a delight as the pitifully inept wretch who undergoes metamorphosis at Sim's finishing school for social misfits, and Terry-Thomas masterfully plummets from one-up to one-down as his exasperated victim.

Janette Scott, a fresh, natural beauty, charmingly plays the object of their attention. Unfortunately for Dennis Price and Peter Jones, they are involved in the weakest passage of the film – a none-too-subtle used car sequence that will disturb Potter purists.

THE SECRET LIFE OF WALTER MITTY

1947, 108 mins, ◇ ⊘ *Dir* Norman Z. McLeod   US

★ **Stars** Danny Kaye, Virginia Mayo, Boris Karloff, Fay Bainter

Some of the deepest-dyed Thurber fans may squeal since there's naturally considerable change from the famed short story on which the screenplay is built. There's a basic switch in the plot that has been concocted around the Mitty daydreams. Thurber's whole conception of Walter Mitty was an inconsequential fellow from Perth Amboy, NJ, to whom nothing – but nothing – ever happened and who, as a result, lived a 'secret life' via his excursions into daydreaming. In contrast, the picture builds a spy-plot

Virginia Mayo and Danny Kaye in one of the latter's many day dream fantasies in **The Secret Life of Walter Mitty.**

around Mitty that becomes more fantastic than even his wildest dream.

Danny Kaye reveals a greater smoothness and polish thespically and a perfection of timing in his slapstick than has ever been evident in the past.

Exceedingly slick job is done on the segues from the real-life Mitty into the dream sequences. Mitty's fantasies carry him through sessions as a sea captain taking his schooner through a storm, a surgeon performing a next-to-impossible operation, an RAF pilot, a Mississippi gambler, a cowpuncher and a hat designer. They're all well-loaded with satire, as is the real-life plot with pure slapstick.

Virginia Mayo is the beautiful vis-a-vis in both the real-life spy plot, and the dreams. She comes a commendable distance thespically in this picture. Karloff wins heftiest yaks in a scene in which he plays a phony psychiatrist convincing Mitty he's nuts.

THE SECRET OF MY SUCCESS

1987, 110 mins, ◇ ⓥ *Dir* Herbert Ross   US

★ **Stars** Michael J. Fox, Helen Slater, Richard Jordan, Margaret Whitton, John Pankow, Christopher Murney

The Secret of My Success is a bedroom farce with a leaden touch, a corporate comedy without teeth. What it does have is Michael J. Fox in a winning performance as a likable hick out to hit the big time in New York.

Fresh off the bus from Kansas, Brantley Foster (Fox) doesn't want to return until he has a penthouse, jacuzzi, a beautiful girlfriend and a private jet he can go home in. His ideals are a yuppie's dream.

Fox encounters the predictable crime-infested corners of New York and his squalid apartment is furnished with roaches and rats. When he meets his dream girl (Helen Slater), he is literally thunderstruck.

After young Brantley lands a job in the mailroom of an anonymous NY corporation his big chance comes when he takes over an abandoned office and sets himself up as a young exec.

Fox, in spite of his inherent charm, lacks a genuine personality and is neither country bumpkin nor city sharpie. Consequently, the film lacks a consistent tone or style.

SEE NO EVIL, HEAR NO EVIL

1989, 103 mins, ◇ ⓥ *Dir* Arthur Hiller   US

★ **Stars** Richard Pryor, Gene Wilder, Joan Severance, Kevin Spacey, Kirsten Childs

With Richard Pryor and Gene Wilder in the lead roles, *See No Evil, Hear No Evil* could only be a broadly played, occasionally crass, funny physical comedy.

How the blind Pryor ends up working for the deaf Wilder at a Manhattan lobby newsstand really is inconsequential, since neither their first encounter, nor anything that fol-

lows, is believable for a minute, including the thing that binds them in the first place – how each denies his limitations.

While Wilder's back is turned, a customer is shot in the back. Pryor is out on the curb listening for the New York *Daily News* to make its morning drop – so he misses hearing anything inside.

By the time Wilder turns around, he's only able to catch a glimpse of the assailant's (Joan Severance) sexy gams. Pryor has missed it all, though he does manage to catch a whiff of Severance's perfume before she slips by him onto the crowded street.

The cops arrive and, in predictable fashion, arrest the only suspects around, the two numbskulls who couldn't possibly coordinate anything, much less a murder.

THE SEVEN YEAR ITCH

1955, 105 mins, ◇ ⓥ *Dir* Billy Wilder   US

★ **Stars** Marilyn Monroe, Tom Ewell, Evelyn Keyes, Sonny Tufts, Robert Strauss, Victor Moore

The film version of *The Seven Year Itch* bears only a fleeting resemblance to George Axelrod's play of the same name on Broadway. The screen adaptation concerns only the fantasies, and omits the acts, of the summer bachelor, who remains totally, if unbelievably, chaste. Morality wins if honesty loses, but let's not get into that. What counts is that laughs come thick and fast, that the general entertainment is light and gay.

The performance of Marilyn Monroe is baby-dollish as the dumb-but-sweet number upstairs who attracts the eye of the guy, seven years married and restless, whose wife and child have gone off for the summer. The acting kudos belongs to Tom Ewell, a practiced farceur and pantomimist who is able to give entire conviction to the long stretches of soliloquy, a considerable test of Ewell's technique.

SHAMPOO

1975, 109 mins, ◇ ⓥ *Dir* Hal Ashby   US

★ **Stars** Warren Beatty, Julie Christie, Goldie Hawn, Lee Grant, Jack Warden, Tony Bill

Late 1960s story about the ultimate emotional sterility and unhappiness of a swinger emerges as a mixed farcical achievement.

Warren Beatty is a Beverly Hills hairdresser who turns onto all his customers including Lee Grant, bored wife of Jack Warden (latter in turn keeping Julie Christie on the side), while Beatty's current top trick is Goldie Hawn.

All the excellent creative components do not add up to a whole. There are, however, strong elements in the film. Warden's performance is outstanding. He makes the most of a script and direction which gives his character much more dimension than the prototype cuckold. Also, Hawn's excellent delineation of a bubbly young actress has a solid under-

A modern-day Casanova of the curling tongs, Beatty's wave to Julie Christie in Shampoo is hardly permanent.

tone of sensitivity which culminates in her quiet dismissal of Beatty from her home and her heart.

SHE'LL BE WEARING PINK PAJAMAS

1985, 90 mins, ◇ Ⓥ   *Dir* John Goldschmidt   UK

★ **Stars** Julie Walters, Anthony Higgins, Jane Evers, Janet Henfrey, Paula Jacobs, Penelope Nice

She'll Be Wearing Pink Pajamas is about a group of British women from mixed backgrounds who gather together, awkwardly at first, but eventually confide in each other and reveal their innermost secrets and problems.

After a slightly off-key opening, in which the characters are introed, we're into the setting of an outdoor survival course for women only, a week-long exercise designed to push the participants physically as far as they can go. The intimate discussions that follow take place against outdoor backgrounds, filmed in England's beautiful Lake District, as the women ford streams, climb mountains, canoe, swing on ropes, or go on a marathon hike.

There's one man around (Anthony Higgins), but he's almost an intrusion. The women are a lively and well-differentiated lot, and there is a bevy of fine actresses playing them. Standout is Julie Walters as a bouncy type who proves surprisingly weak in the crunch.

SHE'S GOTTA HAVE IT

1986, 100 mins, ◇ Ⓥ   *Dir* Spike Lee   US

★ **Stars** Tracy Camilla Johns, Redmond Hicks, John Terrell, Spike Lee

This worthy but flawed attempt to examine an independent young woman of the 1980s was lensed, in Super 16mm, in 15 days but doesn't appear jerrybuilt.

All the elements of an interesting yarn are implicit here – save one: a compelling central figure (played by Tracy Camilla Johns). The young woman who's the focus of the pic is, clearly, trying to find herself. She juggles three beaus, fends off a lesbian's overtures and consults a shrink to determine if she's promiscuous or merely a lady with normal sexual appetites.

The three beaus, an upscale male model, a sensitive sort and a funny street flake, all essayed nicely by, respectively, John Terrell, Spike Lee and Redmond Hicks, serve to keep the scenario moving with interest.

Tracy Camilla Johns and John Terrell in Spike Lee's **She's Gotta Have It***, a comedy with a serious core.*

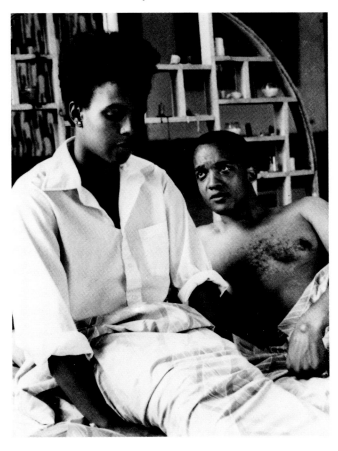

A SHOCK TO THE SYSTEM

1990, 87 mins, ◇ ⓥ *Dir* Jan Egleson   US

★ *Stars* Michael Caine, Elizabeth McGovern, Peter Riegert, Swoosie Kurtz, Will Patton, John McMartin

A Shock to the System is a very dark comedy about escaping the current rat race via murder. An unsympathetic, poorly motivated central character [from a novel by Simon Brett] and flat direction serve to nullify Michael Caine's reliable thesping.

Caine is cast as a Britisher working for a NY firm who's passed over for the post of marketing department head when John McMartin (in an affecting performance) is forced to take early retirement. Upstart Peter Riegert (way too sympathetic for the role) gets the job instead and starts throwing his weight around.

After doing away with wife Swoosie Kurtz by rigging faulty electric wiring in the basement, Caine blows up Riegert (and obnoxious assistant Philip Moon) on his sailboat. Plodding Connecticut cop Will Patton discovers plenty of clues along the way.

Jan Egleson's direction slows to a snail's pace during the middle reels and lacks the style of the classics in this genre.

A SHOT IN THE DARK

1964, 103 mins, ◇ ⓥ *Dir* Blake Edwards   US

★ *Stars* Peter Sellers, Elke Sommer, Herbert Lom, George Sanders, Graham Stark, Douglas Wilmer

Based upon the French farce authored by Marcel Achard and adapted to the American stage by Harry Kurnitz, director Blake transforms Peter Sellers' role from a magistrate, whose activities were limited to judicial chambers, into Inspector Clouseau, where more movement and greater area are possible. 'Give me 10 men like Clouseau, and I could destroy the world!' his superior exclaims in despair, summing up the character played by Sellers, sent to investigate a murder in the chateau of a millionaire outside Paris.

When this chief inspector, portrayed by Herbert Lom, attempts to take Clouseau off the case, powers above return him to his investigations which revolve about chief suspect Elke Sommer, a French maid, whom the dick is convinced is innocent.

The chores takes him to a nudist camp, a tour of Parisian nightclubs, where dead bodies are left in his wake, and to his apartment, where one of the funniest seduction scenes ever filmed unfolds to the tune of three in a bed and an exploding time bomb. It's never completely clear whether the detective solves his case in a windup that doesn't quite come off.

Sometimes the narrative is subordinated to individual bits of business and running gags but Sellers' skill as a comedian again is demonstrated, and Sommer, in role of the chambermaid who moves all men to amorous thoughts and

sometimes murder, is pert and expert. Lom gives punch and humor to star's often distraught superior, George Sanders lends polish as the millionaire and Graham Stark excels as Sellers' dead-pan assistant.

Kirstie Alley and Jami Gertz in Sibling Rivalry, *a lighthearted comedy of fracturous family ties and marital mayhem.*

SIBLING RIVALRY

1990, 88 mins, ◇ ⓥ *Dir* Carl Reiner   US

★ *Stars* Kirstie Alley, Bill Pullman, Carrie Fisher, Jami Gertz, Scott Bakula, Sam Elliott

In her first solo-starring vehicle, Kirstie Alley – who plays the creatively stifled wife of a stuffy young doctor (Scott Bakula) – comes into her own with a flamboyant, highly physical performance.

Her adulterous hop in the sack with mystery hunk Sam Elliott results in his death by heart attack after strenuous lovemaking. What follows involves three sets of siblings: Alley and her slightly ditzy younger sister and rival (Jami Gertz); weird vertical blinds salesman Bill Pullman as the black sheep younger brother of upwardly mobile cop Ed O'Neil; and the massive clan of doctors comprising Bakula, his sister (Carrie Fisher) and brother (Elliott).

The surprise that Elliott turns out to be Alley's brother-in-law is effectively developed and launches several hilarious setpieces. Pullman and Alley are united in crime after Pullman thinks *he* accidentally killed Elliott with his vertical blinds equipment. Both he and Alley attempt to cover up the fatality as a suicide.

Though the rushed happy ending doesn't ring true, *Sibling Rivalry* creates a cheerful mood from morbid material. Carl Reiner directs swiftly and efficiently, getting maximum yocks out of borderline vulgar content.

SILENT MOVIE

1976, 86 mins, ◇ ⓥ *Dir* Mel Brooks   US

★ *Stars* Mel Brooks, Marty Feldman, Dom DeLuise, Bernadette Peters, Sid Caesar, Harold Gould

It took a lot of chutzpah for Mel Brooks to make *Silent Movie* a film with only one word of dialog in an almost non-stop parade of sight gags.

Brooks, Marty Feldman, and Dom DeLuise head the cast as a has-been director and his zany cronies, conning studio chief Sid Caesar into making their silent film as a desperate ploy to prevent takeover of the studio by the Engulf & Devour conglomerate, headed by villainous Harold Gould. The parallels with realities are drolly satiric.

The slender plot of *Silent Movie* [from a story by Ron Clark] is basically a hook for slapstick antics, some feeble and some very fine (notably a wonderful nightclub tango

with Anne Bancroft). Harry Ritz, Charlie Callas, Henny Youngman, and the late Liam Dunn are standouts.

SITTING DUCKS

1979, 90 mins, ◇ ⓥ *Dir* Henry Jaglom   US

★ *Stars* Michael Emil, Zack Norman, Patrice Townsend, Richard Romanus, Irene Forrest, Henry Jaglom

A rather loopy story, *Sibling Rivalry* serves basically to provide a framework for several fabulous character riffs and to give a little momentum to any number of enjoyable crazy situations.

Two small-time hustlers make off with loot siphoned off from a gambling syndicate for which one is working, and majority of the running time is devoted to their haphazard drive down the eastern seaboard to reach a plane that will carry them to a life of kings in Central America.

Along the way, hyped-up pair, acted in a marvel of improvisational style by Michael Emil and Zack Norman, meet up with two young ladies who hitch on for the wild ride.

Interplay among the four constitutes the meat of the film, and every line and every scene springs spontaneously off the screen as if they're being played for the first time.

SLEEPER

1973, 88 mins, ◇ ⓥ *Dir* Woody Allen   US

★ *Stars* Woody Allen, Diane Keaton, John Beck, Mary Gregory, Don Keefer, Don McLiam

Woody Allen's *Sleeper*, is a nutty futuristic comedy, with Allen brought back to life 200 years hence to find himself a wanted man in a totally regulated society. Diane Keaton again plays his foil, and both are hilarious. The Dixieland music score [played by Allen with the Preservation Hall Jazz Band and New Orleans Funeral & Ragtime Orchestra] is just one more delightful non sequitur.

Story opens with Bartlett Robinson and Mary Gregory, two underground scientists, restoring Allen to life from a two-century deep freeze after sudden death from a minor operation. Allen is hunted as an alien. In the course of avoiding capture he becomes first a robot servant to Keaton, later her captor, then rescuer, finally her lover in a fadeout clinch.

Diane Keaton and Woody Allen in one of actor's early directorial romps, the sci-fi'n'slapstick Sleeper.

S

The film is loaded with throwaway literacy and broad slapstick, and while it fumbles the end, the parade of verbal and visual amusement is pleasant as long as it lasts.

The star teaming resembles, on a much more advanced basis, the Bob Hope pix of the 1940s in which he starred with some gorgeous leading women in a series of improbable but delightful escapades.

SMOKEY AND THE BANDIT

1977, 96 mins, ◇ ⊚ *Dir* Hal Needham   US

★ *Stars* Burt Reynolds, Sally Field, Jerry Reed, Jackie Gleason, Mike Henry, Paul Williams

Burt Reynolds stars as a bootlegger-for-kicks who, with Jerry Reed and Sally Field, outwit zealous sheriff Jackie Gleason.

The plot is simple: rich father-son team of blowhards Pat McCormick and Paul Williams offer a reward if Reynolds will truck a load of Coors beer from Texas to Georgia; Reynolds and buddy Reed race to meet the deadline: Field complicates matters as a not-yet-bride who flees beau Mike Henry, son of outraged Gleason, who then chases them all across the southeast.

There is a parade of roadside set pieces involving many different ways to crash cars. Overlaid is citizens band radio jabber (hence, the title) which is loaded with down-home gags. Field is the hottest element in the film.

SOAPDISH

1991, 95 mins, ◇ ⊛ *Dir* Michael Hoffman   US

★ *Stars* Sally Field, Kevin Kline, Robert Downey Jr, Cathy Moriarty, Whoopi Goldberg, Carrie Fisher

Soapdish aims at a satiric target as big as a Macy's float and intermittently hits it. Sally Field and Kevin Kline play a feuding pair of romantically involved soap opera stars in this broad but amiable sendup of daytime TV.

Field, the reigning 'queen of misery' on the sudser *The Sun Also Sets*, is at the peak of her glory but is going to pieces emotionally. Amazonian harpy Cathy Moriarty is scheming to take over the show by using her sexual wiles to convince the slimy producer (Robert Downey Jr) to have Field's character destroy her popularity by committing some unspeakable crime.

To drive Field even more off the edge, Downey surprises her by bringing back her long-ago flame, Kevin Kline, whom she had thrown off the show in 1973. Whoopi Goldberg, the show's jaded head writer, flips when told Kline is coming back because his character was written out by having him decapitated in a car crash.

Field works hard and shows an expert sense of comic timing, but the grittily down-to-earth acting persona Field has developed now makes her seem a bit too reasonable for the zany demands of this script.

Kline is utterly marvelous as a sort of low-rent John

Barrymore type, boozing and carousing his way through the ranks of worshipful young actresses. Moriarty, who acts as if she's been staying up late studying Mary Woronov pics, is a scream as Field's deep-voiced, hate-consumed rival.

S.O.B.

1981, 121 mins, ◇ *Dir* Blake Edwards   US

★ *Stars* Julie Andrews, William Holden, Marisa Berenson, Larry Hagman, Robert Loggia, Robert Vaughn

S.O.B. is one of the most vitriolic – though only occasionally hilarious – attacks on the Tinseltown mentality ever.

Taking its core from part of director Blake Edwards' own battle-weary Hollywood career, pic is structured as an arch fairytale, spinning the chronicle of a top-grossing producer (Richard Mulligan) whose latest $30 million musical extravaganza is hailed by the world as the b.o. turkey of the century, relegating him to has-been status overnight.

With Julie Andrews as his pure-as-driven snow imaged wife prompted finally to leave him for good, while production chief Robert Vaughn plots how to salvage the pic by massive, contract-bending recutting, Mulligan tries several failed variations on the suicide route until a mid-orgy epiphany tells him to cut and reshoot the G-rated failure into an opulent softcore porno fantasy.

Black comedy is a tough commodity to sustain and, after a broad start, Edwards quickly finds a deft balance that paints a cockeyed, self-contained world that comfortably supports its exaggerated characters. Unhappily, about midway through the pic, the tone becomes less certain (especially when it strains for seriousness) and styles begin to switch back and forth.

SO FINE

1981, 91 mins, ◇ *Dir* Andrew Bergman   US

★ *Stars* Ryan O'Neal, Jack Warden, Mariangela Melato, Richard Kiel, Fred Gwynne

So Fine is quite all right. Andrew Bergman, screenwriter on *Blazing Saddles* and *The In-Laws*, has come up with a somewhat less zany concoction this time but makes an impressively sharp directorial debut highlighted by some good bedroom farce.

Ryan O'Neal is a Shakespeare-spouting English professor, implausibly recruited into his father Jack Warden's faltering dressmaking firm upon the unchallengeable demand of Big Eddie, played by the 7' 2" Richard Kiel.

The latter's petite wife, Mariangela Melato, quickly corrals O'Neal into the sack (while Kiel's in it too, no less) and, in his best bumbling manner, Ryan O'Neal inadvertently hits upon a new fashion discovery – skin-tight jeans with seethrough behinds.

Despite his smashing success in the garment district, O'Neal retreats to the world of academia but is pursued by

Melato, who in turn is followed by the jealous Big Eddie. It all ends up in a slapstick, amateur hour operatic production of Verdi's *Otello* remindful of, among other things, *A Night at the Opera*.

SOME LIKE IT HOT

1959, 105 mins, ⊘ *Dir* Billy Wilder   US

★ **Stars** Marilyn Monroe, Tony Curtis, Jack Lemmon, George Raft, Pat O'Brien, Joe E. Brown

Some Like It Hot is a whacky, clever, farcical comedy that starts off like a firecracker and keeps on throwing off lively sparks till the very end.

Story revolves around the age-old theme of men masquerading as women. Tony Curtis and Jack Lemmon escape from a Chicago nightclub that's being raided, witness the St. Valentine's Day massacre and 'escape' into the anonymity of a girl band by dressing up as feminine musicians. This leads

Marilyn Monroe, Jack Lemmon and Tony Curtis in the Billy Wilder tour de force **Some Like It Hot.**

to the obvious complications, particularly since Curtis meets Marilyn Monroe (ukulele player, vocalist and gin addict) and falls for her. Lemmon, in turn, is propositioned by an addle-brained millionaire (Joe E. Brown).

A scene on a train, where the 'private' pullman berth party of Lemmon and Monroe in her nightie is invaded by guzzling dames, represents humor of Lubitsch proportions. And the alternating shots of Monroe trying to stimulate Curtis on a couch, while Lemmon and Brown live it up on the dance floor, rate as a classic sequence.

Marilyn has never looked better. Her performance as Sugar, the fuzzy blonde who likes saxophone players 'and men with glasses', has a deliciously naive quality. It's a tossup whether Curtis beats out Lemmon or whether it goes the other way round. Both are excellent.

Curtis has the upper hand because he can change back and forth from his femme role to that of a fake 'million-aire' who woos Monroe. He employs a takeoff on Cary Grant, which scores with a bang at first, but tends to lose its appeal as the picture progresses.

Lemmon draws a choice assignment. Some of the funniest bits fall to him, such as his announcement that he's 'engaged' to Brown.

But, in the final accounting, this is still a director's picture and the Wilder touch is indelible. If the action is funny, the lines are there to match it.

SPIES LIKE US

1985, 109 mins, ◇ ⊘ *Dir* John Landis   US

★ **Stars** Chevy Chase, Dan Aykroyd, Steve Forrest, Donna Dixon, Bruce Davison, William Prince

Teamed together for the first time in *Spies Like Us*, Chevy Chase and Dan Aykroyd need a subteen audience for their juvenile humor.

Spies is not very amusing. Though Chase and Aykroyd provide moments, the overall script thinly takes on eccentric espionage and nuclear madness, with nothing new to add.

Chase and Aykroyd are a couple of bumbling bureaucrats with aspirations for spy work, but no talent for the job. They unknowingly are chosen for a mission, however, because they will make expendable decoys for a real spy team headed by pretty Donna Dixon.

Much of the time, Aykroyd is fooling with gadgets, Chase is fooling with Dixon and director John Landis is fooling with half-baked comedy ideas.

SPLASH

1984, 111 mins, ◇ ⊘ *Dir* Ron Howard   US

★ **Stars** Tom Hanks, Daryl Hannah, John Candy, Eugene Levy, Dody Goodman, Shecky Greene

Touchstone Films takes the plunge with surprisingly charming mermaid yarn notable for winning suspension of disbelief and fetching by-play between Daryl Hannah and Tom Hanks.

Although film is a bit uneven, production benefits from a tasty look, an airy tone, and a delectable, unblemished performance from Hannah who couldn't be better cast if she were Neptune's daughter incarnate. Hanks, as a Gotham bachelor in search of love, makes a fine leap from sitcom land, and John Candy as an older playboy brother is a marvelous foil.

The mermaid's fin materializes into human legs when she leaves the water and, a la Lady Godiva, blonde tresses covering her breasts.

Screenplay is marred by some glaring loopholes in its inner structure but story is a sweet takeoff on the innocence mythology and sensuality associated with mermaids.

SPRING IN PARK LANE

1948, 91 mins, *Dir* Herbert Wilcox UK

★ ***Stars*** Anna Neagle, Michael Wilding, Tom Walls, Peter Graves, Nicholas Phipps, Nigel Patrick

Great merit of the story is that it seems like a happy improvisation. None of the elaborate and necessary scaffolding is apparent, and when Michael Wilding as a younger son of a noble family, needing money for a return trip to New York, becomes a temporary footman in a Park Lane mansion, he is immediately accepted as such by the audience. And since Anna Neagle plays a secretary in the same house, everybody knows it will be love at first sight and that sooner or later the two will march altarwards.

It's a story in which the trimmings and incidentals are all-important. The gay harmless fun poked at the film stars, the dinner party bore, the housekeeper to whom bridge is a religion, the footman cutting in to dance or discussing art with his boss – incident upon incident carry merry laughter through the picture.

STARTING OVER

1979, 106 mins, ◇ Ⓥ *Dir* Alan J. Pakula US

★ ***Stars*** Burt Reynolds, Jill Clayburgh, Candice Bergen, Charles Durning, Frances Sternhagen, Austin Pendleton

Starting Over takes on the subject of marital dissolution from a comic point of view, and succeeds admirably, wryly directed by Alan J. Pakula, and featuring an outstanding cast.

In fact, *Starting Over* [from the novel by Dan Wakefield] favorably evokes the screwball comedies of the 1930s and the heyday of American screen comedy.

Burt Reynolds plays a mild-mannered writer unwillingly foisted into a 'liberated' condition by spouse Candice Bergen, feeling her feminine oats as a songwriter. Fleeing to Boston and protection of relatives Charles Durning and Frances Sternhagen, he meets spinster schoolteacher Jill Clayburgh, and the off-and-on romance begins.

With unfailing comic timing Reynolds is the core of the film, and underplays marvellously.

STEAMBOAT BILL, JR

1928, 65 mins, Ⓥ ⓥ *Dir* Charles F. Reisner US

★ ***Stars*** Buster Keaton, Ernest Torrence, Tom McGuire, Marion Byron, Tom Lewis

The last comedy Buster Keaton made under his United Artists contract, it was held back for several months, getting itself concerned in several wild rumors. Whatever may have been the real reason why United Artists took its time about releasing this one, it had nothing to do with quality, for it's a pip of a comedy. It's one of Keaton's best.

The story concerns the efforts of an old hard-boiled river captain (Ernest Torrence), to survive on the river in the face of opposition from a brand new modern rival boat, put in commission by his rival (Tom McGuire). The old-timer hasn't seen his son since he was an infant. The son arrives (Keaton), and things begin to happen, fast and furiously.

The son falls in love with the daughter of the rival owner. Matters reach a climax when the old tub of Steamboat Bill is condemned. In a rage, he confronts his rival and accuses him of robbing him. A battle ensues.

An excellent cast gives Keaton and Torrence big league support. Tom Lewis as the first mate, McGuire as the rival owner and Marion Byron as the girl contribute heavily. The windstorm is a gem and the river stuff interesting and colorful.

Buster Keaton, as* Steamboat Bill, Jr*, gives a piggy-back to Marion Byron, daughter of rival steamboat owner.

STICKY FINGERS

1988, 97 mins, ◇ Ⓥ *Dir* Catlin Adams   US

★ *Stars* Helen Slater, Melanie Mayron, Danitra Vance, Eileen Brennan, Carol Kane

Sticky Fingers is a snappy, offbeat urban comedy about two New York gal pals – starving artist types – who get caught up in the shopping spree of a lifetime. Too bad the money isn't theirs.

Story, co-written by debut director Catlin Adams and Melanie Mayron, casts Mayron and Helen Slater as struggling musicians on the verge of eviction from their NY walkup until a bagful of drug money – nearly a million bucks – lands in their laps. They've been asked to 'mind it' for a spacey friend-of-a-friend (Loretta Devine) who's clearing out of town in a hurry.

Initially panicked, they wind up using it to pay their rent; then to replace their instruments. As days pass, the urge to spend becomes insatiable, and they give in with gusto.

Memorable supporting roles abound, including Danitra Vance as a fellow musician and Stephen McHattie as a tough but romantic undercover cop posing as a parking lot attendant across from their building.

Eileen Brennan is right on as the ailing landlady and Carol Kane delightful as her sister, who has a romance with the cop. Christopher Guest is near perfect as Mayron's un- certain boyfriend, a newly published novelist pursued by a spooky ex-girlfriend (Gwen Welles).

STIR CRAZY

1980, 111 mins, ◇ Ⓥ *Dir* Sidney Poitier   US

★ *Stars* Gene Wilder, Richard Pryor, Jobeth Williams, Georg Stanford Brown

Story setup has down-on-their-luck New Yorkers Richard Pryor and Gene Wilder deciding to blow the city for what they think are the promising shores of California. Driving cross-country they land in a small town where they take a job dressing up as woodpeckers in a local bank in order to make some cash. Two baddies they met in a bar use the woodpecker suits to rob the bank, leaving Pryor and Wilder 120-year prison sentences and no alibi.

Majority of the action focuses on the antics of prison life, with Pryor and Wilder at the center of a group of fairly stereotypical jail characters.

Director Sidney Poitier's chief role seems to be provid- ing enough space for Pryor and Wilder to do their schtick without going too far afield from the scant storyline.

In the long tradition of Hollywood prison comedies, Gene Wilder and Richard Pryor get arrested in Stir Crazy.

S

STRIPES

1981, 103 mins, ◇ Ⓥ *Dir* Ivan Reitman   US

★ **Stars** Bill Murray, Harold Ramis, Warren Oates, Sean Young, John Candy, P.J. Soles

Stripes is a cheerful, mildly outrageous and mostly amiable comedy pitting a new generation of enlistees against the oversold lure of a military hungry for bodies and not too choosy about what it gets. There's little in the way of art or comic subtlety here, but the film really seems to work.

Bill Murray, who worked under Ivan Reitman in *Meatballs*, is an aimless layabout whose Sad Sack life prompts him to consider the army as a last-ditch passport to the career, romances, travels and other delights painted in those glossy federal commercials.

Predictably, after he cons buddy Harold Ramis into enlisting, the sexy ads quickly prove to be Madison Avenue fiction, with basic training – under the grizzled glare of drill sergeant Warren Oates – taking the place of fraternity hell week as Murray heads deeper into trouble, cued by his amiably arrogant smart-assedness.

Apart from Murray's focal presence, Ramis and obese John Candy are wildly funny, with Oates treading a good balance between grizzly humor and military convictions (which the film, surprisingly, winds up more honoring than knocking).

TAKE THE MONEY AND RUN

1969, 85 mins, ◇ Ⓥ *Dir* Woody Allen   US

★ **Stars** Woody Allen, Janet Margolin, Marcel Hillaire, Jacquelyn Hyde, Lonny Chapman

A few good laughs in an 85-minute film do not a comedy make. Woody Allen's *Take the Money and Run*, basically a running gag about hero Allen's ineptitude as a professional crook, scatters its fire in so many directions it has to hit at least several targets. But the pic's satire on documentary coverage of criminal flop is over-extended and eventually becomes tiresome.

Bright spots are interviews with parents-in-disguise Ethel Sokolow and Henry Leff; Janet Margolin, as wife, and prison psychiatrist Don Frazier also deliver yocks. Margolin turns in a neat performance as Allen's wife.

Allen, both as director and actor, sustains his own characterization. In such scenes as the robbery when he can't convince bank personnel they are being robbed, or in the chain gang's visit to a farmhouse, he creates genuinely funny moments.

TAKING CARE OF BUSINESS

1990, 103 mins, ◇ Ⓥ *Dir* Arthur Hiller   US

★ **Stars** James Belushi, Charles Grodin, Anne DeSalvo, Loryn Locklin, Veronica Hamel, Hector Elizondo

Charles Grodin and James Belushi come together too late in the plot to prevent a poky start for *Taking Care of Business*, but their mutual chemistry eventually kicks in some jovial jousting. Brash Belushi and befuddled Grodin are perfect casting for yarn about a likable escaped con who assumes the identity of a stuffy, overworked ad agency exec.

At the start, Belushi is still in county jail, and there's some fun there as he high-fives it with fellow inmates and torments warden Hector Elizondo. Mostly familiar schtick. Ditto Grodin's intro as he fusses with his workload and neglects wife Victoria Hamel. Though Belushi is set for release in just days, he can't wait to see the World Series so he escapes just as Grodin arrives in LA to pitch his agency to a Japanese tycoon.

At the airport, Grodin loses his time-planning book – *Business* is one long commercial itself for a particular brand (Filofax, as pic is titled in the UK) – and Belushi finds it. Setting himself up in a Malibu mansion, Belushi proceeds to live Grodin's life just the opposite of how the businessman would do it, romancing the boss's daughter (played with sexy feistiness by Loryn Locklin), beating the potential client (Mako) at tennis, criticizing his products and making sexist remarks to fierce, feminist exec (Gates McFadden).

Inevitably, Grodin catches up with Belushi and the farcical convolutions multiply with the arrival of Hamel. As the action picks up, so does the dialog.

TAKING OFF

1971, 92 mins, ◇ Ⓥ *Dir* Milos Forman   US

★ **Stars** Lynn Carlin, Buck Henry, Linnea Heacock, Georgia Engel, Tony Harvey, Audra Lindley

Taking Off is a very compassionate, very amusing contemporary comedy about a NY couple whose concern for a drop out daughter is matched by her astonishment at their social mores. Milos Forman's first US-made film shows him to be a director who can depict the contradictions of human nature while avoiding tract, harangue and polemics.

The plot peg is the flight to Greenwich Village of Linnea Heacock, who's seeking something not provided in her home life. Lynn Carlin and Buck Henry (as the parents) enliven the many motivated and developing sequences: initial search for the girl conducted with friends Tony Harvey and Georgia Engel; a large meeting of discarded parents where Vincent Schiavelli turns them all on to marijuana; and a funny strip poker game at home which ends abruptly when the runaway girl calmly appears from her bedroom.

Henry tackles his first big screen role and achieves superb results. Carlin seems not an actress in a part, but a real mother, caught by candid camera, who doesn't know whether to laugh or cry about a family crisis.

THE TALL GUY

1989, 92 mins, ◇ Ⓥ *Dir* Mel Smith   UK

★ *Stars* Jeff Goldblum, Emma Thompson, Rowan Atkinson, Emil Wolk, Geraldine James

The Tall Guy is a cheery, ingratiating romantic comedy with Jeff Goldblum putting in a stellar performance as a bumbling American actor in London whose career and romantic tribulations are suddenly transformed into triumphs.

At the film's outset, Yank thesp Goldblum has been performing in the West End for several years as a straight man to popular comic Rowan Atkinson. The insecure but likable goof-ball is earning a living but going nowhere fast when he comes under the care of hospital nurse Emma Thompson.

Immediately smitten, Goldblum spends the time between weekly visits for injections desperately concocting ways to ask her out.

Throughout the entire film, the relationship evolves winningly, with so much believable give-and-take, mutual ribbing and support that one roots for it heavily.

As soon as he has discovered domestic bliss, however, Goldblum is sacked by Atkinson, who resents anyone else in his show getting a laugh, and is thrust into the forbidding world of the unemployed actor.

The fresh, alert performances add enormously to the polished sparkle of the script. Goldblum is in splendid form as the eternally naive American abroad. Thompson makes a wonderfully poised foil for her leading man's volubility. British favorite Atkinson has a great time enacting the most vain and mean-spirited of stars, and Hugh Thomas elicits quite a few laughs in his brief appearance as a wild-eyed hospital medic.

Jeff Goldblum (left) takes a beating in **The Tall Guy** *as popular comedian Rowan Atkinson's straight man.*

TEEN WOLF

1985, 91 mins, ◇ Ⓥ *Dir* Rod Daniel   US

★ *Stars* Michael J. Fox, James Hampton, Scott Paulin, Susan Ursitti, Jerry Levine, Jim Mackrell

Lightweight item is innocuous and well-intentioned but terribly feeble, another example of a decent idea yielding the least imaginative results conceivable.

The Beacontown Beavers have the most pathetic basketball team in high school history, and pint-sized Michael J. Fox is on the verge of quitting when he notices certain biological changes taking place. Heavy hair is growing on the backs of his hands, his ears and teeth are elongating.

Instead of turning into a horrific teen werewolf, however, Fox takes to trucking around school halls in full furry regalia, becoming more successful with the ladies and, most importantly, winning basketball games.

Fox is likable enough in the lead, something that cannot be said for the remainder of the lackluster cast.

"10"

1979, 122 mins, ◇ Ⓥ *Dir* Blake Edwards   US

★ *Stars* Dudley Moore, Julie Andrews, Bo Derek, Brian Dennehy, Dee Wallace, Robert Webber

Blake Edwards' *"10"* is a shrewdly observed and beautifully executed comedy of manners and morals.

"10" is theoretically the top score on Dudley Moore's female ranking system, although he raves that his dream girl is an '11' after he first spots her. Frustrated in his song writing and in his relationship with g.f. Julie Andrews, diminutive Moore, 40-ish, four-time Oscar winner, decides to pursue the vision incarnated by Bo Derek despite fact that she's on her honeymoon with a jock type seemingly twice Moore's size.

Long build-up to Moore's big night with Derek is spiced with plenty of physical comedy which displays both Moore and Edwards in top slapstick form.

THAT SINKING FEELING

1979, 80 mins, ◇ Ⓥ *Dir* Bill Forsyth   UK

★ *Stars* Robert Buchanan, John Hughes, Billy Greenlees, Douglas Sannachan, Alan Love

The first wholly Scottish feature for many a year proves debuting filmmaker Bill Forsyth has an entertaining touch.

Forsyth's screenplay, largely set in the city's dank demolition areas, plots a motley bunch of unemployed lads, amiably led by Robert Buchanan, who heist a hundred stainless steel sinks in a boisterous bid to embark on an essentially light-hearted life of crime.

first New York escapade of Theodora in a dashing blade's apartment is a high point of light-and-shade farce. Melvyn Douglas is an excellent romantic partner for Dunne. She, rather than he, gets the real acting chances but he is consistently intelligent.

An adult comedy of manners, "10" teams diminutive Dudley Moore with the statuesque Bo Derek.

The central joke – the absurdity of seeing sinks as likely hot sellers – is hardly strong enough to carry a full-length film. But Forsyth's incidental observations, and the generally high standard of playing by non-professionals, help to offset the fact that most scenes could be pruned to advantage. Technical credits are remarkable considering the almost invisible production budget.

THEODORA GOES WILD

1936, 94 mins, *Dir* Richard Boleslawski   US

★ **Stars** Irene Dunne, Melvyn Douglas, Thomas Mitchell, Spring Byington, Elisabeth Risdon, Margaret McWade

A comedy of steady tempo and deepening laughter. Irene Dunne takes the hurdle into comedy with versatile grace.

Theodora may superficially be compared to the *Mr Deeds Goes to Town* (1936) character in that both come from small New England villages. Quaint and eccentric figures and customs are exploited for laughs and background in both cases. And the experiences of the small-town character when hitting Manhattan form the main content of the story [from the novel by Mary McCarthy].

Painstaking direction of Richard Boleslawski brings out the nuances. His direction and Dunne's playing of the

THERE'S A GIRL IN MY SOUP

1971, 94 mins, ◇ ▼ *Dir* Roy Boulting   UK

★ **Stars** Peter Sellers, Goldie Hawn, Tony Britton, Nicky Henson, John Comer, Diana Dors

There's a Girl in My Soup is a delightful surprise: a rather simple legit sex comedy (by Terence Frisby) transformed into breezy and extremely tasteful screen fun.

Peter Sellers is a TV personality whose roving eye misses few femme specimens. Accidental encounter with Goldie Hawn, who is having some free-love domestic problems with mate Nicky Henson, blossoms into unexpected love and compassion between the unlikely pair.

Henson is excellent in giving depth to the limited part, and adds immeasurably to the general moral tone. In superior support also are Tony Britton as Sellers' publisher-confidante; John Comer as Sellers' envious doorman; and Diana Dors in a good offbeat character casting as Comer's shrewish wife.

THEY ALL LAUGHED

1981, 115 mins, ◇ *Dir* Peter Bogdanovich   US

★ **Stars** Audrey Hepburn, Ben Gazzara, John Ritter, Colleen Camp, Dorothy Stratten, Patti Hansen

Rarely does a film come along featuring such an extensive array of attractive characters with whom it is simply a pleasure to spend two hours. Nothing of great importance happens in a strict plot sense, but this *La Ronde*-like tale is intensely devoted to the sexual and amorous sparks struck among some unusually magnetic people.

In fact, pic could be considered a successful, non-musical remake of *At Long Last Love*, as the dynamics of the partner changes are virtually identical.

It takes a little while to figure out just where the story is headed, but basic framework has Ben Gazzara, John Ritter and Blaine Novak working for the Odyssey Detective Agency, which is truthfully advertised by the line 'We never sleep'. Gazzara's been assigned to track Gotham visitor Audrey Hepburn by her husband, while Ritter and Novak trail Dorothy Stratten as she slips away from her husband to rendezvous with young Sean Ferrer.

Hepburn doesn't have a line to speak for the entire first hour (much of the film is devoted to vaguely voyeuristic pursuit and observation on the part of the detectives), but ultimately she emerges winningly as the most mature and discreet character in the group.

Certain plot contrivances bear eerie resemblances to the cirumstances leading up to Stratten's real-life 1980 mur-

Goldie Hawn in one of her earliest leads in **There's a Girl in My Soup,** *a British outing with Peter Sellers.*

der, as she too, had been followed by a detective hired by a husband suspicious of her fidelity. A palm reading sequence in which Ritter predicts that her marriage will come to a quick end – and she wonders if she has much time left – is chilling for those familiar with the Stratten case.

THEY MIGHT BE GIANTS

1971, 91 mins, ◇ ⊛ *Dir* Anthony Harvey   US

★ **Stars** George C. Scott, Joanne Woodward, Jack Gilford, Lester Rawlins, Rue McClanahan, Ron Weyand

They Might Be Giants starts off splendidly and hilariously, with George C. Scott at his intense and imposing best as a former jurist who thinks he's Sherlock Holmes, and Joanne Woodward charmingly harried as the psychiatrist who's delighted to encounter a 'classic paranoid', and who just happens to be named Dr (Mildred) Watson.

After that it's all downhill. It's not only unfunny, but increasingly preachy and sentimental – hammering at the cliched tale of the good-hearted nut who's basically saner, and certainly nicer, than the pack of meanies who attempt to defeat him.

Scott and Woodward battle the script valiantly. Scott has the easier time of it by virtue of his character's self-contained system. But both are buried eventually under a pile of loose ends, and they're not helped much either by Anthony Harvey's visually unimaginative direction.

THINGS CHANGE

1988, 100 mins, ◇ ⊛ *Dir* David Mamet   US

★ **Stars** Don Ameche, Joe Mantegna, Robert Prosky, J.J. Johnston, Ricky Jay, Mike Nussbaum

Direct by David Mamet, *Things Change* is a dry, funny and extremely intelligent comedy about an innocent mistaken for a Mafia don.

Pic opens in Chicago as the elderly Gino (Don Ameche), a shoeshine boy, is 'invited' to meet a Mafia boss whom he physically resembles. The boss has killed a man and there were witnesses. The latter wants Gino to confess to a murder and take the rap and as a reward he can have his heart's desire, which turns out to be owning a fishing boat back in Sicily.

Gino is handed over to Jerry (Joe Mantegna), a very junior member of the Mafia clan. All Jerry has to do is coach Gino in his story for two days, then deliver him to the law. Instead, Jerry decides to give the oldster a final fling, and takes him to Lake Tahoe where, unknown to him, a Mafia convention is about to take place.

Gino is instantly mistaken for a senior Don and given royal treatment: lavish hotel suite, credit, girls, limo. He's also invited to meet the local Mafia kingpin (Robert Prosky) with whom he instantly strikes up a close rapport while Jerry sees himself getting into deeper and deeper trouble.

This comedy of mistaken identity centers around a beautifully modulated starring performance from Ameche as the poor but painfully upright and honest Gino. As the dimwitted young Jerry, Mantegna is consistently funny and touching.

Rock music hasn't attracted as much sending-up as it deserves, but **This Is Spinal Tap** *helped reset the balance.*

THIS IS SPINAL TAP

1984, 82 mins, ◇ ⓥ *Dir* Rob Reiner   US

★ *Stars* Rob Reiner, Michael McKean, Christopher Guest, Harry Shearer, R.J. Parnell, David Kaff

For music biz insiders, *This Is Spinal Tap* is a vastly amusing satire of heavy metal bands. Director Rob Reiner has cast himself as Marty DiBergi, a filmmaker intent upon covering the long-awaited American return of the eponymous, 17-year-old British rock band. Pic then takes the form of a cinema-verité documentary, as Reiner includes interviews with the fictional musicians, records their increasingly disastrous tour and captures the internal strife which leads to the separation of the group's two founders.

Reiner and co-writers have had loads of fun with the material, creating mock 1960s TV videotapes of early gigs and filling the fringes with hilariously authentic music-biz types, most notably Fran Drescher's label rep and Paul Shaffer's cameo as a Chicago promo man.

THREE FUGITIVES

1989, 96 mins, ◇ ⓥ *Dir* Francis Veber   US

★ *Stars* Nick Nolte, Martin Short, Sarah Rowland Doroff, James Earl Jones, Alan Ruck

Three Fugitives marks the Hollywood helming debut of French director Francis Veber, remaking his own 1986 comedy *Les fugitifs* American-style. Clever premise starts pic off on a roll, as master bankrobber Lucas (Nick Nolte) gets out of the slammer determined to go straight, only to get involved in another heist in the very first bank he enters.

This time, he's an innocent bystander taken hostage by a hysterically inept gunman (Martin Short). But who's going to believe that?

Short, once he figures out Nolte's predicament, blackmails him into aiding and abetting his escape from the country. To make things even stickier. Short's got an emotionally withdrawn little girl (Sarah Rowland Doroff) who latches onto Nolte like a stray kitten.

As for the Nolte–Short pairing, it'll do, but it's no chemical marvel. Nolte, not really a comic natural, gruffs and grumbles his way through as hunky straight man to Short's calamitous comedian. Short runs with the slapstick style.

3 MEN AND A BABY

1987, 102 mins, ◇ ⓥ *Dir* Leonard Nimoy   US

★ *Stars* Tom Selleck, Steve Guttenberg, Ted Danson, Nancy Travis, Margaret Colin

3 Men and a Baby is about as slight a feature comedy as is made – while at the same time it's hard to resist Tom Selleck, Ted Danson and Steve Guttenberg shamelessly going goo-goo over caring for an infant baby girl all swaddled in pink.

This is an Americanized version of the 1985 French sleeper hit *3 hommes et un couffin* and parallels the original's storyline almost exactly.

The lives of three confirmed bachelors – the studly sort who live, play and scheme on voluptuous women together – is thrown into confusion when a baby is left at their front door. As it happens, actor and suspected father of the infant (Danson) is conveniently out of town on a shoot, leaving architect and super pushover Peter (Selleck) and cartoonist Michael (Guttenberg) all in a quandary what to do with the precious little thing.

Big macho men tripping all over themselves trying to successfully feed, diaper and bathe a bundle of innocence and helplessness is ripe for comic development, and it certainly helps that these three are having a blast seeing it through.

Film is a good showcase for the comic abilities of this threesome, all of whom seem to have their one-liner timing down pat.

3 MEN AND A LITTLE LADY

1990, 100 mins, ◇ ⓥ *Dir* Emile Ardolino   US

★ *Stars* Tom Selleck, Steve Guttenberg, Ted Danson, Nancy Travis, Robin Weisman, Christopher Cazenove

Back in their places for this two-dimensional sequel are the three bachelor dads of the waif who landed on their doorstep in part one: vain actor Ted Danson and biological dad, and architect Tom Selleck and illustrator Steve Guttenberg, the honorary dads.

What's news is that hunk Selleck has fallen in love with the baby's mom, Sylvia (Nancy Travis), the actress who shares their new appartment, although he hasn't admitted it to her or himself.

Crisis occurs when baby turns five and enrolls in preschool, thereby encountering other children. Mom decides she must marry. She accepts a proposal from her director friend, Edward (Christopher Cazenove), and plans to move to England with little Mary (Robin Weisman), all because bachelor No. 2 (Selleck) is too confused to pop the question.

Rest of the pic is standard romantic comedy. Script [story by Sara Parriott and Josann McGibbon] spoonfeeds the audience with a plodding script that seems based more on demographic research than on any wisp of a creative im-

pulse. Emile Ardolino directs with the same degree of competent but calculated non-risk. As for the actors, they have nothing to play.

THE THRILL OF IT ALL

1963, 108 mins, ◇ ⓥ *Dir* Norman Jewison   US

★ *Stars* Doris Day, James Garner, Arlene Francis, Edward Andrews, ZaSu Pitts, Reginald Owen

Carl Reiner's scenario, from a story he wrote in collaboration with Larry Gelbart, is peppered with digs at various institutions of American life. Among the targets of his fairly subtle but telling assault with the needle are television, Madison Avenue, the servant problem and such specific matters as the sharp points at the rear extremities of the modern Cadillac and the maitre d' who has immediate seating for celebrities only.

But these nuggets and pinpricks of satiric substance are primarily bonuses. Ultimately it is in the design and engineering of cumulative sight gag situations that *Thrill of It All* excels. In addition to a running gag about a suspiciously similar weekly series of live TV dramas, there is a scene in which a swimming pool saturated with soap gives birth to a two-story-high mountain of suds and another in which James Garner, coming home from work one evening, drives his convertible into his back yard and straight into a pool that wasn't there in the morning.

Doris Day scores as the housewife with two children who is suddenly thrust into an irresistible position as an $80,000-a-year pitch woman for an eccentric soap tycoon who is impressed by her unaffected quality. Bearing the brunt of these soap operatics is Garner as the gynecologist whose domestic tranquillity is shattered by his wife's sudden transition to career girl.

Arlene Francis and Edward Andrews are spirited in the key roles of a middle-aged couple suddenly expectant parents. ZaSu Pitts does all she can with some ridiculous shenanigans as a fretful maid.

THROW MOMMA FROM THE TRAIN

1987, 88 mins, ◇ ⓥ *Dir* Danny DeVito   US

★ *Stars* Danny DeVito, Billy Crystal, Anne Ramsey, Kim Greist, Kate Mulgrew

Throw Momma from the Train is a fun and delightfully venal comedy. Very clever and engaging from beginning to end, pic builds on the notion that nearly everyone – at least once in life – has the desire to snuff out a relative or nemesis, even if 99.9% of us let the urge pass without ever acting on it.

Here, it's the idle death threats of a frustrated writer and flunky junior college professor (Billy Crystal) against his ex-wife that are overheard by one of his dimwitted and very impressionable students (Danny DeVito).

Billy Crystal (top) and Danny DeVito get on the right track for grim laughter in Throw Momma from the Train.

DeVito's limited creative abilities are further stifled by his crazy, overbearing momma (Anne Ramsey), a nasty, jealous old bag whom he loathes and fears. He seeks out Crystal for help on his writing and instead is told to go see Alfred Hitchcock's *Strangers on a Train*, which he does – coming away with a ridiculous scheme on the film's plot to kill Crystal's wife and then ask for a like favor in return.

Crystal's talent as a standup comic comes through as it appears he got away with a fair amount of ad-libbing. His tirades on his ex-wife, a routine he does several times, get funnier with each delivery and are a good counterbalance for DeVito's equally comical dumb-impish schtick.

If there were to be a first place prize for scene stealing, however, it would to to Ramsey, whose horrible looks and surly demeanor are sick and humorous at the same time.

TIN MEN

1987, 112 mins, ◇ Ⓥ *Dir* Barry Levinson   US

★ **Stars** Richard Dreyfuss, Danny DeVito, Barbara Hershey, John Mahoney, Jackie Gayle, Stanley Brock

The improbable tale of a pair of feuding aluminum siding salesmen, *Tin Men* winds up as bountiful comedy material in the skilful hands of writer-director Barry Levinson.

Film is packed with laughs, thanks to taut scripting and superb character depictions by Richard Dreyfuss, Danny DeVito and a fascinating troupe of sidekicks. These fast-buck hustlers collectively fashion a portrait of superficial greed so pathetic it soars to a level of black humor.

Central storyline finds Dreyfuss and DeVito tangling from the start after an accident damages both of their Cadillacs. Conflict between the two strangers – who don't find out until later they're both tin men – escalates to the point where Dreyfuss seeks to get even by wooing DeVito's unhappy wife (Barbara Hershey) into bed.

While each of the tin men is revealed as a compelling, off-center type in his own right, the one played by Jackie Gayle especially shines.

THE TITFIELD THUNDERBOLT

1953, 84 mins, ◇ Ⓥ *Dir* Charles Crichton   UK

★ **Stars** Stanley Holloway, George Relph, Naunton Wayne, John Gregson, Godfrey Tearle, Hugh Griffith

Titfield is a small English village which gets worked up when the government decides to close the unprofitable branch railway line. The vicar and the squire are both railway enthusiasts and are heartbroken at the news. The only ones cheered by the decision are the partners of a transport company who can see big profits by organizing a bus service. The railway enthusiasts, however, persuade the village tippler to provide the cash by telling him he will be able to start drinking far earlier if they install a buffet car on the train.

The *Thunderbolt* is the railway engine involved in the story. Once the basic situation is accepted, the entire yarn concentrates on the feuding between the rival factions with the opposition stopping at nothing in their efforts to block the train service.

Stanley Holloway gives a polished performance as the village soak. George Relph does a fine job as the vicar; Naunton Wayne's contribution as the town clerk is in typical vein while John Gregson does very nicely as the earnest squire. A gem from Godfrey Tearle as the bishop and a powerful performance by Hugh Griffith are among the pic's strong characterizations.

TOOTSIE

1982, 116 mins, ◇ Ⓥ *Dir* Sydney Pollack   US

★ **Stars** Dustin Hoffman, Jessica Lange, Teri Garr, Dabney Coleman, Charles Durning, Bill Murray

Academy Award 1982: Best Picture (Nomination)

Tootsie is a lulu. Remarkably funny and entirely convincing, film pulls off the rare accomplishment of being an in-drag comedy which also emerges with three-dimensional characters.

Dustin Hoffman portrays a long-struggling New York

*Dustin Hoffman in **Tootsie**: an absolute rarity, a drag comedy without camp overtones.*

stage actor whose 'difficult' reputation has relegated him to employment as a waiter and drama coach.

Brash but appealing actor's solution: audition for a popular soap opera as a woman. Becoming a hit on the show, 'Dorothy Michaels' develops into a media celebrity thanks to her forthright manner and 'different' personality. Hoffman finds it hard to devote much time to sort-of-girlfriend Teri Garr, and all the while is growing more deeply attracted to soap co-star Jessica Lange.

Hoffman triumphs in what must stand as one of his most brilliant performances. His Dorothy is entirely plausible and, physically, even reasonably appealing. But much more importantly, he gets across the enormous guts and determination required of his character to go through with the whole charade.

TOP SECRET!

1984, 90 mins, ◇ Ⓥ *Dir* Jim Abrahams, David Zucker, Jerry Zucker   US

★ *Stars* Val Kilmer, Lucy Gutteridge, Christopher Villiers, Omar Sharif, Peter Cushing, Jeremy Kemp

Top Secret! is another bumptious tribute to all that was odd in old movies. Followers of the *Airplane!* trio will probably be happy and satisfied with this effort, yet short of overjoyed.

The attempted target this time is a combination of the traditional spy film and Elvis Presley musical romps, which in and of itself is funny to start with. And Val Kilmer proves a perfect blend of staunch hero and hothouse heartthrob.

But in a deliberate effort to do something different, the directors have unfortunately discarded the cast of matinee idols so closely identified with the originals.

Other than that, *Secret!* shares the same wonderful wacky attitude that allows just about any kind of gag to come flowing in and out of the picture at the strangest times.

A TOUCH OF CLASS

1973, 106 mins, ◇ Ⓥ *Dir* Melvin Frank   UK

★ *Stars* George Segal, Glenda Jackson, Paul Sorvino, Hildegard Neil, Cec Linder, K. Callan

Academy Award 1973: Best Picture (Nomination)

A Touch of Class is sensational. Director, writer and producer Melvin Frank has accomplished precisely what Peter Bogdanovich did in *What's Up, Doc?* – revitalizing, updating and invigorating an earlier film genre to smash results.

Segal herein justifies superbly a reputation for comedy ability while Jackson's full-spectrum talent is again confirmed. An accidental London meeting between George Segal and Glenda Jackson leads to a casual pass by Segal, thence (through a series of hilarious complications, including wife, in-laws, and old friends) to a frustrated rendezvous in a Spanish resort. Pair's romance flourishes into

a full-blown affair at home, with Segal wearing himself out dashing between two beds.

The visual and verbal antics are supported by just enough underlying character depth to keep the film on a solid credible basis, setting up the plot for its tender, bittersweet climax.

TRADING PLACES

1983, 106 mins, ◇ ⊘   *Dir* John Landis   US

★ *Stars* Dan Aykroyd, Eddie Murphy, Ralph Bellamy, Don Ameche, Denholm Elliott, Jamie Lee Curtis

Trading Places is a light romp geared up by the schtick shifted by Dan Aykroyd and Eddie Murphy. Happily, it's a pleasure to report also that even those two popular young comics couldn't have brought this one off without the contributions of three veterans – Ralph Bellamy, Don Ameche and the droll Englishman, Denholm Elliott.

Aykroyd plays a stuffy young financial wizard who runs a Philadelphia commodities house for two continually scheming brothers, Bellamy and Ameche.

Conversely, Murphy has grown up in the streets and lives on the con, including posing as a blind, legless veteran begging outside Aykroyd's private club.

Dan Aykroyd and Eddie Murphy, with Jamie Lee Curtis, unwittingly swap lifestyles in Trading Places.

On a whim motivated by disagreement over the importance of environment vs breeding, Bellamy bets Ameche that Murphy could run the complex commodities business just as well as Aykroyd, given the chance. Conversely, according to the bet, Aykroyd would resort to crime and violence if suddenly all friends and finances were stripped away from him.

So their scheme proceeds and both Aykroyd and Murphy are in top form reacting to their new situations.

The only cost, however, is a mid-section stretch without laughs, still made enjoyable by the presence of Jamie Lee Curtis as a good-hearted hooker who befriends Aykroyd.

TRAIL OF THE PINK PANTHER

1983, 97 mins, ◇ ⊘   *Dir* Blake Edwards   UK

★ *Stars* Peter Sellers, David Niven, Herbert Lom, Richard Mulligan, Joanna Lumley, Capucine

A patchwork of out-takes, reprised clips and new connective footage, *Trail of the Pink Panther* is a thin, peculiar picture unsupported by the number of laughs one is accustomed to in this series. Stitched together after Peter Sellers' death, this is by a long way the slightest of the six Inspector Clouseau efforts.

Story's structure is strange, to say the least. The fabulous Pink Panther gem is stolen yet again from its vulnerable resting place in an Arab museum, which sparks immediate interest from the haplessly effective French detective.

Opening two reels are devoted to supposed out-take footage of Sellers trying on a disguise and on attempting to relieve himself in an airplane lavatory despite the encumbrance of an ungainly cast.

After about 40 minutes, Clouseau's Lugash-bound plane is reported missing. French television reporter Joanna Lumley sets out to interview many of those who had known the inspector in earlier pics, including David Niven, Capucine (looking great), Burt Kwouk, Graham Stark and Andre Maranne, as well as his father, Richard Mulligan, and a Mafia kingpin, Robert Loggia.

TRAVELS WITH MY AUNT

1972, 109 mins, ◇ *Dir* George Cukor   UK

★ **Stars** Maggie Smith, Alec McCowen, Lou Gossett, Robert Stephens, Cindy Williams, Robert Flemyng

Travels with My Aunt is the story [based on the Graham Greene bestseller] of an outrageous femme of indeterminate years cavorting in a set of outrageous situations which spell high comedy. Of course, it may also be regarded as utter nonsense in a hammed-up set of overly-contrived circumstances.

Maggie Smith plays the title role in an overdrawn but thoroughly delightful manner. Film opens quietly enough at the funeral services of her nephew's mother, but the disrupting arrival of the over-dressed, over-cosmeticked Aunt Augusta sets the stage for a comedy spree.

George Cukor's direction is quite up to meeting the demands of the script, and it is he who is responsible for a tempo attuned to his unusual characters. Alec McCowen's characterization of the nephew is subtle and expansive as he gradually withdraws from his former stuffy, priggish, ex-bank manager style.

TROUBLE IN STORE

1953, 85 mins, ◉ *Dir* John Paddy Carstairs   UK

★ **Stars** Norman Wisdom, Margaret Rutherford, Moira Lister, Derek Bond, Lana Morris, Jerry Desmonde

This British piece of slapstick marks the debut of Norman Wisdom. He clowns his way through the whole thing, playing in his inimitable way the most humble member of a big department store who falls foul of his new boss. But he gets his girl and also rounds up some gangsters.

Apart from one or two brief exteriors, the entire action takes place in the department store, but there is plenty of movement and an ample slice of broad comedy in *Trouble in Store*. Margaret Rutherford has some nice comedy scenes as an inveterate shoplifter and Moira Lister is a very lush manageress who's in league with the gangsters led by Derek Bond. Lana Morris pleasantly offers the romantic interest. Jerry Desmonde is little more than a comedy stooge, as the boss, but plays the role for all it is worth.

THE TUNNEL OF LOVE

1958, 98 mins, *Dir* Gene Kelly   US

★ **Stars** Doris Day, Richard Widmark, Gig Young, Gia Scala, Elisabeth Fraser, Elizabeth Wilson

The Broadway hit on which this is based has been transferred virtually intact to the screen.

Richard Widmark is a would-be cartoonist for a *New Yorker*-type magazine, whose gags are good but whose drawings are not. He and his wife (Doris Day) want a child and cannot catch. They live in a remodeled barn (naturally) adjacent to the home of their best friends (Gig Young and Elisabeth Fraser) whom they envy in many ways. Young is an editor of the magazine Widmark aspires to crack, and is a parent. While Young adds to his and Fraser's brood as regularly as the seasons, Widmark and Day are planning to adopt a baby.

Meantime, back at the barn, Young, whose homework has been stimulated by extracurricular activities, urges his system on Widmark. With this suggestion in the back of his mind, Widmark is visited by an adoption home investigator (Gia Scala). When he wakes up in a motel after a night on the town with her, he assumes the thought has been father to the deed in more ways than one. Just a little over nine months later, the adoption agency presents a baby to Day and Widmark.

The only important change Joseph Fields has made in the screenplay, from the play by him and Peter DeVries (based on DeVries' book), is to explain at the very end that the child is not actually Widmark's.

Day and Widmark make a fine comedy team, working as smoothly as if they had been trading gags for years. They are ably abetted by Young, one of the greatest flycatchers in operation, and Scala, who displays a nice and unexpected gift for comedy.

This is the first time Gene Kelly has operated entirely behind the camera, and he emerges as an inventive and capable comedy director.

TURNER & HOOCH

1989, 100 mins, ◇ ◉ *Dir* Roger Spottiswoode   US

★ **Stars** Tom Hanks, Mare Winningham, Craig T. Nelson, Reginald VelJohnson, Scott Paulin

Until its grossly miscalculated bummer of an ending, *Turner & Hooch* is a routine but amiable cop-and-dog comedy enlivened by the charm of Tom Hanks and his homely-assin canine partner.

Hanks plays a fussy smalltown California police investigator whose life is disreputed by a messy junkyard dog with a face only a furry mother could love.

In the numbingly unoriginal plot, the dog named Hooch (delightfully played by Beasley), witnesses a double murder and is Hanks' only means of catching the drug smug-

glers responsible for the slayings. The rather mechanical style of director Roger Spottiwoode (who took over the film after original director Henry Winkler departed) fails to enliven the stereotypical criminal proceedings.

THE TWELVE CHAIRS

1970, 94 mins, ◇ ⓥ *Dir* Mel Brooks   US

★ **Stars** Ron Moody, Frank Langella, Mel Brooks, Andreas Voutsinas, Vlada Petric, David Lander

The Twelve Chairs is a nutty farce, frequently slapstick and often tongue-in-cheek. Mel Brooks, who directed, scripted, plays a leading role and authored a song, has turned a search for jewels into a cornpop – circa 1927, Russia, when all men were comrades – and the result is a delightful adventure-comedy.

Based on the novel by Ilf & Petrov, exteriors were lensed in Yugoslavia, which provides some novel and picturesque backdrops. The steps in Dubrovnik, vistas of the Dalmatian coast and mountains in the interior lend fascinating atmosphere.

Simple story thread is of three men trying to locate 12 dining-room chairs, once owned by a wealthy woman who confesses separately to her son-in-law and village priest on her deathbed that years before she had secreted all her jewels in the upholstery of one of them. Voila, the plot.

TWINS

1988, 112 mins, ◇ ⓥ *Dir* Ivan Reitman   US

★ **Stars** Arnold Schwarzenegger, Danny DeVito, Kelly Preston, Chloe Webb, Bonnie Bartlett

Director Ivan Reitman more than delivers on the wacky promise of *Twins* in this nutty, storybook tale of siblings separated at birth and reunited at age 35.

Arnold Schwarzenegger plays Julius Benedict, a perfect specimen of a man in both body and soul, raised as an orphan in pristine innocence on a tropical isle. Created in a genetic experiment, he has a twin brother on the mainland. Lionhearted Julius, filled with familial longing, rushes off to LA to search for bro – only to discover he'd have found him faster by looking under rocks.

Danny DeVito's Vincent Benedict is a major creep, a guy you wouldn't mind seeing get hit by a car. To him, Julius is a dopey nut who makes a good bodyguard. They finally set out to locate their mother, but Vincent still is on his incorrigible path.

Schwarzenegger is a delightful surprise here in this perfect transitional role to comedy. So strongly does he manage to project the tenderness, nobility and puppy-dog devotion that make Julius tick that one is nearly hypnotized into suspending disbelief.

DeVito is a blaze of energy and body language as Vince, articulating the part as though he's written it himself.

THE ULTIMATE SOLUTION OF GRACE QUIGLEY

1984, 102 mins, ◇ ⓥ *Dir* Anthony Harvey   US

★ **Stars** Katharine Hepburn, Nick Nolte, Elizabeth Wilson, Chip Zien, Kit Le Fever, William Duell

In this black comedy dealing with voluntary euthanasia by the Geritol set, casting Katharine Hepburn as the spry, entrepreneurial mother figure who arranges for her peers' demise and Nick Nolte as the gruff, hard-bitten and sarcastic hitman she hires, the two actors impart a light-hearted and whimsical tone to otherwise unpleasant subject matter.

Pic opens with Hepburn as a lonely and economically strapped pensioner who lost her immediate family in a pre-war auto accident, but who has a zestful embrace for life nonetheless. Sitting across from her apartment one day, she inadvertently witnesses Nolte put a bullet into her money-grubbing landlord, and subsequently enlists him in her scheme to provide a 'service' for her aging compatriots who wish to meet the hereafter ahead of schedule.

There are some marvelous supporting performances by Elizabeth Wilson as the spinster who can't get arrested trying to get Nolte to put her out of her misery, William Duell as the nerdy neighbor of Hepburn, and Kit Le Fever as Nolte's girlfriend hooker.

UNCLE BUCK

1989, 100 mins, ◇ ⓥ *Dir* John Hughes   US

★ **Stars** John Candy, Amy Madigan, Jean Louisa Kelly, Gaby Hoffman, Macaulay Culkin

John Hughes unsuccessfully tries to mix a serious generation gap message between the belly laughs in *Uncle Buck*, a warm-weather John Candy vehicle.

On paper the rotund Second City veteran seems ideal for the title role: a ne'er-do-well, coarse black sheep of the family suddenly pressed into service when his relatives (Elaine Bromka, Garrett M. Brown), a suburban Chicago family, have to rush off to visit Bromka's dad, stricken with a heart attack.

Enter Uncle Buck, put in charge of the three youngsters for an indefinite period. The kids wear down Buck's rough edges and he teaches them some seat-of-the-pants lessons about life.

Unfortunately, Candy is too likable to give the role any edge. When called upon to be tough or mean he's unconvincing, as in the slapstick dealings with the precociously oversexed boyfriend Bug (Jay Underwood) of eldest daughter Jean Louisa Kelly.

John Candy is **Uncle Buck,** *the slobbish and coarse relative brought in to look after his brother's children at short notice.*

UP IN SMOKE

1978, 86 mins, ◇ Ⓥ *Dir* Lou Adler   US

★ **Stars** Cheech Marin, Tommy Chong, Stacy Keach, Edie Adams, Tom Skerritt, Zane Buzby

Up in Smoke is essentially a drawn-out movie version of the drug-oriented comedy routines of Tommy Chong and Cheech Marin.

Script by the two comedians has hippie rich kid Chong teaming up with barrio boy Cheech in a confused search for some pot to puff on, presumably to aid them in putting together a rock band. Pursuit takes them to Tijuana, where they end up driving back a van constructed out of treated marijuana called 'fibreweed'.

In diligent pursuit is narcotics detective Stacy Keach, saddled with the usual crew of incompetent assistants. The trail eventually leads to popular LA nitery, The Roxy, (in which Adler is partnered) where the dopers' band engages in a punk rock marathon. They take top prize when the high-grade van, catching on fire, inundates the club with potent smoke.

What's lacking in *Up in Smoke* is a cohesiveness in both humor and characterization. Once the more obvious drug jokes have been exhausted, director Lou Adler lets the film degenerate into a mixture of fitful slapstick and toilet humor.

VICTOR/VICTORIA

1982, 133 mins, ◇ Ⓥ *Dir* Blake Edwards   UK

★ **Stars** Julie Andrews, James Garner, Robert Preston, Lesley Ann Warren, Alex Karras, John Rhys-Davies

Victor/Victoria is a sparkling, ultra-sophisticated entertainment from Blake Edwards. Based on a 1933 German film comedy [*Viktor und Viktoria*, written and directed by Rheinhold Schunzel] which was a big hit in its day, pic sees Edwards working in the Lubitsch–Wilder vein of sly wit and delightful sexual innuendo.

Set in Paris of 1934 gorgeously represented by Rodger Maus' studio-constructed settings, tale introduces Julie Andrews as a down-on-her-luck chanteuse. Also suffering a temporary career lapse is tres gai nightclub entertainer Robert Preston, who remakes her as a man who in short order becomes celebrated as Paris' foremost female impersonator.

Enter Windy City gangster James Garner, with imposing bodyguard Alex Karras and dizzy sexpot Lesley Ann Warren in tow. Not knowing he's in one of 'those' clubs, the tough guy falls hard for Andrews, only to experience a blow to his ego when it's apparent that she's a he.

While the central thrust of the story rests in Andrews–

Garner convergence, everyone in the cast is given a chance to shine. Most impressive of all is Preston, with a shimmering portrait of a slightly decadent 'old queen'.

Andrews reaffirms her musical talents and Garner is quizzically sober as the straight man, in more ways than one.

WHAT'S NEW PUSSYCAT

1965, 108 mins, ◇ Ⓥ   *Dir* Clive Donner   US

★ **Stars** Peter Sellers, Peter O'Toole, Romy Schneider, Capucine, Paula Prentiss, Woody Allen

What's New Pussycat is designed as a zany farce, as wayout as can be reached on the screen. It's all that, and more . . . it goes overboard in pressing for its goal and consequently suffers from over-contrived treatment.

The Charles K. Feldman production is peopled exclusively by mixed-up characters. Peter Sellers is a Viennese professor to whom Peter O'Toole, editor of a Parisian fashion magazine, goes for psychiatric help in solving his women problems, which keep piling up as he finds more pretty girls. On his part, Sellers has a jealous wife and a roving eye which keeps getting him into trouble.

Original screenplay by Woody Allen, who plays an undresser for strippers at the Crazy Horse Saloon and similarly afflicted with girl troubles – provides a field day for gagmen, who seldom miss a trick in inserting a sight gag.

Sellers' nuttiness knows no bounds as he speaks with a thick German accent, and O'Toole proves his forte in drama rather than comedy.

Trio of femmes who chase O'Toole have the proper looks and furnish as much glamor as any one man can take.

WHAT'S UP, DOC?

1972, 94 mins, ◇ Ⓥ   *Dir* Peter Bogdanovich   US

★ **Stars** Barbra Streisand, Ryan O'Neal, Kenneth Mars, Austin Pendleton, Sorrell Booke, Stefan Gierasch

Peter Bogdanovich's *What's Up, Doc?* is a contemporary comedy [from his own original story] in the screwball 1930s style, with absolutely no socially relevant values. This picture is a total smash.

The script and cast are excellent; the direction and comedy staging are outstanding; and there are literally reels of pure, unadulterated and sustained laughs.

Gimmick is a quartet of identical suitcases which of course get into the wrong hands. Barbra Streisand is discovered conning some food out of a hotel, where Ryan O'Neal and fiancee (Madeline Kahn) are attending a musicologists'

convention. There is an unending stream of opening and closing doors, perilous balcony walks, and two terrific chases through San Francisco streets.

The humor derives much from the tradition of Warner Bros. cartoons, with broad visuals amid sophisticated ideas. One of the hilarious car chases is virtually a *Road Runner* storyboard, and there's absolutely nothing wrong about that.

WHEN HARRY MET SALLY . . .

1989, 95 mins, ◇ Ⓥ   *Dir* Rob Reiner   US

★ **Stars** Billy Crystal, Meg Ryan, Carrie Fisher, Bruno Kirby, Steven Ford

Can a man be friends with a woman he finds attractive? Can usually acerbic scripter Nora Ephron sustain 95 minutes of unrelenting cuteness? Can the audience sit through 11 years of emotional foreplay between adorable Billy Crystal and Meg Ryan?

Abandoning the sour, nasty tone of some of her previous writing about contemporary sexual relationships, Ephron cuddles up to the audience in this number about the joys and woes of (mostly) platonic friendship.

Two characters who seem to have nothing on their minds but each other (even though they won't admit it), Harry and Sally are supposed to be a political consultant and a journalist, but it's hard to tell from the evidence presented.

Rob Reiner directs with deftness and sincerity, making the material seem more engaging than it is, at least until the plot mechanics begin to unwind and the film starts to seem shapeless. The only thing that's unpredictable about the story is how long it takes Harry and Sally to realize they're perfect for each other.

WHISKY GALORE!

1949, 82 mins, Ⓥ   *Dir* Alexander Mackendrick   UK

★ **Stars** Basil Radford, Joan Greenwood, Gordon Jackson, James Robertson Justice, Bruce Seaton, Gabrielle Blunt

Compton Mackenzie's novel, on which the pic is based, is unfolded on a Hebridean island in 1943. Only sign of the war is the local Home Guard, but a major disaster occurs when the island runs out of whisky. After some days a freighter with 50,000 cases of Scotch runs aground off the island. The natives organize a midnight expedition and lay in a tremendous store for future consumption.

Sustained comedy treatment successfully carries the film forward to the point where the islanders outwit the Home Guard captain who regards the adventure as the worst type of looting.

Basil Radford gives a flawless performance of the misunderstood Home Guard chief whose zealousness leads to trouble in high quarters. Bruce Seton and Joan Greenwood as well as Gabrielle Blunt and Gordon Jackson provide the slight romances of the film.

WHO FRAMED ROGER RABBIT

1988, 103 mins, ◇ Ⓥ *Dir* Robert Zemeckis   US

★ *Stars* Bob Hoskins, Christopher Lloyd, Joanna Cassidy, Stubby Kaye, Alan Tilvern

Years in the planning and making, *Who Framed Roger Rabbit* is an unparalleled technical achievement where animation is brilliantly integrated into live action. Yet the story amounts to little more than inspired silliness about the filmmaking biz where cartoon characters face off against cartoonish humans.

Pic opens appropriately enough with a cartoon, a hilarious, overblown, calamitous scene where Roger Rabbit, a famous contract Toon player (as in car*toon*) for Maroon Studios, is failing in his attempt to keep Baby Herman (voice by Lou Hirsch) from the cookie jar.

Things aren't going well for poor Roger. Ever since he became estranged from his voluptuous human character Toon wife Jessica (sultry, uncredited voice courtesy of Kathleen Turner, and Amy Irving for the singing) he just can't act.

This is the context from which scripters, in adapting Gary Wolf's story, try to work up a Raymond Chandler-style suspenser where Roger becomes an innocent murder suspect, with a disheveled, alcoholic private eye (Bob Hoskins) being his only hope to help him beat the rap.

The real stars are the animators, under British animation director Richard Williams, who pull off a technically amazing feat of having humans and Toons seem to be interacting with one another. It is clear from how well the imagery syncs that a lot of painstaking work [two years] went into this production – and clearly a lot of money [$70 million].

WILT

1989, 91 mins, ◇ Ⓥ *Dir* Michael Tuchner   UK

★ *Stars* Griff Rhys Jones, Mel Smith, Alison Steadman, Diana Quick, Jeremy Clyde

There is a good deal of enjoyment to be derived from *Wilt*, [based on Tom Sharpe's novel] mainly thanks to a uniformly excellent cast and unpretentious, straightforward direction by Michael Tuchner, as well as the charmingly honest urban provincial settings.

Rhys Jones is the title character, a disillusioned college lecturer, who spends his spare time walking his dog and dreaming about murdering his domineering wife (Alison Steadman).

She has made friends with upwardly mobile couple Diana Quick and Jeremy Clyde. When Steadman and Rhys Jones attend a party at their posh country home Rhys Jones gets dead-drunk, and due to Quick's machinations finds himself locked in a naked passionate embrace with a life-size inflatable doll named Angelique.

He drunkenly roams the town trying to get rid of the doll. The next day, Steadman goes missing and Rhys Jones' nocturnal activities are noted – especially by ambitious inspector Mel Smith.

The most amusing scenes are those with Rhys Jones and Smith indulging in the banter they are known for from their TV appearances.

WORKING GIRL

1988, 113 mins, ◇ Ⓥ   *Dir* Mike Nichols   US

★ *Stars* Melanie Griffith, Harrison Ford, Sigourney Weaver, Joan Cusack, Alec Baldwin, Philip Bosco

Academy Award 1988: Best Picture (Nomination)

Working Girl is enjoyable largely due to the fun of watching scrappy, sexy, unpredictable Melanie Griffith rise from Staten Island secretary to Wall Street whiz. She's the kind with an eye for stock figures – the numeral kind and the real kind (Harrison Ford).

Griffith stands apart, both for her eagerness to break out of her clerical rut and her tenacity dealing with whomever seems to be thwarting her, at first a lecherous brokerage house exec, whom she very cleverly and humorously exposes, and then a much more formidable and disarming opponent, femme boss Sigourney Weaver.

Although they're both 'girls' trying to make their way amidst a sea of men it doesn't make them friends.

This is not a laugh-out-loud film, though there is a lighthearted tone that runs consistently throughout, Griffith's innocent, breathy voice being a major factor.

YOUNG EINSTEIN

1988, 89 mins, ◇ Ⓥ   *Dir* Yahoo Serious   AUSTRALIA

★ *Stars* Yahoo Serious, Odile Le Clezio, John Howard, Pee Wee Wilson, Su Cruickshank

This wild, cheerful, off-the-wall comedy showcases the many talents of Australian satirist Yahoo Serious, who not only directed and plays the leading role, but also co-wrote (from his own original story), co-produced, edited and handled the stunts. Quite a lot to take on for a first-time filmmaker.

Pic posits young Einstein as the only son of eccentric apple farmers from Australia's southern island, Tasmania. He has a fertile mind, and is forever discovering things: it's not his fault that, by 1905 when the film's set, gravity has already been discovered by someone else.

The lad discovers accidentally how to split the atom while experimenting methods of injecting bubbles into home-brewed beer. He sets off for mainland Australia (a comically lengthy journey) to patent his invention, and meets French genius Marie Curie (Odile Le Clezio) on a train; he also meets villain and patents stealer Preston Preston (John Howard), scion of a family of Perth entrepreneurs.

The entire production rests on the shoulders of its director/star. Fortunately Serious (born Greg Pead), a long-haired gangly clown, exhibits a brash and confident sense of humor, endearing personality, and a fondness for sight gags.

YOUNG FRANKENSTEIN

1974, 108 mins, Ⓥ   *Dir* Mel Brooks   US

★ *Stars* Gene Wilder, Peter Boyle, Marty Feldman, Madeline Kahn, Cloris Leachman, Gene Hackman

Young Frankenstein emerges as a reverently satirical salute to the 1930s horror film genre. The screenplay features Gene Wilder as the grandson of Baron Victor Frankenstein, creator of the monster. Wilder, an American medical college teacher, is lured back to Transylvania by old family retainer Richard Haydn. Wilder's assistant, the namesake descendant of Igor, is played by Marty Feldman.

Teri Garr is a curvaceous lab assistant, while Cloris Leachman is a mysterious housekeeper composite of Una O'Connor and Mrs Danvers. Wilder's fussy fiancee Madeline Kahn turns up importantly in the final reels. Peter Boyle is the monster, an artistically excellent blend of malice, pity and comedy.

ZELIG

1983, 84 mins, ◇ Ⓥ   *Dir* Woody Allen   US

★ *Stars* Woody Allen, Mia Farrow, Garreth Brown, Stephanie Farrow, Will Holt, Sol Lomita

Lampooning documentary tradition by structuring the entire film as a meticulously crafted bogus docu, Woody Allen tackles some serious stuff en route (namely the two-edged sword of public and media celebrityhood) but manages to avoid the self-oriented seriousness that's alienated many of his onetime loyalists. More positively, *Zelig* is consistently funny, though more academic than boulevardier.

Allen plays the eponymous Leonard Zelig, subject of the 'documentary' that traces this onetime legend of the 1920s-30s whose weak personality and neurotic need to be liked caused him to become the ultimate conformist.

Through the use of doctored photos and staged black and white footage cannily – and usually undetectably – matched with authentic newsreels and stock footage of the period, Allen is seen intermingling with everyone from the Hearst crowd at San Simeon, Eugene O'Neill and Fanny Brice to the likes of Pope Pius XI and even Adolf Hitler.

The narrative that does emerge limns the efforts of a committed psychiatrist (played with tact and loveliness by Mia Farrow) to give Zelig a single self, a relationship that blossoms, predictably, to love by fadeout.